Praise for *Happiness Now!*

'If you could do just one thing that will immediately enrich your life and improve the world at large, it would be to take the advice of this book. I recommend it wholeheartedly!' Paul Wilson, author of *The Little Book of Calm*

'*Happiness Now!* offers a passport, map and compass to true joy. It teaches us it is never too late to be happy and to recognise that happiness is actually our true state of being, our natural inheritance. This excellent book really can help you to transform your life' Jerry Jampolsky MD, author of *Love is Letting go of Fear*

'Full of Robert Holden's own anecdotes and humour, this book is about living in the moment, "being" what you want, and allowing yourself rightful happiness. *Happiness Now!* sets the record straight on true happiness – go get it now' Stuart Wilde, author of *Life Was Never Meant to be a Struggle*

'I think the most revolutionary act a person can commit today is to be publicly happy. Robert's new book offers great insight, encouragement and vision on how to do just that. The idea is that happiness is not some prize that comes after lots of work, suffering or sacrifice, but, rather, happiness is a choice – a choice made with gratitude, love and a desire to help others. Bless you, Robert, for your example and for your willingness to add to the dialogue!' Patch Adams MD, author of *House Calls*

'If you only buy one book on happiness in your life, then make it this one! Robert Holden's profound work offers a ray of hope and a beautiful guiding vision for all who want to be happy, peaceful and free' James Twyman, author of *Emissary of Light*

'*Happiness Now!* is a wonderful guide to living joyfully' Colin Turner, author of *The Eureka Principle*

'Brilliant! Profound wisdom neatly packaged. Robert Holden's *Happiness Now!* is a clearly written treatise of what most people consider a complex, unreachable goal. Happiness is our birthright. Robert puts it right!' Eddie and Debbie Shapiro, authors of *Meditation for Inner Peace*

'More than a "feel good" guide, *Happiness Now!* offers a whole new way to see yourself and the world. It can bring more than a smile to your life!' Tom Carpenter, author of *Dialogue on Awakening*

Also by Robert Holden

Living Wonderfully
Laughter: the Best Medicine
Stress Busters
What Number Are You? (with Lilla Bek)

HAPPINESS NOW!

Timeless Wisdom for Feeling Good Fast

Robert Holden

Hodder & Stoughton

First published in 1998 by Hodder & Stoughton
A division of Hodder Headline PLC

10 9 8 7 6 5 4

A CIP catalogue record for this title is available
from the British Library

ISBN 0 340 71308 9

Typeset by Palimpsest Book Production Limited,
Polmont, Stirlingshire
Printed and bound in Great Britain by
Mackays of Chatham PLC, Chatham, Kent

Hodder and Stoughton
A division of Hodder Headline PLC
338 Euston Road
London NW1 3BH

Dedicated to those who dare to
sprinkle kindness,
radiate love
and scatter joy.

ACKNOWLEDGEMENTS

Gratitude inspires joy. It is with great joy, therefore, that I make the following acknowledgements. First, to my wife, Miranda, acting midwife for the birth of this book! Next, to The Happiness Project team: thank you, David Holden, for your 'Mr Big' love and skill; thank you, Ben Renshaw, for your vision and support; thank you, Alison Atwell, for your joy and creativity; and thank you, Candy Constable, for stepping into the spirit of this project so gracefully.

Thank you to Tom and Linda Carpenter. This book is so thoroughly inspired by our friendship. Thank you to Diane Berke and Tony Zito, for you are truly The Presence of Love. Thank you to Avanti Kumar for the wake-up call! Thank you to Helen Schucman, author of *A Course In Miracles*. Thank you also to the other teachers of love and joy who have so enriched my life. They include Marika Burton, Deirdre Ahern, Graham Taylor-Chilton, Nick and Anne Davis, Mark Reynolds, Brian Little, Eddie and Debbie Shapiro, Nick Williams, Robert and Anne Redfern, Bob and Cathy Colman, Stephanie Bennett, Ian Patrick and Jacqueline Heron.

For this book in particular, thank you to Robert Norton whose inspirational album, 'Painting the Ocean', played continually whilst I wrote. Thank you again to Candy Constable for your help with research. Thank you to my editor, Rowena Webb, for your enthusiasm, support and patience. Thank you also to Laura Brockbank and Rachel Connolly for the same.

Thank you to my mother, my father, my family, my friends, my clients, my two cats, Great and Wonderful, and to everyone else who has taught me about happiness and love!

Note: Every case-history in this book appears with the agreement of the people involved. Names have been altered where requested.

No one who comes here but must still have
hope, some lingering illusion, or some dream
that there is something outside of himself that
will bring happiness and peace to him. If
everything is in him this cannot be so.
And therefore by his coming, he denies
the truth about himself, and seeks for
something more than everything,
as if a part of it were separated
off and found where all the rest of
it is not. This is the purpose he bestows
upon the body; that it seek for what he
lacks, and give him what would make
himself complete. And thus he wanders
aimlessly about, in search of something
that he cannot find, believing that
he is what he is not.

A Course In Miracles

CONTENTS

CHAPTER ONE

꧅

Happy Already!

꧅

Picture the following scene:

I am at my friend's house. It is mid-afternoon. We are having tea, and Jane and I are engaged in a deep and meaningful conversation. Her two boys run into the room. They are young, full of energy, lively and noisy. Tom is four years old, and Ben is three years old. Ben follows Tom everywhere.

Jane and I continue to talk, but soon we cannot hear each other speak. The boys are in dispute. 'What's the problem?' Jane asks. Tom throws Ben off himself, takes a deep breath, and says, 'It's *my* turn to play on *my* bike, but Ben won't leave me alone, and he's already ridden *my* bike once today.' A few more things were said. No agreement was reached. 'Go outside and sort this out. Robert and I are talking,' said Jane. The boys were dismissed.

1

After only a minute or two the boys ran into the room again, with the bike! Before Jane could tell the boys off for bringing it into the house, Tom said, 'We've worked it all out.' 'Good,' we both said. Tom went on, 'Today the bike belongs to me all day, and tomorrow the bike belongs to Ben all day.' Both boys nodded their heads with great enthusiasm. 'Are you both agreed?' asked Jane, sounding quite surprised. 'Yes,' they both said. 'Good, now go along and play,' said Jane. The boys turned around to leave, and just before they left the room, Ben piped up at the top of his voice, '*I know – let's pretend it's tomorrow!*'

How I love this story. It illustrates so well the power of what preacher Robert H. Schuller calls 'possibility thinking'[1]. Young children – the younger the better – are great possibility thinkers. Give a child any household object, a wooden spoon for example, and possibility thinking instantly turns the spoon into a microphone, a tennis racket, a guitar, a mobile phone, a magic wand, ET's cousin from outer space, a delicious ice cream, or anything else you care to imagine! With possibility thinking, *children can make anything out of anything*.

Adults are also very good at possibility thinking. We too can think 'possibility thoughts', instinctively *making anything out of anything*. Using possibility thinking, we can choose to make a meaning out of any situation or event. A failed job interview, for instance, could mean 'This is a tragedy', 'I'm not good enough', and 'My life is over', or conversely, 'This job was not for me', 'This was good practice for next time', and 'Let's go out and celebrate anyway!' Indeed,

it is a key to great happiness to know that you can make anything out of anything.

Tom and Ben's story also illustrates perfectly how children use possibility thinking to enjoy happiness *now*! I believe that, contrary to popular opinion, a baby's favourite toy is not a thing, it's a moment – a moment called *now*. Children are born only with an awareness of *now* – past and future are meaningless at first. In the beginning, *now* is the whole world to a child, his or her entire playground. This fascination and reverence for *now* is entirely natural; it is neither learned nor fabricated.

Children, like Tom and Ben, are completely unimpressed by the idea of 'future happiness' – above all, they want happiness *now*! They, who are yet to be indoctrinated or conditioned fully by meaningless 'laws of time', do not know how to wait for happiness. Why wait for heaven, when the possibility for heaven exists right here and now?

I believe that as a young child you too were alive to the infinite possibilities of the present moment. Like other children, you were full of wonder, imagination, awe and appreciation for the precious present. *You got so much from 'now' because you gave so much to 'now'* – and for all the while you were engaged with the present you were happy to leave past and future exactly where they were. *Now* was your treasure island, and you believed whole-heartedly that happiness was here and now, waiting to be seen. The more you believed this, the more you would look; and the more you looked, the more happiness you found. Here again, then, is another key to happiness.

3

Milking the 'Sacred *Now*'

The world has changed greatly in recent times in an effort to accommodate our desire for happiness *now*. Everything has speeded up. We live life fast – faster than ever. Fast technology, fast travel, fast careers, fast relationships and fast results are all the go in our 'I want it *now*' world. Indeed, the world is fast becoming a vast convenience store where you can get everything in an instant – instant coffee, microwave foods, minute-meals, half-hour film developing, 24-hour banking, drive-thru funerals, quickie divorces, television shopping, home delivery on everything, and, of course, instant credit. We are sold on signs which read 'No queues', 'No need to wait', 'One stop', 'Open all hours' and 'Buy now – pay later'.

One way of looking at our 'I want it *now*' world is to see it as a highly egotistical and selfish pursuit of happiness that is fuelled by impatience, violence and greed, doomed from the very start to 'end in tears'. Indeed, many people are voicing their concerns at 'the way the world is going', believing that traditional values and morals are fast being corroded and obliterated by the chase for happiness *now*.

Another way of seeing our 'I want it *now*' world is that this clamour for happiness *now* reflects an instinctive wisdom and a great spiritual truth which states that

everything – absolutely everything – is available to you 'now'.

There is a famous story from the Zen tradition which tells of an encounter between a young, eager student and a well

4

respected Zen Master, noted especially for his perpetual grace and happiness:

'Master, I dream of an everlasting happiness. What is the highest wisdom you can teach me?' asked the student.

The Master smiled. He took his brush and wrote, as if for the first time, 'Attention.'

'Wonderful,' said the student, 'And what comes next after attention?' he asked.

The Master smiled. He took his brush and wrote, as if for the first time, 'Attention. Attention.'

'Yes,' nodded the student, utterly perplexed. 'Anything more?' he asked.

The Master smiled. He took his brush and wrote, as if for the first time, 'Attention. Attention. Attention.'

'Okay, so what does "attention" mean?' asked the student, unable to see.

The Master spoke: 'Attention means attention.'

'Is that all?' said the student, obviously dispirited.

'Attention is all,' said the Master. 'Without attention, happiness is nowhere; with attention, happiness is now here. Attention is freedom from all. Attention offers all.'

Every authentic school of wisdom and spirituality teaches you that *now* is the most abundant moment of your life. The bibles of the world, be it the *Old Testament* or the *New*, the *Koran* or the *Bhagavad Gita*, the *Dhammapada* or the *Tao te Ching*, indeed any true spiritual text, all agree that *now* is an eternal treasure chest dripping with beautiful everlasting gifts of peace, happiness, love and joy freely available to all on a 24-hour 'Don't pay now – Don't pay later' basis.[2]

'Now' is sacred! This is what the Zen Master is trying to tell the eager young student in the story above. Indeed, talk to any spiritual teacher or guru worth their mantra, so to speak, and they will tell you, *'now' is always sacred*. But why and how is *'now' always sacred*, you may ask? What if you've just been stood up on a date, or you've just opened a bill, or you've just chipped a tooth, or your football team has lost again – *how sacred is that?*

One approach to milking the 'sacred *now*' is to place your attention on what is happening around you right at this minute and aim to appreciate, respect and value it as much as you feel is possible. You can do this right now. Before you read on, look around you and appreciate fully for a moment what your senses pick up. When you do this you will experience first hand how pleasurable appreciation can be. Events sometimes seem to make this exercise hard, but willingness can overcome this.

In my workshops for The Happiness Project I often show a slide which reads 'HAPPINESSISNOWHERE'. When I ask people to call out what they can see, I always get two distinct answers, one being *happiness is nowhere*, the other being *happiness is now here*. Often, then,

the difference between 'happiness is nowhere'
and 'happiness is now here' has something to do
with the event and everything to do with how
you see the event. Your perception is key.

The real secret to milking the 'sacred *now*' is to place

your attention not out in the world about you, but within yourself – your inner, unconditioned *self*. In truth, the *sacred now* is an inner potential. It is eternal, abundant and its geography is spiritual, not physical. In other words, the *sacred now* represents a permanent potential within you to experience love, freedom and joy regardless of time, place or circumstance.

The gift of happiness is wrapped in your heart, not the world. Thus, your happiness will never be mailed to you! And it can never get lost in the post! In truth, your happiness has already been delivered, sitting in your inner mail box – your heart – waiting to be opened. This is what the *sacred now* is really all about. In essence, then, *you are the key to happiness*. More than what happens to you, it is your perceptions, your thoughts, your beliefs and your overall response that are essential; your Self, your whole Self, is the real key.

The real reason *now* is so naturally abundant is because when you allow yourself to be unrestrained by fear and uninhibited by worry, it is *you* who is so naturally, originally abundant. In truth, then:

> Now *has enough wisdom to last you forever,*
> *because within you, right now, there is all*
> *the wisdom you listen out for in others.*

> Now *has enough love to last you a lifetime,*
> *because within you, right now, there is the*
> *love you continually cry out for.*

> Now *has enough peace to last you an eternity,*
> *because within you, right now, peace of mind*
> *is one thought away at most.*

And now *has enough joy to outlast the world,
because within you, right now, the joy you
chase is not in things – it is in* you.

The problem with our 'I want it *now*' society is not that we want happiness *now*; but that we have lost sight of how to experience it now. In particular, we say 'I want it *now*' but we doubt and do not really believe 'it is here *now*'. We have lost faith in *now* and placed all of our faith in some imagined future. Similarly, we have lost faith in our *self* and placed all our attention on the world outside. Now it is the world, it seems, that must 'make us happy' – *herein lies the source of all our misery*.

For as long as you believe it is the world that must make you happy you leave yourself open to great disappointment and much sadness. Why? Because for as long as you refuse to see your inner potential for happiness *now* you will not see it in the world. *How can a mirror change the way you look?* Think on that, for the world is only a mirror. You will only see in the world what you are prepared to see in yourself, nothing more and nothing less.

Know, therefore, that the journey to true happiness and to happiness *now* is not a journey of physical distance or time; it is a journey of personal 'self-recovery' where we learn again, re-member and re-connect consciously to an inner potential for joy – a paradise lost – waiting to be found. One moment we look within and we see *happiness nowhere*; the next moment we look within and this time we see *happiness now here*. This is revelation. This is enlightenment. This is joy!

The faster we chase the world and the future, the quicker we appear to overlook the possibility that happiness is here already. Every morning as we wake the alarm clock sings *'now'*, and from that moment on we do not give *now* another thought as we desperately chase our future. But are you so sure happiness is not already here within you now? Have you really looked? I mean, *really* looked?

Milking the 'sacred *now'* is excavation work. It is about re-discovering an inner potential for original joy – a potential that already exists but has been buried beneath a pile of fears, worries, doubts, conditioning and history. Think of this potential for original joy not as something to arrive at but as something you bring with you wherever you go. Re-cultivating this potential is our task, and the task begins with the realisation that

joy waits on welcome, not on time[3].

Diving For Treasures of the Soul

Psychology school taught me a lot about our potential, in particular, our potential for unlimited amounts of misery, pain, weakness and despair! We studied every affliction, every neurosis and every mental dis-ease available at the time. In a nutshell, my psychology training consisted of: year one, an introduction to basic suffering; year two, the study of advanced suffering; year three, a qualification in inspired suffering.

The focus was entirely on our inner potential to mess life up. My curriculum was the A–Z of suffering, from anger to zoophilia, including stress, depression, anxiety, neurosis, psychosis, neurotic-psychosis and psychotic-neurosis, hysteria, schizophrenia, obsessive-compulsive disorders, phobias, inferiority complexes, kleptomania, suicide, insanity and delusion. At no time did we consider our potential for joy, love, or peace of mind. In effect, I was studying for a PhD in misery!

Studying suffering full-time had a big impact on my way of thinking. I once read that history has no evidence there ever lived a happy psychologist. I can see why now. After a while, I was able to work out just how low I was going to feel on any given day by looking at my lecture time-table. For instance, when we studied depression for a week, I remember the entire class eventually felt totally depressed by the end. The same was true for any and all of the complexes, afflictions, disorders and fixations. Getting an unexpectedly low mark for my paranoia essay didn't help at all!

Do you remember when at primary school or kindergarten you were given a lecture on the importance of bodily hygiene and the dangers of head-lice? And do you remember how, after twenty minutes of listening to this woman who showed you great big blown-up slides of head-lice with six-inch teeth, you became absolutely convinced you had a nest of these things in your hair? Well, that's what it was like in my psychology lectures. Junior doctors will tell you their experience was also the same.

I learned a very important lesson about perception and focus during those years which is,

be careful what you look for because you will find it.

I immersed myself thoroughly in the study of misery. I

received distinctions for the most part in every study I undertook. As I increased my focus, I soon realised there was not one type of depression, but one hundred. Furthermore, there was not one sort of schizophrenia, but thirty, forty or more. Whatever you focus on expands. Each day I hoped we might dive for pearls, but instead we merely collected crabs!

After a full six years of study, I still had not been given a single lecture on our potential for joy, peace, unity, wholeness and success. Psychology, originally defined as *the study of the soul*, had been reduced to a study of illness and neurotic behaviour. Freud and Behaviourism, in particular, reduced human beings to no more than a pitiful bag of blood and bones housing a mind full of neurotic defences and endless psychotic potential for aggression and psycho-sexual hang-ups. Never was there any mention of the soul, of spirit, of divinity, of God, of love.

My training in psychology, with its almost exclusive focus on pain, is a very common story. It also reflects a tendency in our society to focus on negatives. Doctors, for instance, study illness, not health. Business leaders analyse failure, not success. Economists study cost, not value. Philosophers mostly debate original sin, not original blessing. Christians talk endlessly about crucifixion, not resurrection. Mental health organisations publish books on 'Understanding Depression', 'Understanding Stress', 'Understanding Bereavement', but not on 'Understanding Joy' and 'Understanding Love'. The media is full of journalists suffering from an addictive, anti-social, obsessive-compulsive need to communicate and make up bad news. Literature and art is full of depressed poets and painters – can you name three joyful poets?

What you focus on most often becomes familiar, and what is familiar feels real to you. In our society, we focus on pain before joy, tears before laughter, fear before love, and so gradually we grow blind to our inner, ever-present potential for happiness. I remember well how my lecturers frowned on happiness. What they taught me essentially was, 'If you find you are experiencing happiness – don't worry – you are just in denial and the pain will return soon!'

Happiness appeared to have no value, other than it offered a temporary respite between periods of pain and trauma. It was defined simplistically as the absence of pain. Other messages I received included, 'happiness is superficial, pain is deep', 'laughter is a common symptom of manic depression', 'smiling a lot means you are suppressing a hidden pain', 'optimism is often unrealistic and delusional', and 'talking to God is the first sign of a nervous breakdown'.

Of greater concern to me, though, is the large body of thought within the psychology profession which suggests that happiness is in some way a dysfunctional behaviour in light of all the suffering in the world. The idea is, 'if you have normal blood pressure living in our troubled world you are not taking it seriously enough.' There have been several recent studies which have tried to suggest that happiness is only an avoidance of real issues, a selfish coping strategy, or a superficial form of escape. This thinking does not take into account that your happiness is an inspiration, a gift to others, and a way out of suffering[4].

When I asked my lecturers why we didn't study happiness, they usually challenged me to look at my resistance

to embracing my pain more fully! The most common expla-
nation given, however, for why happiness, love, peace and
God are not studied by psychologists is that they cannot
be measured as easily as fear and pain. In other words,
they are inner potentials that do not show up on laboratory
measuring apparatus designed to measure externals[5].

Just because psychologists choose not to focus on joy,
however, does not mean to say joy does not exist. We can
refuse to look at the sun, for example, but that will not
make it go away. One problem, though, with not focusing
directly on happiness is that what has emerged in place
of the truth is a myth of happiness where happiness has
become *a potential time forgot*, clouded in misperception,
superstition, doubt and cynicism.

The Oasis in the Desert

It was whilst studying Communications, that I met a man in
my class who was to change my life forever. His name was
Avanti Kumar. Avanti was an Asian gentleman, a mature
student of about twenty-four years old, and the spitting
image of the actor Danny Devito – short build, stocky, no
hair directly on top of his head but wild curly bushes of
growth either side, big bronzed cheeks, a great smile, and
a beautiful radiant light in his eyes.

Avanti always sat at the back of the class, and in the early
weeks he was always last in and first out. 'Who is he?' we
all wondered. All we knew about him was that he was quiet
and that he was always smiling. In fact, he was never not

smiling. It was as if he had a private joke running in his head all the time.

I was deeply intrigued by Avanti from the very first moment I laid eyes on him. It was as if I somehow knew him already. There was a familiarity I felt but could not explain. I remember wanting to talk to him but feeling, unusually for me, too nervous to approach. Our first conversation I will never forget. I asked him why he had chosen this course to study. His answer was, 'To meet you, of course.' His smile really was infectious.

After that, I made sure we drank coffee together most days. I asked questions, he gave me cryptic clues. I remember asking him one day, 'What are you?' 'A yogi,' he replied. 'A what?' I asked. 'A student of yoga,' he said. 'Oh! You mean Jane Fonda?' Fortunately, we enjoyed each other's humour. Soon, another student, Phil, joined our coffee sessions. We became inseparable. We were one.

It was as if Avanti was fresh out of some Himalayan cave or esoteric monastery, where, I imagined, he had been sitting for centuries in blissful meditation. He was my first direct experience of someone consciously connected to and aware of the inner potential for joy anywhere, anytime. Over the next few months, he carefully and lovingly re-acquainted Phil and I with this inner awareness as we talked about yoga, metaphysics, spiritual wisdom and the more enlightened schools of psychology.

'What you have been learning about is a psychology of the ego, or lower self,' Avanti explained, 'which is immersed in separation, fear and suffering. If you would like, I will teach you about another psychology, a psychology of wholeness and of the Higher Self, which teaches you how to allow your inner joy to shine on the world once more.' It was with Avanti, then, that I first began to focus directly on happiness. It was Avanti who first taught me that happiness is not just the absence of pain, but that

true happiness is an inner power, natural,
healing, abundant and always available.

Like all great teachers, Avanti loved to tell stories. One day he introduced me to the story of two birds, first written in an ancient Hindu text called the *Mundaya Upanishad*[6]. It reads:

Two birds
  inseparable companions
  perched on the same tree.
One eats fruit,
  the other looks on.

The first bird is our individual self,
  feeding on the pleasures and
  pains of this world;
The other is the universal Self,
  silently witnessing all.

'Think of the two birds as two thoughts flying about in the sky of your mind,' said Avanti. 'The first bird, *the individual self*, is your ego. It "desires" happiness, and it tells you you must search the world to find it. The second bird, *the universal Self*, is your spirit. It "knows" happiness, and it tells you you are happy already, that you were created happy, that all the happiness you have ever dreamed of rests in the centre of your *Self* right now.

'Like an oasis in the desert, the *universal Self* is wholly joyous, wholly abundant and wholly peaceful,' said Avanti.

It is home to the *sacred now*, your inner potential for immediate peace and joy anywhere, anytime. With Avanti's guidance, I immersed myself in Eastern and Western literature in an effort to understand further the concept of *individual self* and *universal Self*. There are many names for these two selves, some of which I have listed opposite in *Table A*.

Today, many years later, I now think of the *universal Self* as your *unconditioned Self* – the Self that exists behind the mask of your personal history, your conditioning, your learned limitations, the roles you play, your persona, your defences, your doubts and your fears. This *unconditioned Self* is the original you, untouched by the world, completely safe and whole. It is who you really are, and not who you have been taught you are by parents, teachers, friends, lovers, anybody else, and most of all, by yourself.

Your *unconditioned Self* is the presence of peace. Three words, in particular, describe the *unconditioned Self*, and they are 1) wholeness; 2) love; 3) joy. The oriental mystics called the *unconditioned Self* the 'uncarved block'. Other names for the *unconditioned Self* include the Zen term 'the original face', the Buddhist phrase 'the sacred happiness', the North American name 'free spirit', the Taoists' 'inner smile', and the Christian mystics' 'inner Eden'.

E.G.O. – Everything Good is Outside

The following story helps to describe the plight of the ego, or *conditioned self*:

conditioned self	Unconditioned Self
learned self	original Self
false self	real Self
fearful self	loving Self
critical self	creative Self
lower self	higher Self
dissociated self	unified Self
ego	holy spirit
split self	whole Self
body/mind	spirit/soul
persona	atman
flesh	christos
nothing	'I am'
sin	source
hell	heaven
fallen self	divine Self

Table A

Every day at 4 am, Brother Daniel would be the first to rise in the monastery. He did so out of choice, and was proud to do so. Whilst his teacher and all of his brothers slept peacefully, Brother Daniel busily exerted great effort in his prayer, study and meditation. Enlightenment was his goal.

Every day, Brother Daniel would pray longer and louder for enlightenment. He worked hard at improving his physical posture for meditation, and, above all, he would labour to memorise all of the ancient spiritual texts at the monastery. Rarely, if ever, did

Brother Daniel rest, eat or sleep, for he wanted to get to enlightenment and he wanted to get there fast.

Brother Daniel liked to meditate and pray, but most of all he immersed himself in scriptures. Brother Daniel liked to be quiet and still, but he rarely had time, for he found there was always so much to do. Brother Daniel liked the silence, but he would rather hear his teacher talk of the silence.

Brother Daniel's teacher, a gentle, peaceful man, who was always smiling, would encourage him to slow down, enjoy the sun and watch the grass grow. But Brother Daniel was too keen and in too much of a hurry to heed the advice. 'Why do you rush, speed and hurry so?' his teacher asked. 'I am after enlightenment,' said Brother Daniel. 'When will you get there?' his teacher smiled. 'Oh, one more prayer perhaps, my next meditation hopefully, or an act of service maybe,' replied Brother Daniel. 'Why are you so sure enlightenment is running on ahead of you?' asked his teacher. 'Perhaps if you stood still awhile, you would find enlightenment is here right now – but you are too busy running away from it!'

In this story, the monastery is a symbol for your mind, the teacher is a symbol for your unconditioned Self, or spirit, which is always smiling, and Brother Daniel is a symbol of your conditioned self, or ego. The unconditioned Self experiences wholeness, while the conditioned self searches for wholeness.

Much has been written about the ego, or conditioned self. The phrase 'the ego' can be misleading, for when we say 'the ego' it sounds as if we are talking about a person, a child, or something real. Essentially put, the ego is just a thought. It is a small idea, and nothing more. And the idea is, *Everything Good is Outside*. So conditioned and convinced are we by this frightening thought, that we chase the world, just like Brother Daniel, searching for success, happiness, love and peace of mind. And we dare not look within ourselves, for what if all we find is nothing, or, worse still, something rotten?

I remember once reading, though I'm not sure where now, that the word 'ego' also stands for *Edging God Out*. Here is a similar idea to *Everything Good is Outside*. Your conditioned self is acting on information that something is missing inside you and that you have to search outside of yourself to find it. This thought of lack, *of not being enough*, is very frightening, and it leaves us needy, disorientated and chasing shadows.

The ego is fear. It is also the denial of inner happiness. The ego's prayer therefore is always *Look out!* 'Look out, look out,' cries the ego, but the ego is blind because it does not believe. It looks, but never finds; it asks but it does not receive. In effect,

the ego is like a thirsty fish – it is confused!

Imagine a thirsty fish – a fish dying of thirst that is born in water, made of water, surrounded by water! Just because the fish refuses to drink, it does not mean there is no water. Another analogy is to think of the ego as a bird flying high and trying to reach the sky, while all the time being in the sky. And a final analogy would be to think of the ego as a sparkle in a diamond whilst insisting there is no diamond.

The ego is a doubt that you are whole, i.e. your conditioned self doubts that there even is an unconditioned Self. The unconditioned Self declares 'I am whole', but the conditioned self asks 'Am I whole?', as I have shown in *Figure 1*. This doubt in your essential goodness, your essential beauty and essential wholeness is where all your pain and suffering stems from.

Our unconditional Self is forgotten but not entirely lost as we roam the world. Every now and then we catch its fragrance, its melody, its taste. In childhood we are told stories, the significance of which hits us much later on[7]. For instance, Hans Christian Anderson's tale of 'The Ugly Duckling' is a wonderful description of the ego (the duckling) and the spirit (the swan). What is the ego other than a mistaken identity?

Figure 1

> *Just like the ugly duckling, we are afraid we are*
> *not good enough, wrong, bad and nothing; and*
> *just like the ugly duckling, we will eventually*
> *learn this is not true.*

'Sleeping Beauty' is a tale that encourages us to wake up to our inner beauty, i.e. our unconditioned Self. 'Beauty and the Beast' show us how love (beauty) can help us transform our ego-thinking (beast). 'Peter Pan' beckons us to remember, to imagine and to fly free again. Pick any children's tale, 'Aladdin', 'The Lion King' and 'Pinocchio', for instance, and we are told of a spiritual journey that moves from ego to Self, fear to love, pain to joy.

One final thought about our conditioning: *it is all made up!* It has been made up and it is not true. What you think about yourself, and what other people have told you about you, is just an opinion, not a fact. It is helpful, therefore, to remember that the ego is just a thought, a thought of limitation, *that is not true.* The final verdict of the ego is that it is a mistake. It offers a small, poor, dull, limited likeness, a bad snapshot that does not capture the real you. In other words, *the ego is not real.*

Michelangelo, God and Miracles

When the great Italian artist, Michelangelo, was asked by a great admirer, 'How do you create your beautiful sculptures?', he gave a reply that became famous and is still told around the world to this day. He said, 'The beauty is already there, my friend. I do not create beauty;

God creates beauty. I merely chip away the surrounding marble so as to reveal the beauty. The beauty is already within. It is already perfectly in place.'

The surrounding marble Michelangelo refers to is like our conditioning, and the beauty already within the marble is like our true, unconditioned self.

Avanti encouraged me to read poetry whenever I could, particularly the metaphysical poets like William Wordsworth, William Blake and Robert Browning, and also the Indian poet Rabindranath Tagore and the Sufi bard, Rumi, to name just a few[8]. In one of Robert Browning's works he refers to our 'imprisoned splendour' in much the same way as Michelangelo talks of the beauty already within the marble. He writes:

Truth is within ourselves, it takes no rise
From outward things, whatever you may believe.
There is an inner centre in us all
Where truth abides in fullness; and around
Wall upon wall the gross flesh hems it in
That perfect, clear perception which is Truth.
A baffling and perverting carnal mesh
Binds all and makes all error, but to know
Rather consists in finding out a way
For the imprisoned splendour to escape
Than in achieving entry for a light
Supposed to be without.[9]

Alongside Avanti's tutoring, I also began to investigate schools of psychology and psychotherapy that are not so well covered in university syllabuses. My research showed me that since the end of World War II, in particular, many new schools have emerged which go way beyond Freud and Behaviourism in their definition of what it means to be human. Freud, particularly, maintained that humans have two basic drives, *sex* and *aggression*, and that our goal in life is to be as sexy and as aggressive as politely possible. There was no higher Self according to Freud.

The idea of a higher, spiritual, unconditioned Self is now re-emerging. More and more schools of psychology now see that healing is about outgrowing your limited self-concept of the ego to embrace your true Self, a Self that is not conditioned or altered in any way by the world (see *Table B* over the page). The terminology varies from school to school, but the basic principles and understanding are very similar.

An increasing number of psychologists are changing their minds about the limited models and concepts that have so governed human understanding. It is of interest to note that even Sigmund Freud changed his mind about many of his ideas towards the end of his life. In one of my books, *Stress Busters*, I quote from Freud, who just before he died wrote, '*In the final analysis, we must love in order not to fall ill*'[10]. Psychology is finding its soul once more. And now all that remains, it seems, is for us to change our minds about ourselves.

I also became absorbed in Eastern philosophy with its rich, vibrant and poetic vision. Although many of these authors describe the unconditioned Self using mystical images and deeply spiritual metaphors, they are at pains to point out that an experience of this whole Self is a natural, normal, commonplace, everyday possibility. The Buddhist term, 'satori', for instance, refers to instant enlightenment, *available for all and to all.*

I found the works of Sri Ramakrishna, a nineteenth-century mystic, to be particularly fascinating. Every word

Psychologist	School	Ego	Spirit
Alfred Adler	Individual Psychology	Guiding Fiction	Creative Self
Carl Jung	Analytical Psychology	Persona	Self
Fritz Perls	Gestalt Therapy	Self-image	Self
Roberto Assagioli	Psychosynthesis	Sub-personalities	I
R. D. Laing	Primal Integration Therapy	False Self	Real Self
Janov	Primal Integration Therapy	Unreal Self	Real Self
Eric Berne	Transactional Analysis	Adapted Child	Free Child
Dr. J. L. Moreno	Psychodrama	Conserved Roles	Spontaneity

Table B

seemed strangely familiar to me. He wrote extensively about the unconditioned Self which he referred to as the Divine Self. In one passage, he explains:

Know thyself, and thou shalt then know the non-self and

the Lord of All. What is my ego? Is it my hand, or foot, or flesh, or blood, or muscle, or tendon? Ponder deep, and thou shalt know that there is no such thing as I. As by continually peeling off the skin of the onion, so by analysing the ego it will be found that there is not any real entity corresponding to the ego. The ultimate result of all such analysis is God. When egoism drops away, Divinity manifests Itself.[11]

Over and over during my search for greater understanding I felt I was being pulled along by a golden thread of teaching which made a connection between the unconditioned Self and God within: 'Search not in distant skies; in man's own heart God lies,' said one Japanese text. In the Sikh bible, *The Granth*, it is written, 'God is in thy heart, yet thou searchest for him in the wilderness.' In the Psalms it is written, 'You too are gods, sons of the most High, all of you.' Jesus tells us in *The Bible*, 'Ye are Gods.' Islam purports, 'Those who know themselves know their God.' And in Buddhism, it is written, 'Look within, you are the Buddha.'[12]

The god I first learned about as a child was like a huge inflated ego, living in the sky, very jealous, a big beard, middle-aged, has an anger problem, very aloof. This god blesses bombs, fixes football matches, finds you car parking spaces, and helps you win the lottery. It is a special god that loves and hates some people more than others.

The ego-sized god apparently needs and enjoys sacrifices of live animals, young babies, tobacco, drugs and beer. It is clearly a god of fear, and therefore, a god of punishment, attack, vengeance and judgement. Clearly,

great unhappiness is caused by our misperceptions of our Self and God.

Slowly, but surely, with the help of Avanti and many other teachers and mentors I met along my spiritual path, I began to heal my misperceptions of my Self and of God[13]. Layer by layer I let go of my conditioning. It is enough to say here that I now relate to God as pure unconditional love, and that I now see no difference between unconditional love and the unconditional Self.

It was approximately nine years after meeting Avanti that I sat down together with my wife, Miranda, to read a book called *A Course In Miracles*, that changed my life forever. It is a remarkable book which offers a spiritual psychology training in transforming our fearful thoughts into loving thoughts, and in giving up the ego for our real unconditional Self[14].

I did not get on too well with this book at first – it was so big, bigger than *War and Peace*, more than 1200 pages long, and full of religious metaphor. If truth be known, Miranda and I had both bought this book long before we met each other, and it had sat on both our shelves idle for five years! Every time I had tried to read it my eyes would glaze over and I'd soon be asleep, no matter what the time of day.

Other than being a great remedy for insomnia, I discovered *A Course In Miracles* had other uses too. It made an excellent door-stop, for instance, a great paper-weight, and, most importantly, it looked very impressive on the book shelf. Finally, one day, Miranda and I returned to the book, opened a page at random, and began to read.

The words we read were, *'The self you made [the ego] is not the Son of God [your unconditioned Self].'* This message is repeated many, many times throughout the entire book. Later, there is a meditation that reads:

My true Identity is so secure, so lofty, sinless, glorious
and great, wholly beneficent and free from guilt,
that Heaven looks to It to give it light. It lights
the world as well. It is the gift my father gave to me;
the one as well I give the world. There is no gift
but This that can be either given or received. This
is reality, and only This. This is illusion's end. It is
the truth.
My Name, O Father, still is known to You. I have
forgotten it, and do not know where I am going, who
I am, or what it is I do. Remind me, Father, now,
for I am weary of the world I see. Reveal what You
would have me see instead.

A Course In Miracles is a constant affirmation that you are
created by an unconditional thought of love that appears
to have lost itself in a world of fear. Freedom, joy and
peace of mind are yours again when you re-member and
re-connect to your unconditioned Self. As the book says,
'Salvation requires the acceptance of but one thought; you are as
God created you, not what you made of yourself.'

Choosing to Remember or to Forget

You are, in any given moment, either re-membering or
forgetting about your unconditioned Self, your true spiritual identity. Nothing else is really happening. When you
re-member you are free, you feel happy, hopeful, trusting,
generous, loving and, above all, safe. When you doubt,

however, and you forget the truth about yourself, you become afraid, isolated and desperate, you go it alone, you protect and defend, you strive and you attack.

Perhaps you know this famous passage by William Wordsworth:

Our birth is but a sleep and a forgetting:
The soul that rises with us, our life's Star,
Hath had elsewhere its setting,
And cometh from afar:
Not in entire forgetfulness,
And not in utter nakedness,
But trailing clouds of glory do we come
For God, who is our home:
Heaven lies about us in our infancy!
Shades of the prison-house begin to close
Upon the growing Boy,
But He beholds the light, and whence it flows,
He sees it in his joy;
The Youth, who daily farther from the east
Must travel, still is Nature's Priest
and by the vision splendid
Is on his way attended;
At length the Man perceives it die away,
And fade into the light of common day.[15]

Unhappiness is a symptom of forgetfulness, as much as joy is a symptom of re-membering. When we are unhappy, balance gives way, perspective collapses, faith falters, communication often breaks down, doubt doubles, panic ensues, and a thousand different symptoms spill all around us. The disharmony we feel is ultimately a disharmony with our

Self. We have stepped out of our centre, and we 'lose heart', 'lose spirit', and lose our Self.

Healing is re-membering. It is what author Marianne Williamson calls a return to love[16]. Much of my therapeutic work with clients is, therefore, about helping people to rediscover the *trailing clouds of glory* within. We talk, we meditate, we laugh, we cry, we pray, we sing, we dance, we do whatever is necessary to help us remember the truth and let go of the pain.

At my seminars hosted by The Happiness Project, I occasionally share a poem of mine that helps me to remember what my own healing and my work is all about. It reads:

There once was a moment,
a mad, forgetful moment, that slipped
past eternity into time.
And in that moment, mad and
forgetful as it was, out of nowhere
an entire world, separate from God,
was dreamed up.
And although it was only a moment,
it felt like forever.
And although it was only a dream,
it felt so real.
In this mad, forgetful world, the
Ocean prayed to God,
'Give me water. I want water.'
The Sun, brilliant and bright, would
pray, 'Dear God, fill me with light.'
And the mighty, powerful, roaming Wind
would plea, 'Set me free, set me free.'

One time, all of sudden, and I don't quite
know why, the Silence began to speak,
'God grant me peace, grant me peace.'
Then, Peace Itself, fell to its knees,
'Dear God, please, what can I do to be
more peaceful?'
Now, looking quite perplexed, prayed,
'Dear God, what next?'
Even Eternity began to pray,
'I want to last forever and ever and ever.'
Infinity felt small,
'Dear God, help me to grow.'
And Life itself, began to cry,
'I don't ever want to die!'
And You and I, who are essence of Love,
we cried out for love,
'God please love me,' we prayed.
'God, fill me with love,' we prayed.
'God, grant me love.'
Mad and forgetful as it was, that moment
in time soon slipped, tripped and fell
away back into eternity.
It's all over now, save the memory,
a mad, forgetful memory, it too ready
for eternity.

In the Buddhist scripture, *The Dhammapada*, there is the famous 'Eight Fold Path' which refers to eight spiritual freedoms, one of which is *right remembrance*, or right mindfulness[17]. Disciples of Buddhism are called upon to 'Arise! Watch. Remember and forget not.' In a similar way, Jesus asked us to 'Watch and pray.'

To be happy, it is good to make a point of knowing what it is in your life that helps you to re-member truth. What is it that helps you to love, to be real, to be free? What is it that helps you to awake from the slumber of your conditioning? As for myself, I love the sounds of laughter and of friendship. I love to look at the stars, to walk in nature, to listen to the river's song, to smell the heavenly scent of star-gazer lilies, to watch a roaring fire, to feel its warmth and see its light. I love to be still, to smile, to meditate and to pray. How about you?

It is important to re-member what helps you to re-member! For I guarantee that the next time you are ill or unhappy you will move away from everything that supports you, strengthens you and inspires you. Indeed, you must already have moved away or you would not be so unhappy. How curious it is that we abandon our greatest sources of strength when we are stressed or challenged in some way. We tell ourselves, 'First I must work my problems out', and only then will we ask for help.

Remembering to remember 'now' is the key!

For four years I worked with the BBC as a counsellor and personal performance trainer. There was a church opposite the main building which had a prominent sign outside that never changed in all the time I was there. The sign read, '*O God, show me what is wrong with me*'. This was, I imagine, a call to worship. It often struck me that this church needed a new marketing manager!

I was once introduced to a truly beautiful prayer, the exact opposite of this church sign, which I believe offers a perfect example of how to re-member and re-connect to our true, unconditioned Self. It is a prayer by a woman called Macrina Wiederkehr, and it reads:

> *'O God, help me to believe the truth about myself,*
> *no matter how beautiful it is.*
> *Amen.'*[18]

This is real prayer. Try it. Give yourself seven days. Say this prayer each day, first thing in the morning, and then sit and listen for guidance. This prayer offers a wonderful frame of mind for re-membering and re-connecting to your unconditioned Self. As you take hope into your silence you will surely draw hope from that silence. Try this prayer for a week and you will see what I mean.

Seeing the Light!

> *First, you believe, and then you see the Light.*
> *Next, you go toward the Light. Soon, you*
> *are in the Light. Now you are the Light.*

Paul was a self-made multi-millionaire. He told me so the first time we met. He talked and I listened. He told me about his wife, his life, his work and, most of all, his children. 'I have three children who I love more than anything,' he said. 'I want to give them everything I didn't have when I grew up. I tell them constantly they can be what they want. I encourage them to strive, to work hard, to give everything every effort, to be the best they can. I always remind them

they can do better, they can give more, they can be more –
there are no limits.'

I listened to Paul talk about his children for almost thirty
minutes. Eventually, I asked, 'Paul, what are you trying to
tell me?' Paul paused a moment. He bowed his head. His
bullish confidence and upbeat mood vanished. I think I
even saw a tear. 'The problem is,' he said, 'my children hate
me. I have given them everything, and they hate me.'

'Have you ever told your children that they are wonderful, right now, just the way they are?' I asked Paul.
He obviously had not. 'Paul, your children do not need
to be told how great they are going to be; what they
really need is to be told how loved and how wonderful
they are *now*,' I said. I also suggested that by telling his
children how wonderful he thinks they are now he is also
investing wisely in their future.

Paul had only one hesitation: 'What if I tell them they
are complete and whole as you say and then they get
complacent!' We explored this common fear for a while.
'Would you have become complacent if your father had
ever once told you he loved you,' I asked. 'Certainly not,'
said Paul. 'Well, you have your answer then. See the Light
in your children now Paul. See the Light in them, for their
sake and yours. Trust in their Light, for their sake and yours.
See the Light,' I said.

As a psychologist, I had originally been trained to be a
problem spotter. In fact, initially, I prided myself on how
good I was at being able to spot people's weaknesses,
neuroses, fears and hang-ups. You see, I wanted to be a
really good psychologist, and, as everyone knows, a really
good psychologist is someone who can always find more
wrong with you than an average psychologist can!

My original training was, therefore, (1) to spot the problem you had that you were going to tell me about; (2) to spot the problem you had that you were *not* going to tell me about; (3) to spot the problem you had that you didn't even know about yet! That's how creative psychology can be – you come in with a few minor problems and you leave with some major ones!

Over time, I began to have a change of heart. I began to realise that the greatest psychotherapy of all is not in pointing out people's problems and failures, but rather in pointing people towards their Light. You see, I really do believe now that

a true healer helps you to re-member and re-connect consciously to your inner Light.

By 'Light' I mean your innate unconditional potential to be happy, to be loving, to be free of fear, to be creative beyond your greatest imagination. You can never really lose your Light because your Light is you – your unconditioned Self – but you can forget about it. This Light feels so real when you are happy, and so unreal when you are unhappy. Hence, the pain, the fear, the loneliness and the grief of unhappiness. When in darkness, we wonder if we will ever see Light again.

I can remember the exact day when I first realised the absolute necessity of being able to see the Light of the unconditioned Self in healing. I was at my Stress Busters Clinic, a clinic I had been running through the National Health Service in West Birmingham for a couple of years[19]. I looked out on a sea of people who had gathered for another two-hour session. This time I didn't actually see people, though. All I saw was a group of alcoholics, depressives, heart attack victims, cancer sufferers, drug addicts, AIDS victims, people suffering phobias, and one schizophrenic.

At first, I felt a wave of absolute hopelessness. I remember thinking, 'How can I help all these people – their problems are so huge and so completely different from one another?' It occurred to me that what I really needed to do was set up an individual clinic for each illness, a clinic for depression, a clinic for anxiety, etc. Before I could really panic, I instinctively said a quick prayer, 'Dear God, help me to see this differently.' Then, in true British fashion, I had a sip of tea. As I opened my mouth to speak, I quickly shut it again before any words could spill out. My mind was on to something. A new idea was formulating, coming through like a fax or e-mail. I had another sip of tea while the downloading continued.

It dawned on me that although these people's illnesses certainly appeared very different, they were in fact all symptoms of one single illness. Essentially put, these people were ill because they were unhappy. Each of them had somehow become unhinged from the happiness of their *unconditional Self*. I realised, therefore, that they had come not just to de-stress but to re-member and re-connect to happiness. They had come to see the Light.

Years earlier I had read the works of the Greek philosopher, Pythagoras, who had said, 'There is no illness, only ignorance'[20]. Now, at last, I was beginning to see that maybe the ignorance he was referring to was the forgetting and separating from the Light of our unconditioned Self. I also began to see that my work at Stress Busters was probably, like the Tower of Pisa, slightly off-centre.

Until that time, the emphasis of my work had been, like

my psychology training, problem-orientated. I had hosted days studying every illness, dis-ease and stress-related problem I could find. And, although I had mentioned happiness many times, I had never given a workshop specifically on happiness. The same was true for love, for peace of mind, for success, for joy. Now it occurred to me that if these people could remember how to be happy again, maybe they would not be ill. Sometime later, I wrote in my daily journal some words that I still call upon to this day for inspiration. They read:

Know Love; no fear
Know Joy; no pain
Know Light; no darkness
Know Wholeness; no dis-ease
Know Now; no past
Know Truth; no lies
Know God; no separation
Know Self; no other

A true healer takes into account any darkness, but their real task is to see the Light in their client so as to help the client remember and consciously re-connect to their own inner Light. In this way, both healer and client are healed together. Parenting is the same. The ultimate gift of a parent to a child is to care for the inner Light of a child until they can care for it themselves. True friends are friends who believe in you through thick and thin. They still see the Light in you even when your moods and behaviour are dark and low. Mentors, managers, leaders, visionaries, peacemakers and everyone who truly serves – they all see the Light.

CHAPTER TWO

꧁

Giving Up The Search

꧁

One day, at the beginning of another new session at the Stress Busters Clinic, I decided to try a completely new tack. The room was full. Thirty people or so were chatting, drinking tea, waiting for me to begin. 'Welcome everybody to Stress Busters. Have you had a good week since we last met?' I asked. 'Not bad,' said someone. 'Not too bad, thanks,' said another. 'Oh, can't complain,' came a voice from the back. This opening was not my new tack, by the way. That came next.

'What I would like you to do is tell everybody about your good week,' I said. I then asked the entire group to stand up, and I explained to them that I wanted them to meet each other one-to-one and share a piece of good news, anything happy, that had happened to them over the last seven days. The only rule was that they had to come up with a different piece of good news for each person they met.

I noticed that as I was explaining the game to the group,

most people had begun to stop breathing. The room was full of tension, nervous laughter, defensive postures and on-the-spot prayers like, 'Oh, God!', 'Christ!', 'Good Lord', and 'Heaven help us!'. 'What, you mean like twenty bits of good news in the last week?' asked someone. 'Yes, twenty or more things that made you smile, lifted your spirits, helped you feel good, and you were grateful for,' I explained. 'But what if you can't find anything?' asked someone. 'Let's start looking and then maybe we will begin to see,' I said.

What I had asked the group to do was very simple, yet highly significant. Most previous sessions at the Clinic had seemed to slip automatically into a round-up of bad news, setbacks and new problems. No report was ever made of good news and personal breakthroughs. And yet I knew people were benefiting from our time together. Indeed, the Stress Busters Clinic had won national recognition over the previous couple of years for its effective support and care.

Looking back, I see now it was as if we had all agreed to follow an unspoken rule of 'problems only'. Just like in my own psychology and psychotherapy training, we had put happiness and love on the back burner for the moment, and we were now fully preoccupied – and I have to say, strangely comfortable – with our problems. Worse than this, I also noticed from time to time that certain people in the group were competing for who had had the worst week.

In a sort of sad, macabre way, it was as if we were trying to prove our personal worth by how much suffering we were enduring. In our minds, an unofficial points system had developed along the way, i.e. five points for headaches, ten points for migraines, depression fifteen points, anxiety only seven points, but anxiety plus a phobia attack was worth twenty points! The more points, the more self-worth, plus more air-time in the group.

In fairness, I suppose we were only doing what we thought we were supposed to do, which is talk problems. That's what psychology is all about, isn't it? There was a strong overall reluctance to discuss happiness. The assumed rule in the Clinic was: if you have a problem, speak up; if you are happy, be quiet. Happiness didn't appear to have any value. No one had actually ever said happiness is allowed.

Now, for the very first time, everyone was talking about good news. By the end of the good news game, which I now call 'Blessings', the energy of the group had been transformed. Everyone looked like sunshine, radiating a spirit of warmth and joy that filled the room. One or two people had found the exercise close to impossible, but most people were truly astonished to find how much good news there was in their life.

Feedback from the good news game was spontaneous. 'That was wonderful,' said someone. 'Thank you,' said another. 'Great!' said someone else. One woman stood up and said, 'All of your good news helped me to remember all my good news that I had forgotten or overlooked.' Another woman said, 'I've had a far better week than I realised!' There was a natural pause, and then an old man called Graham, known by all at the Clinic for his simple wisdom, said, 'It has occurred to me that maybe we are all a lot happier and more blessed than we realise.'

Don't Give Up On Happiness

Happiness will always bring out the best in you. You were born to be happy. Happiness is natural. It suits you entirely. You look good and you feel good when you let happiness ooze from within you. Your step is light, your mind is free and your spirit soars when you let happiness happen. The whole world responds well to you.

When you are truly happy you are radiant and you function fully. Above all, you are loving, for the essence of happiness is love. You are also naturally kind, generous, open, warm and friendly. This is because where there is true happiness, there is no fear, no doubt, no anxiety. You are unrestrained and uninhibited. You are fully present, here now, and not lost in some past or future.

When you are truly happy you are on song and on purpose. You are also very real. It is, after all, impossible to be happy and play small, to be happy and hide, to be happy and inauthentic, to be happy and defensive. Indeed, the real reason why happiness feels so good is that when you are truly happy you are being your Self – your unconditioned, original Self.

Like a fragrance to a flower, true happiness is an expression of your unconditioned Self – the real You.

True happiness is also very attractive in that it literally attracts great things. Happiness, by its very nature, encourages trust, spontaneity, optimism and enthusiasm, all of which bring great gifts. In particular, when you dare to be happy, you find people instinctively gravitate to you and like you, though they may not know why. Maybe it's something to do with your smile. Whatever it is, your happiness is an inspiration and a gift to everyone. *Everyone benefits from true happiness – everyone benefits from your happiness.*

Not surprisingly, then, happiness is clearly very important to us. It is, along with love, *the* goal of life. Everybody wants to be happy. Can you think of anyone in your life who would genuinely refuse an offer of true happiness? No! The question is, then, if happiness is the common goal, why is happiness so uncommon in our world? Hands up, who knows more than three genuinely happy people? When I ask this question in a room full of a thousand people, I see only about five or six hands go up.

No one talks happiness. Happiness is edited out of most conversation. In my workshops I often ask participants to recall specific conversations on happiness that they have had with their parents. What follows is usually a profound silence. All parents want their children to be happy, but so few parents talk about happiness.

Also, judging by our day-to-day conversations with friends, family and colleagues, no one is happy; either that, or if they are, they are certainly not letting on. 'How are you?' we ask, when we greet one another. The replies arrive thick and fast – 'Not bad', 'Not so bad', and 'Not too bad'. Some slightly more creative people say:

'Could be better.'
'Could be worse.'
'Bearing up.'
'Oh, so-so.'
'Fair to middling.'
'Hanging in there.'

41

'Soldiering on.'
'Surviving.'
'Can't complain.'
'Mustn't grumble.'
'Okay.'
'I'm still here.'
'Don't ask.'
'Getting by.'
'Keeping my head above water.'
'Hanging by a thread.'
'No news is good news.'
'Not dead yet.'

How about that! I call this type of inane conversation 'Not-so-badder-itis'. It is like a 'near-life experience', as opposed to a 'near-death experience', in that there is no happiness, no sadness, no commitment, no nothing. In our fast and furious world, where no one appears to have the time to engage in mindful conversations, 'Not so bad' has become a learned response, a type of social shorthand. It's quick, it's easy, and we have no idea what we are talking about.

The point is, though, even when we do have the time, and even when there has been some good news, or we feel genuinely happy, we still respond with 'Not so bad'. We have given up talking about happiness. Furthermore, we have grown accustomed to hiding our happiness as if in fear. But what on earth are we so afraid of? What is there to fear about happiness?

I first became aware of the fear of happiness in my one-to-one psychotherapy private practice, where I experienced three repeating patterns with clients, patterns which my training had in no way prepared me for.

In the first pattern, I would help a person to address a particular fear or problem to the point of letting it go. Then, when I was convinced they were now ready to let go of their pain and be happy, they would suddenly stop coming. Without notice, they would disappear. All my telephone calls would go unreturned. Where I was able to follow up, my clients would most often say, 'I'm just too busy to come' or 'I've got no money'. The offer of payment later was always declined. Sometimes my clients would simply say, 'I'm just not ready'.

The second pattern I called 'the familiar devil', derived from the common saying, 'better the devil you know'. In this pattern, a client would get to the point where he or she was ready to let go and move on past something painful and destructive, only to decide at the very last minute to stay put. One client, Jonathan, came to see me after having a heart attack whilst working in a highly demanding and very unrewarding job. He spoke often of looking for a more fulfilling job, something that suited him better, once he was healthy enough to work again. Come the time, he went straight back to his old job. 'It's all I know,' he said.

Susan's case illustrated perfectly the third repeating pattern. Susan was single, in her late twenties, living with a boyfriend who was consistently abusing her both emotionally and physically. 'I have come to see you to get the strength to leave my boyfriend,' she told me on our first meeting. Susan did eventually leave her boyfriend, despite great hurt and fear to herself. Happiness *now* beckoned. Her friends had hardly got the celebrations underway, however, before Susan had moved in with a new boyfriend who also started to abuse her.

By witnessing these three patterns, I began to see that

helping people to resolve a problem is not the same thing as helping people to experience personal happiness. One obvious reason for this is that happiness is quite clearly much more than just the absence of pain or problems. More than that, though, I began to realise that until you develop a healthy conscious, creative and unconditional relationship to happiness you will always experience unhappiness and illness.

Facing Your 'Happychondria'

Happiness feels so natural and so normal to us, and yet we often relate to happiness as something special, odd, lucky, a bonus or a win. Instead of greeting happiness with open arms, as we would a dear and intimate friend, we shy away from happiness, our thoughts full of suspicion, doubt, cynicism and fear, 'waiting for the fall'.

Clearly, we want happiness, but we do not trust happiness. Certainly, we allow ourselves trickles of delight every now and then, but when the experience of happiness is more vivid, real and long term, we are often racked with self-doubt and thrown about by our fears. We doubt happiness as much as we doubt ourselves.

In short, we are afraid of happiness.

The greatest irony is that we are actually afraid of everything we like. For instance, according to fear, success will corrupt you, money is the root of all evil, fame will ruin you, love makes you blind, happiness is selfish, retirement will be the death of you. Strangely, *that which we most desire frightens us the most.*

'Happychondria' is the term I use to describe the fear of happiness, and, in particular, the utterly morbid superstitions we have gathered and placed before happiness. Happiness is so natural to our unconditioned Self, and yet our conditioning has somehow taught us to cloud our experience of happiness with endless misperceptions, fearful beliefs, false pre-requisites and unnecessary dogma.

The next time you experience genuine happiness, watch your thoughts awhile and see how unconditional you can be in your acceptance of this happiness. Notice, for instance, how your unconditioned Self rushes to greet this happiness, full of love and deep gratitude. Watch also, though, how your conditioned self may be tempted to question your happiness, to control it in some way, to hold it at arm's length, or even to tighten the grip for fear the happiness might fly away.

Have you ever noticed that when you are happy you think highly fearful conditioned thoughts like, 'watch for the fall', 'what did I do to deserve this?', and 'this is too good to be true'? Keep looking, and you may also notice other fears like, 'what have I forgotten?', 'this can't last', 'what's the catch', 'maybe I've left the stove on', 'I'll have to pay for this', 'unbelievable', 'did I lock the back door?', 'all good things must come to an end', 'there will be tears before bedtime', and more. Take a moment, before reading on, and add to this list if you can. Awareness of these fearful, limiting thoughts (plus a big smile!) is an important step to undoing them and outgrowing them.

When happiness happens, we experience a mix of great gratitude and nagging self-doubt. Fear's advice is, *when happy, hide it*. We are afraid to show our happiness for fear of being thought of as conceited, selfish, juvenile, or an irresponsible air-head, perhaps. We fear especially that too much happiness will endanger our professional status. Many people work in highly fearful, uncreative cultures, in which appearing to be happy twice in one week is definitely not good for the career.

We somehow have it wired up in our conditioned thinking that *happiness is blasphemy*. We fear that if we are too happy, then we will somehow upset others, draw envy, and invite rejection. We have come to believe that, the moment we step out of 'not-so-badder-itis' territory, we will be hated and persecuted for our happiness.

Not only have we learned to feel very afraid when we are happy, we have also learned to feel very guilty. Too much happiness, far from being seen as a gift for all, is targeted as an enemy that will lead to hedonism, no moral restraint, a collapse of values, no order or control, and the death of the world. It is as if we have learned to believe that happiness reveals an innate 'badness' rather than our natural unconditioned goodness. Furthermore, there is an implied fear that, if there is too little suffering, the world will not be able to work as it is!

We have also been taught to believe that whilst the gods will tolerate occasional happiness, anything over half an hour or so will evoke high payment at least and terrible wrath at worst! Fate is also a real kill-joy, it seems. Hence, when happy, we keep our fingers crossed, hold our breath, avoid walking under ladders and look out for lucky black cats.

The fear of happiness has been passed from generation to generation, each one carefully elaborating on the myths,

46

superstitions and trickery that went before. We too have played our part, so that now, according to 'happychondria', happiness no longer begets happiness; rather, happiness merely heralds the onset of further suffering. No wonder we have learned to be afraid of happiness.

Several years ago I had the pleasure of meeting and counselling a priest called Harold. Harold was about sixty-five years old at the time. He was medium height and medium build, his shoulders slightly hunched, as if he was carrying a weight of some kind. Harold had big bushy eyebrows, a half-smile and a face full of character lines. There was an air of sadness all around him.

'I have come to see you, Robert, because I am unhappy and I have been for a long time.' Harold had a wife, fifteen years younger, whom he described as 'lovely, lively and active'. 'We seem to be growing apart lately,' he said. In truth, Harold had been cutting himself off from the world. He felt increasingly isolated, unable to make much sense of anything, and very sad.

'Talk to me about happiness, Harold,' I said one day. It is too long ago for me to remember Harold's exact answer. I do remember him saying, though, 'Happiness is something I fully expect to experience through the grace of our Lord in the hereafter.' I asked him, 'What about before then? Is it acceptable for you to be happy before you die?' Harold always looked down at the floor when we talked. I could tell he was puzzled. 'I don't know,' he replied.

Because Harold was a Christian, I reminded him that the gospel of Jesus is a gospel of joy. I encouraged Harold to read again how the *New Testament* speaks of the 'joy of thy Lord', and how it refers to joy as 'the fruit of the spirit' and heaven as 'a kingdom of joy'. My challenge to Harold was that heaven is not a place in the sky, but rather, heaven is a choice, a consciousness available to him now. 'You can have heaven *now* if you like Harold, for heaven, like love and happiness, waits on welcome, not on time,' I said.

Harold and I met together quite a few times. Harold was a perfect gentleman. He would always express gratitude for our time together, and he would always nod profusely in agreement with everything I said. At least intellectually, he liked these 'new ideas' as he called them. I tried to convince him that my ideas were not so new. I remember Harold saying on one of our last visits together, 'I don't know Robert, maybe I am just not worthy of happiness.' Here, I believe, was the crux of the matter.

I do not know how much I was able to help Harold. I often think of him, though. He taught me so much. Not least, he taught me that unless we believe we are entirely worthy of happiness, we cannot accept happiness fully, for we will always attempt to question it, control it and ultimately push it away. In essence, happiness is perhaps the greatest challenge of all, then, in that

happiness challenges us to make peace with ourselves.

Undoing the Confusion

We are certain we want happiness, but we are confused about what happiness is.

How many times have you bought what looked like a ticket to certain happiness, only to discover later that the ticket was invalid? How many times have you chased something – a career, a relationship, a possession – absolutely convinced that happiness must be there, only to find that the happiness somehow went missing soon after you arrived? For a lifetime, *we work hard at happiness without ever really working out what happiness is.*

One very telling measure of how confused we have become about happiness is the language we use to convey our joy. Our language reveals our thinking, and our thinking is obviously very confused or we would not *use the language of pain to describe our joy*. Look at the following phrases, for instance:

> 'I had a hell of a time.'
> 'It was terribly good.'
> 'Like a house on fire.'
> 'What a blast.'
> 'To die for.'
> 'It was mad.'
> 'Bad!'
> 'Wild!'
> 'It was awfully nice.'
> 'It went frightfully well.'
> 'Crash hot!'
> 'Really wicked.'

49

'I nearly died!'
'Drop-dead gorgeous.'
'It was dead good.'
'Damn good.'
'So good it's a sin.'
'Dying to see you.'
'Let's get wasted.'
'Unreal!'

Our confusion is compounded by our *dis-illusion*. Our present perception of happiness has become clouded and misted up with the unresolved pain and disappointment of our past. Thus, we still dream of happiness, but we have also become afraid and cynical. Confusion reigns. It knows no bounds. The comedian, Woody Allen, reveals the full extent of our learned neurosis when he writes:

To love is to suffer. To avoid suffering one must not love, but then one suffers from not loving. Therefore, to love is to suffer, not to love is to suffer, to suffer is to suffer. To be happy is to love. To be happy then is to suffer. But suffering makes one unhappy. Therefore, to be unhappy one must love or love to suffer. Or suffer from too much happiness.

Somehow we appear to have lost our mooring to the happiness that is our unconditioned Self. Much in the same way humankind has so divorced itself from Mother Nature, we appear to have distanced ourselves from our own inner happiness to a point at which we are no longer really certain what happiness is. In fact, we feel so distanced that we even question the existence of an *inner happiness* for it feels so foreign, unreal and untrue.

Our confusion is conditioned. It is learned. It is a forgetfulness. It is in no way inherent to our unconditioned Self. To the unconditioned mind, happiness is natural; to the ego, or conditioned mind, happiness is special. To the unconditioned mind, happiness is within; to the ego, everything good is outside. To the unconditioned mind, happiness is constant; to the ego, happiness never lasts. To the unconditioned mind, happiness is free; to the ego, happiness requires suffering, sacrifice and payment.

In a nutshell, then, our conditioning has confused us. The conditioned mind is a confused consciousness. Thus, your conditioned self is not only confused about happiness, it is confused about *everything*, including love, life, God, purpose and your true identity. This learned confusion essentially takes three routes, as shown in *Figure 2*.

Route one is about our misperceptions of what happiness really is. What is happiness? Is it physical pleasure, a worldly pursuit, a cognitive choice, a spiritual joy, or something else? Route two is about the unnecessary conditions and pre-requisites we have created that say happiness must first be 'earned', 'worked for' and 'deserved'. Route three is about the fearful beliefs we have about happiness, i.e. our 'happychondria'.

All of your conditioning about happiness is both learned and unreal. In fact,

> **nothing real stands between you and your happiness, only illusion and your own confusion.**

Figure 2

I know that many times you have felt as if happiness is so very far away from you, somewhere on the other side of the world perhaps, or even on another planet. I have experienced the same myself many times. Although these painful moments feel very real, it is important to realise that they are not the truth. This pain is illusory (i.e. it is not the truth about you). Indeed, *all pain comes from holding on to illusions about your Self.*

After spending several years dedicated to the study of happiness, I now know that there is, in truth, no distance between us and our happiness. I believe, therefore, that the healing journey is not a physical journey as such. Rather, it is a journey of consciousness, of truth emerging from illusion, of light dawning through darkness, of love replacing fear. This journey is an unfolding of that which is already within.

To be happy, therefore, you must first be willing to undo

and un-learn your misperceptions, false conditions and fearful beliefs. I have two friends, Eddie and Debbie Shapiro, both wonderfully enlightened healers, who describe this undoing process as 'Undoism'. I remember well the first time Miranda and I went to a gathering of theirs in the heart of the English countryside. From the front of the room, Eddie proclaimed, 'I have a new religion for you – "Undoism" – unlearning your fears of joy!'[1]

Still Getting There!

One of my clients, Michael, was a perfect example of what psychologists sometimes call 'the successful malcontented'. He was rich, famous, powerful, middle-aged and deeply unhappy. All of his life he had 'gone for *it*' but had never in his opinion ever quite 'got *it*'. That was why he had come to see me. We met maybe a dozen times. We made quick progress.

It was on our last session together that I asked Michael, 'What is the most important lesson you have learned about happiness?' Michael paused. He did not speak for a full two minutes or so. Then he smiled. 'In my twenties, I worked so damned hard I hoped I'd be happy in my thirties; in my thirties, I struggled every day so that I might be happy in my forties; in my forties, I sacrificed everything so as to be happy in my fifties. Now that I am fifty, I don't want to wait until my sixties! All my life I have been struggling and searching for happiness, instead of just being happy. I am ready to give up the search and be happy *now*.'

The search for happiness has brought with it much unhappiness.

Since the beginning of time, we have searched the world for our happiness. Over the centuries we have listened to countless stories of the Holy Grail, the Philosopher's Stone, Excalibur, the Golden Fleece, the Ark Covenant, secret manuscripts of truth, hidden sacred temples, universal elixirs, soul mates, alchemy and magic, pots of gold at the end of rainbows, yellow-brick roads, and more.

All of these stories testify to a belief in a happiness 'out there' and to a distinct absence of happiness within. This is where fear enters. Indeed, the source of all our fears stems from the erroneous belief, *happiness is somewhere else.*

So convinced are we that the world holds our happiness, we roam the earth hunting down anything that looks like happiness. We strive, we struggle, we suffer more than our neighbour, more than our parents, more than anyone we know in an effort to get ahead. The more we get ahead, the more we lose the heart of happiness in the process. In other words, *the more we pursue happiness, the more we forget how to be happy.*

With our almost exclusive focus on the world, Self-knowledge is eclipsed by the need for world acknowledgement; authentic Self-expression is tempered by a need for approval and popularity; Self-realisation is sacrificed as we bid to make the world realise how deserving we are of happiness. Gladly we sell our soul to the world, for we believe the soul has nothing to offer and the world has everything.

So addicted do we become to the pursuit of happiness we will justify any means to 'get there'. We will cheat, lie, steal, even murder. Soon the pursuit of happiness becomes the goal rather than happiness itself. A further irony is that

as we become even more strongly addicted to the pursuit of happiness, we are in no way prepared for happiness when it happens.

Look at the society and the lifestyles we have created. We are too busy to be happy *now*. We are in too much of a hurry to be happy *now*. We are too focused on our bright futures to be happy *now*. We haven't enough time to be happy *now*. Our schedules won't allow us to drop out of the race and be happy *now*. We are too busy 'getting there', and yet, the more we chase happiness, the more it flees.

The pursuit of happiness is our greatest mistake[2]. It is a fabrication, an illusion, a lie, an invention of the ego or conditioned Self, that believes everything good is outside. The world does not have your happiness; you have your happiness. Certainly, events, experiences and people can help you to recover your happiness, if you let them, but they cannot give you what you are refusing to see in yourself.

The pursuit of happiness is essentially the denial of happiness. And, in effect,

the pursuit of happiness must always fail because it is based on a lie – happiness is not outside you.

Until you change the belief that *happiness is somewhere else*, you will only ever experience a life in which you are always 'getting there' but are never quite 'there'! You will always be striving, but never arriving. You will always be looking, but never seeing. You will always be busy, and you will never be at rest. How can you afford to rest if you insist on believing peace is not already within you?

One more thought. Has it ever occurred to you that the pursuit of happiness stems, deep down, from a lack of Self-acceptance? In other words, *whatever it is you pursue, be it peace, happiness, love or God, is what you currently cannot accept.* Thus, you pursue happiness because (1) you cannot accept it for your Self right now; (2) you cannot accept that it may already be in your Self – your unconditioned Self.

It is ironic that the only joy you ever experience whilst pursuing happiness is when you very occasionally allow yourself to rest, relax and stop pursuing happiness. Think what joy you would experience if you dared to stop pursuing happiness completely. Think how fearless you would be, how creative and at peace you would be, and how free you would be to enjoy the world more fully, if you were to stop pursuing happiness and simply start accepting and allowing happiness to happen.

Just One More Thing!

Happiness is not in things;
happiness is in you.

The most significant education of my childhood had nothing

to do with my school. School was academic. It was my family who taught me the most valuable lessons of life, and most especially my grandparents.

The marriage of my mother and father shouldn't have happened according to many. It was a marriage of 'wealth and poverty', not to be confused, by the way, with *War and Peace*! My mother was born into the English aristocracy, the landed gentry, a family of the British Empire. She was young and beautiful. My father was not what my mother's family had in mind for their daughter. Not least, he worked for a living. His family was distinctly working class.

Everyone had a theory about my parents' marriage: it was ill-advised, blessed, wrong, true love, doomed from the start, an act of rebellion by my mother, opportunism by my father, and so on. For marrying my father, my mother was instantly cut off from her financial heritage, as both punishment and caution, I suppose.

Lack of money was a recurrent theme of my childhood. Three memories stand out in particular – one was a string of rented accommodations, including a miserable one-bed unit in a heavily vandalised tower block situated next to a busy railway line; another was being invited by mum and dad to attend an emergency family financial budget meeting on the eve of my eleventh birthday; and another was the huge dirty, ripped, brown leather sofa we had picked up from an auction for fifty pence. That sofa was our pride and joy.

Visiting both sets of grandparents was a bewildering experience. My father's parents lived on the south coast of England, in a town called Seaford, near Brighton. They lived in a council flat over a fish and chip shop. I remember three smells in particular – (1) cigarettes – my grandparents smoked like chimneys; (2) Guinness – my grandpa loved it; (3) the stale smell of old oil from the fish and chip shop down below. We would spend many of our summer holidays with my father's parents.

My mother's parents lived in the heart of the English countryside in Twyford, near Winchester. We would visit much more regularly, almost every other weekend, as we lived only a few miles away. Granny and grandpa lived in a huge mansion with acres of gardens, farmland all around, a beautiful river and an exotic kitchen-garden full of peaches, nectarines, strawberries, raspberries, goose-berries and more. The gardens were so beautiful they were often opened to the public. My mother had two elder sisters and one elder brother who lived in equally beautiful stately homes. We would visit them every now and then. The disparity between 'us' and 'them' was truly shocking and bewildering.

One side of my family appeared to have everything the world could offer, and the other side of my family appeared to have very little indeed. And yet I swear, with hand on heart, *there was no more happiness in those huge mansions than there was in that little council flat*. On the contrary, the laughter I remember most bounced off the walls of the council flat and not the mansions.

Please note, I am not suggesting as some people do that money makes you miserable. I carry no 'Money is the root of all evil' banners. On the contrary, I appreciate money greatly! What I did learn, however, from a very early age indeed, is that no amount of money can make you happy. More precisely, I would say, *money can encourage you to be happy, but it cannot make you happy*[3].

This leads me to another very important principle of

happiness that forms a central part of my teaching at The Happiness Project:

**Nothing in the world can make you happy;
everything in the world can encourage you
to be happy.**

We live our life in the hope that *just one more thing* will complete our happiness. The ego's conditioned thought is *something is missing*. And so we look for the missing piece to bring us salvation. And, yet, no matter how many *things* we purchase, gather and collect, we still feel as if something is missing. Indeed, there is – the thing that is truly missing is the unconditional awareness that nothing is missing. We are, in truth, complete and whole already.

Nothing can make you happy if you will not accept for yourself that happiness rests within you. You see:

I know people with dishwashers who are not happy.
I have met people with Nicam stereo sound television sets, complete with remote control, who are absolutely miserable.
I know men who wear Armani and still feel inferior.
I know women who can afford to buy a dozen Gucci watches but still have no time for themselves.
I have friends who are married and happy, and I have friends who are married and unhappy.
I have friends who are famous and loved by millions, and yet they cannot bear to love themselves; I have friends who can afford a house-cleaner, but still all their life is a chore.

I have counselled people with extreme wealth, and yet they feel as if they have nothing.

I have worked with directors of vast international corporations who are still looking for their first really meaningful achievement.

I have friends who hoped parenthood would bring happiness – to some it did and to some it did not.

I know women who wear real diamonds, but still have no real sparkle in their lives.

I know men who drive sports cars to nowhere in particular.

It is the conclusion of the most extensive psychology and sociology research into happiness, or 'subjective well-being' as it is termed, that *nothing can make you happy.* Just as it is true that the pursuit of happiness fails to make you happy, so too does materialism fail to make you happy. Social psychologist David Myers has written an excellent study called *The Pursuit of Happiness,* in which he collates much of the most recent research into the how of happiness. He concludes:

> . . . whether we base our conclusions on self-reported happiness, rates of depression, or teen problems, *our becoming better-off over the last thirty years has not been accompanied by one iota of increased happiness and life satisfaction.* It's shocking, because it contradicts our society's materialistic assumptions, but how can we ignore the hard truth: *once beyond poverty, further economic growth does not appreciably improve human morale.* Making more money – the aim of so many graduates and other

American dreamers of the 1980s – does not breed bliss.[4]

Perhaps you have heard the old joke – 'Nothing makes me happy: I've tried poverty and wealth and they've both failed!' Materialism is not bad or evil, it is simply not enough to replace the happiness within. The world is not here to meet your needs; the world is here to show you you have no needs.

When people are depressed they often say, 'Nothing makes me happy.' This is the truth! Indeed, the first stage of depression is very often dis-illusion with the world. The world gives us the appearance of happiness, but not the source. It is like a hyped-up, glossy holiday brochure that fails to deliver. The way out of depression is therefore to know (1) the world cannot make you happy; (2) your happiness exists within.

To sum up, nothing can actually make you happy, but everything can encourage you to choose happiness. Money can't buy you happiness, but it can certainly help you choose happiness. A sense of security is important, but again it is no real pre-requisite or guarantee of happiness. Health helps, but it cannot make you happy. Exercise can inspire well-being, and it is highly recommended[5]. So too is a good diet[6] and a healthy sleep pattern[7]. However, it is possible to be physically fit, full of vitamin C, have eight hours of sleep, and still feel miserable. Nothing can *make* you choose happiness. Choosing happiness is your function.

There is also a reverse of the principle that *nothing in the world can make you happy; everything in the world can encourage you to be happy*. And that is,

> *nothing in the world can make you sad;*
> *everything in the world can encourage you to*
> *be sad.*

The world cannot take away from you your right to happiness or sadness. The world may often appear to be trying very hard to take this choice away, but truly it cannot. Events of life can so conspire that you may lose sight of this choice, but never is the choice destroyed. In truth, the decision to be happy or sad always rests with you, whether you can see it or not. It is when we temporarily lose sight of this choice that we must ask for help.

Happiness is a Decision Only You Can Make

Whenever I meet somebody new away from work – on a golf course, at a party, or on holiday, perhaps – conversation usually gets around to the 'So, what do you do?' question. I often hesitate to answer, but I usually end up saying, 'I study the psychology of happiness'. What tends to follow is a very long, profound silence, several nonplussed looks, some awkward body language, and, eventually, a comforting word of reply such as 'Oh' or 'Gosh!' or 'That's nice'. Often I am also asked, 'But isn't happiness just happiness?'

Society parades three broad ideas about happiness: (1) happiness is luck; (2) happiness is circumstance; (3) happiness is a decision.

The Oxford Dictionary of English defines happiness as

'fortunate; lucky; feeling or expression of satisfaction'. I have interviewed thousands of people about happiness over the years for various radio and television programmes, and always the most common answers to the question 'What is happiness?' are 'Winning the lottery', or 'Winning on the horses', or 'Winning the football pools'. Happiness appears to be a bet, and luck is the answer.

The problem with the belief that *happiness is luck*, is that there is no role left for you to play in your own life. With luck as your great hope, your life and your happiness is on hold whilst you wait for the dice to roll your number. Luck denies you any responsibility or influence on how your life may turn out. Your life is determined for you, not by you. Most often those people who gamble on luck see themselves as unlucky victims of the world.

The second view, that *happiness is a circumstance*, is very common. Certain circumstances, particularly those you judge to be 'good' and 'right', can be satisfying, but once again I would refer you to the principle that *nothing in the world can make you happy; everything in the world can encourage you to be happy*. In other words, there is no one circumstance that can completely guarantee happiness.

The belief that *happiness is a circumstance* also suggests, as with luck, that the attainment of happiness is ultimately out of our hands. In other words, your happiness is 'good' only so long as you judge that the circumstances in your life are 'good'. But what happens to your happiness when you spill red wine on your shirt, when your car breaks down, or when your child crams another ginger biscuit into the video player? How strong is your happiness?

I once made friends with a man called Christopher after spending a day training staff at a local hospice. Christopher was 108 years old. He was the oldest and most lively patient on the ward. At his last birthday party I asked Christopher, 'What is the secret of life?' I will never forget his reply, both for its humour and its wisdom. He said, 'Well, Robert, I tell everyone that the first one hundred years of life are definitely the most challenging – after that it gets easier! I also tell people that life is 10% circumstance and 90% your response to circumstance.'

The view that, *happiness is a decision* is both radical and true. I was once given a quotation by a workshop participant which I like very much. The words belong to a gentleman called John Homer Miller:

> **Circumstances and situations do colour life, but you have been given the mind to choose what the colour shall be.**

Life is powerful, but your thoughts about life are even more powerful. In one of my books, *Living Wonderfully*, I wrote:

> *There is a fantastic force in life that has a miraculous power to transform fatigue into energy, despair into delight, and anxiety into action. This force can make 'bad' things 'good', and 'wrong' things 'right'. An 'upset' can become a 'set-up', a 'misfortune' can lead to 'fortune' and a 'failure' can become a prelude to 'success'. This miraculous force has the power to decide.*
>
> *The great news is that you are perfectly entitled to use this fantastic force, if you so choose. If you do, you may well find that, quite miraculously, obstacles turn into opportunities, adversity into advantage, breakdowns into*

breakthroughs, and unhappy endings into bright new begin-
nings. This force, if you haven't already guessed, is the
power of thought.[8]

The second half of the twentieth century has seen a rapid
rise in the number of cognitive schools of psychology which
very much support the idea that happiness is a decision[9]. In
other words, *whatever the picture, it is your frame of mind that*
ultimately counts. Circumstances can be helpful, attitude is
crucial, for as Hugh Downs once wrote:

A *happy person is not a person in a certain set*
of circumstances, but rather a person with a
certain set of attitudes.

The perception that *happiness is a decision* affirms that attitude is first, circumstance is second. It teaches you that
whatever is happening, you always carry the casting vote
when it comes to happiness, success, love and peace of
mind. Sometimes this is easy to remember; other times it
is not so easy. Once again, it is when you forget that you
must ask for help.

Happiness is a decision feels good and empowering, but
even this philosophy offers a limited perception of true
happiness. For example, have you ever thought what happens to happiness when you are low and your attitude is
suffering? Does happiness disappear like a pathetic wisp of
smoke? Can happiness be pulled around so easily by the
world? Is happiness really that weak?

Contrary to popular belief, true happiness is not a fickle,
little something, a dizzy little air-head, that finds it hard to
keep a commitment, always coming and going, appearing

and then disappearing, waving 'Hello!' one minute and then shouting 'Goodbye' the next. True happiness is faithful – it does not and it cannot leave you.

True happiness is constant, not transient; it is strong, not weak. Try not to think of happiness as something external that travels to you or away from you, but think of happiness as a potential you carry within you always – a potential you are, in any given moment, either opening to or withdrawing from. In truth,

> *happiness does not come and go, what comes and goes is your attunement to happiness.*

Above all, my work has taught me that, no matter how much pain you are in, how low, how hurt, how hopeless, how consumed by anger, how bitter, how fearful or how awful you feel, the potential to experience peace and happiness never goes away. Just as clouds in the sky can eclipse the sun but not destroy it, so too can fear and pain eclipse your happiness but not destroy it. The potential for happiness is with you permanently. Happiness is only ever a thought away.

The reason for this is that happiness is the very nature of your unconditioned Self. Happiness is the make-up of existence itself. Thus, happiness is not a peak experience, it is central. It is not the top of the mountain, it is the heart of the mountain. As you throw off your conditioning, you reveal a joy that exists independent of the world. I think the writer J. Donald Walters described this joy beautifully when he wrote, *'It is the gold of our inner nature, buried beneath the mud of outward sense-cravings.'*

This joy is not in you, it is you. I remember being deeply moved reading a passage in *A Course In Miracles* which highlighted this idea. It states:

> *It is hard to understand what 'The Kingdom of Heaven is within you' really means. This is because it is not understandable to the ego, which interprets it as if something outside is inside, and this does not mean anything. The word 'within' is unnecessary. The Kingdom of Heaven is you.*

A more accurate perception of happiness, then, is that happiness is the nature of your unconditioned Self. Hence,

> ***when you are truly happy, you are being your Self.***

Rumi, the Holy Grail, and Your True Identity

The great Sufi mystic and poet, Rumi, told a story of how he once knocked on the door of his beloved God. 'Who's there?' came the answer. 'It is I, your lover, Rumi,' he said. From inside came the voice, 'Go away, there is no room for the two of us in here.' Rumi left, completely dispirited. He meditated and he prayed, and later he returned to the house of his beloved once more and knocked again. 'Who is it?' the beloved asked. 'It is You.' With a welcome, the door was thrown wide open[10].

When we chase happiness we are really chasing our unconditioned Self, for the experience of true happiness is really the experience of the Self. The world, with all its transitory pleasures, cannot make up for that which is always within you. The more you can accept the idea that happiness is your nature, the more joyful will be your experience of the world. *With less needs, you will be more free.*

The author, John Pepper, writes a beautiful passage in his book, *How to be Happy,* that I cannot improve upon. He states:

> *What we do know is that when we have travelled the world over in search of the Holy Grail, ransacked the texts of the saints and sages for clues as to its whereabouts, pleaded with the night to yield it to us, abased ourselves in rituals, followed the light paths of romantic love and relationship and the dark ones of drugs and disorder, and done the million and one things it appears we have to do before finally we grind to a halt in exhaustion, our happiness still tantalisingly out of reach; then we see with a snort of absurdity that there is nowhere left to reach out to; that all the words have gone. The running, brother and sister, is done. The answer is contained here in this frail being in this dark night on this lasted heath; here or nowhere. The Holy Grail is us.*[11]

Every time you say 'yes' to happiness you are saying 'yes' to your unconditioned Self. By making it your intention to be happy, you are throwing off all of the defences, doubts and fears you have learned to value. You are letting go of the pain of your past, pain that would keep you in your past and would prevent you from experiencing happiness *now*.

Over the years I have created many prayers and affirmations that help to strengthen the intent to be happy and free. Intention is the key. One prayer that is a particular favourite of mine is addressed to the God that sits in the centre of your unconditioned Self. It reads:

Dear God,
I know not by myself how to be truly happy.
Teach me, in this moment, how to allow the
spirit of true happiness to shine through.
In this moment, I give to You all my fearful
misperceptions of happiness.
In this moment, I give to You all the false
conditions I have placed between myself
and happiness.
And in this moment, I give to You my fear
of happiness.
Teach me, Dear God, to accept happiness
easily, effortlessly and naturally.
Teach me, Dear God, to radiate happiness
easily, effortlessly and naturally.
Teach me, Dear God, to accept and radiate
happiness in equal measure.
So be it.

Welcome to the Laughter Clinic!

About three years after setting up the Stress Busters Clinic, I was ready to make a radical change in my work, which had so far been very problem-focused. I followed a philosophy of, first resolve all problems, and see about happiness later.

Now, a new philosophy was emerging of putting happiness first. I was beginning to see that

making a whole-hearted commitment to being happy is a powerful medicine.

Happiness is not just the absence of problems; happiness is the power that helps you heal your problems. And if illness and dis-ease are symptoms of unhappiness, then surely a return to happiness *now* will help you to heal. I was beginning to see that, just as a block of ice will melt if you expose it to the sun, so too will our fears disperse before our inner happiness. Above all, happiness helps us to be unconditional and free once more.

The upshot of this change was that in September 1991 I opened the doors to the first ever official Laughter Clinic in Great Britain. I received the backing of the government and the National Health Service to set up a clinic that focused first and foremost on natural, unconditional medicines of love, laughter, happiness and joy[12].

Our approach was four-fold – (1) we would run at least one workshop a week for members of the public on anything to do with unconditional happiness; (2) we would collect, collate and make available as much research on happiness as possible from the fields of medicine, psychology, philosophy and religion; (3) we would hold professional training events for any health professionals who would like to develop their work; (4) we would spread messages of love, joy and laughter through the world's 'more bad news' media of television, radio and press.

Within a month of opening, the Laughter Clinic had received over five hundred enquiries. This compared to less than ten enquiries during the first month of the Stress Busters Clinic. We were overwhelmed by people's enthusiasm and interest. The Laughter Clinic had caught people's imagination. This new approach obviously appealed. The Laughter Clinic ran for three years before it became known, as it is today, as The Happiness Project.

The workshops were an instant success. Well over one thousand events have now been run through The Happiness Project, addressing audiences of five or six people to a thousand or more. Several workshops became very popular, such as *Angels Can Fly Because they Take Themselves Lightly*, which looks at the art of Self-acceptance; *How To Be So Happy You Almost Feel Guilty, But Not Quite!*, which looks at the relationship between happiness and self-esteem; *Happiness Is A Way of Travelling* which focuses on happiness *now*; and *Let There Be Laughter*, which looks at the relationship between spirituality and joy[13].

Well over twenty thousand doctors, nurses, psychologists, counsellors and other therapists have attended professional training held by The Happiness Project. We have also contributed directly to several thousand media features around the world.

One of the peak experiences for me personally was in August 1996, when the BBC broadcast a 40-minute QED documentary on my work entitled 'How to be Happy', which followed three volunteers, Carol, Dawn and Keith, as they took my 'Eight Week Personal Happiness Programme'. Approximately five million viewers tuned in that night to see the progress Carol, Dawn and Keith each made, as verified by independent scientists who conducted a battery of extensive physiological and psychological tests[14].

I have enjoyed great help and support through the years.

My wife, Miranda, has helped to evolve the project in countless ways. More recently, my brother, David, has helped to manage both The Happiness Project and another of our projects called The Deep & Meaningful Training Company. The Happiness Project is also blessed to have great workshop facilitators in Ben Renshaw and Alison Atwell. The list goes on!

The Happiness Project has been, and still is, a most marvellous journey. I now see how the study of happiness is really a most intimate journey of Self-discovery. By looking so closely at happiness, particularly the desire for happiness and at times the resistance to happiness, we can help ourselves and others no end.

CHAPTER THREE

✵

Being Good Enough

✵

Claire had spoken most eloquently for 45 minutes about everything that was wrong with her. Eventually, I was moved to interrupt her pattern of thought: 'What do you love about yourself Claire?' I asked. 'What?' she replied. 'Objectively speaking, what is there to love about you?' Claire looked stunned. Now there were no words, only a bemused smile. 'Can you answer my question?' I asked. 'I don't know,' she said. 'No one has ever asked me to think that way before.'

I have seen many hundreds of clients over the years through my work with the clinics, my private practice and The Happiness Project. *In one way,*

> *every client was different and yet in another way they were all the same.*

Someone who is experiencing alcoholism, for instance, looks very different to someone who is experiencing anorexia. Similarly, someone who is experiencing depression looks very different to someone who has just survived a heart attack. And someone with agoraphobia looks very different to someone who feels totally stressed, and so on. They all look different, their conditions have different names, and, yet, deep down, their illness is the same.

No *dis-ease* happens by itself. Alcoholism does not happen by itself. Alcoholism is an effect, not a cause. It is a symptom, not an illness. Alcoholism is not the primary *dis-ease*; the primary *dis-ease* is the excessive self-judgement and constant self-criticism that pressures someone into taking a drink in the first place. The same is true, in one degree or another, of depression, stress, burnout and every other *dis-ease* ever 'named' by the medical and psychology professions. *Self-judgement is the dis-ease.*

It has been my experience that behind every pain, illness and unhappiness there is, hard at work, a fearful, relentless self-judgement, a distinct lack of love and acceptance, that perpetuates and complicates symptom after symptom. We do not get ill when we are wholly joyous because our joy is free of fear and judgement. Illness does ensue, however, when we judge, berate and criticise ourselves too harshly.

In one way or another, we are all the same in that

we all 'suffer' from a highly critical condition of C.S.J. – constant self-judgement.

Your unconditioned Self, being completely whole, has no need to judge. What is there to judge if all you know is wholeness and love? You know for yourself that when you feel completely happy and whole you do not think to judge. Wholeness is joyful, not judgemental. Thus, self-judgement is not natural to your unconditioned Self. It is learned. It belongs to the conditioned self, the ego, that suspects 'everything good is outside', that fears 'something is missing', that doubts 'Am I whole?'

You have learned to judge, criticise and condemn yourself. No matter how hard anyone else has ever judged you, you judge yourself the hardest. In fact, *you save your most severe standards, judgements, criticisms and punishments for yourself.* This constant self-judgement is something you have learned. It is not natural to you. Once, you were completely accepting of yourself and you were free, but now

no one is harder on you than you are.

Whilst your unconditioned Self continues to be free, your ego continues to judge and imprison itself. Your ego-self accepts nothing and judges everything, including happiness. Judgement is more than a habit, it is a way of life. Your judgements stain the windows of your perception. They filter everything you see so that, in truth, *you see nothing as it really is; you see only your judgements*. Thus, you do not see your own beauty, wholeness and Light within, you see only that you 'could do better' and 'could be more'.

Your conditioned self, or ego, judges, pushes, drives and punishes you so incessantly to compensate for its fear that deep down you are inadequate and incomplete, i.e. *your happiness is somewhere else*. This is not the truth, but you have learned to believe that it might be. Your ego is an addict. Indeed,

the belief in 'not being good enough' is your ego's greatest addiction.

The addiction to this belief feeds all other addictions, including over-dependency in relationships, extreme competitiveness, punishing social comparison, envy and jealousy, pained perfectionism, constant self-judgement, lack of assertiveness, and a desperate never-ending pursuit of happiness. This addiction also feeds other more physical addictions that provide temporary comfort and escape, such as over-eating, alcoholism, compulsive sex and illegal drugs.

Health, love and wholeness cannot flourish where there is constant self-judgement. The starting point, then, with any of my clients, is not necessarily the 'named' *dis-ease*, i.e. stress or depression, it is to address the underlying fears and judgements that may have given rise to that *dis-ease* in the first place. What I often end up prescribing is *a course in kindness, love and true self-acceptance* as an antidote to the learned criticism, fear, judgement and self-hatred of the ego. This is real healing.

In all my years, I have never had a client who suffered from being too kind to themselves!

The ego-self resists kindness, for it believes that judgement buys you something. It is convinced that without judgement you will 'fall behind' and become complacent, slack, disadvantaged, and, more particularly, 'wrong', 'bad', 'nothing' and 'not good enough'. *The cycle of constant self-judgement can only end with love.* In order not to be ill, we must learn to love again. All illness and unhappiness is, therefore, a call for love.

Like my client Claire, I was equally stunned when I was first asked, 'Robert, what do you love about you?' I was at a seminar on health and healing at the time, and I remember vividly how that simple question seemed to set a million chemical reactions bursting instantaneously and simultaneously through my body; my throat went dry, my heart skipped several beats, I stopped breathing, I began to perspire, my stomach churned, my bladder felt full all of a sudden, I couldn't speak, and for all I know my ears probably started to flap as well!

Self-acceptance is as natural to your unconditioned Self as constant self-judgement is to your ego. You must choose between your conditioning and your freedom. Until you are willing to accept your Self – your unconditioned Self – you will not be able to accept all that you long for. The happiness, the peace and the love you crave cannot happen without Self-acceptance.

Home Alone: horror film or love story?

> 'All men's miseries derive from not being able
> to sit quiet in a room alone.'
> Blaise Pascal

We each of us experience moments in our life which become turning points. I had one such turning point one weekend whilst in my second year of studying Communications. I was nineteen years old at the time, and what happened to me that weekend was to change my life forever.

Weekends are everything to students. It's a time for dates, dinners, parties, friendship, bands, going home, romance, being cool, being wild, being whatever you want. Looking back, I recall how most weeks, from Wednesday afternoon onwards attention would turn to the forthcoming weekend. 'What are you going to do?', 'Who are you seeing?', 'Have you been invited to the party?', etc.

I think it was one Thursday morning when I first began to panic a little. My friend Avanti told me he was going to be away for the weekend. He was taking a trip to London. I also found out later that morning that Philip was going home to Lancashire, James was off somewhere and Paul was going to an all-day 'Fight for Peace' event. By Friday afternoon I realised all of my friends, without exception, would be out of Birmingham for the weekend. Now I was really panicking.

I remember going home on Friday afternoon and phoning around looking for anybody to spend some time with that night. First, I tried the 'A' list of friends, then the 'B' list, and then the list of people I barely knew – 'Hello, it's Robert here. Robert Holden. Robert Holden with brown hair, six foot tall, sits at the back in psychology . . .' No one, absolutely no one, was available. Around 7 o'clock that evening I eventually had to face what to me was a terrifying concept – *time alone with myself*.

The idea of a little bit of time 'home alone' I could handle, but an entire weekend, an entire sixty-five hours until my first class on Monday – that was terrifying! Until now, I had deliberately planned my entire life in such a way as to ensure that I was never left alone with myself for too long. Initially, I was afraid, then I became a little panicky, and finally I was completely terrified. It was like I was in a horror movie!

I remember thinking to myself, 'Something is not quite right here. Surely I shouldn't be this frightened to be with me!' It also occurred to me that if I found the prospect of spending time with me to be so very awful, why would it be reasonable to expect anyone else to find that same prospect wonderful? I knew I was in deep trouble.

It was the decision I made next that was to change my life forever. I decided to stop running from myself. I took the plug out of the television set, I then also unplugged the radio, the hi-fi, and the phone. I then went and lay on my bed, and stared up at the ceiling. I soon began to cry and cry and cry. I cried for so long that I remember having to drink some water to rehydrate! I felt wave upon wave of what I can only describe as self-hatred wash over my body. My stomach in particular felt awful. I barely slept that night.

All through Saturday morning, I continued to struggle and wrestle free from my own company. The temptation to watch television, listen to the radio or call my family was at times overwhelming, but I knew somehow this would only be a distraction. I felt as if these feelings of self-doubt and self-hate had been chasing after me all my life, and now, finally, I didn't want to run any more.

I took one breath at a time, and one feeling at a time. I simply decided to watch every awful judgement and feeling I had stored up against myself. I decided there would be no more defences and no more distractions. The supply of awful judgements and criticisms seemed inexhaustible. Still, I took one breath at a time, and one feeling at a time. I also said a lot of prayers.

It was on Sunday afternoon, when time had already become a blur, that I eventually began to experience what I would call a miracle. I became aware of a stillness in the apartment. I was also feeling strangely peaceful. This peace seemed to emerge from the same place in my belly where all the pain had come from. As each moment passed, I felt more and more peaceful. For some reason, I no longer felt lonely being on my own.

For the first time in my life I found my own company to be totally acceptable. I was not just putting up with me, I was actually liking being with me. I even remember thinking how lovely it would be if Monday morning could be put back a little! I emerged that weekend from what felt like an emotional fever in which I faced, with grace, some very dark fears. At last I knew what it felt like to be happy with myself.

You And The #1 Happiness Principle

The story of my weekend serves to illustrate a most funda-mental principle of happiness, a principle that is at the heart of The Happiness Project's philosophy. This #1 Happiness Principle states that

unless you are happy with yourself, you will not be happy.

This Principle quite clearly has some far-reaching implica-tions. It is pivotal to the whole subject of happiness. To understand it better, it is possible to divide the #1 Happiness Principle into four main parts. Each part throws light on the fundamental importance of Self-acceptance and inner peace for experiencing happiness *now*[1].

1. 'What You Do'

Part one of the #1 Happiness Principle predicts quite unequivocally that

> *unless you are happy with yourself, you will not be happy with what you do.*

Your ego projects its self-judgements on to every one of your achievements, without exception. Thus, your judgements about you and about what you do will always be identical. If, therefore, you judge yourself as 'not good enough', whatever you do, no matter how good it looks to others, will never ever be quite 'good enough' to you. No amount of achievement can change this[2].

In my twenties, I was what you might call a typical 'high-achiever'. Two clinics, four published books, deputy editor of the country's leading holistic health journal, my own radio series, thousands of media features world-wide, hundreds of keynote conference speeches and workshops, were all added to my personal CV, which, like a bodybuilder's biceps, bulged rather too big!

Like many 'high achievers' it was my sincere hope that enough achievement would someday bring me a bit of peace and happiness. Some of my achievements were literally for the joy of it all; but most of my achievements were driven by a need to prove myself. Indeed, all through my twenties, I was so busy proving myself, I had no time to accept myself.

Success seemed like salvation. So I set out to be a success, hoping that enough success would drown out the noise of my ego. Achievement was meant to offer respite from my constant self-judgement and 'not good enough' script. At the very least, achievement kept me busy. Being busy is like a behavioural valium – you don't feel your feelings and you don't notice your judgements when you are busy 'doing'. You have to keep 'doing' though, or the self-hatred returns when you try to rest.

Achievement for the *joy* of it is healthy, for your motive is love and your worth is never questioned. Achievement because you *need* it is problematic. What I have slowly come to learn, only to forget again periodically is,

> ### *no amount of 'doing' can compensate completely for a lack of 'being'.*

Over the last few years, I have had the privilege of working with many highly accomplished people, particularly in the world of business, whose CV's bulge much bigger than my own. Time and time again I have witnessed how massive amounts of personal achievement still amount to 'nothing' as long as there is little or no Self-acceptance. Achievement, it seems, can be a wonderful boost to the ego, but

> ### *in no way is achievement a complete solution for low self-esteem.*

Go ahead and achieve by all means. It can be great fun,

especially when you do so for the joy of it. But make no mistake – *'X' amounts of achievement will not buy you 'X' amounts of happiness.* Indeed, no amount of achievement will do for you what you are not prepared to do for you, i.e. accept your Self. Achievement can be fun, but it is not salvation.

Happiness happens naturally when you change your mind about yourself, when you give up your conditioning and accept your Self – your whole Self. Once you can accept that you are indeed 'good enough', all of your achievements will also be 'good enough', but not until then.

2. 'Where You Are'

The second part of the #1 Happiness Principle focuses on the relationship between happiness and environment. It states that

> **unless you are happy with yourself, you will not be happy with where you are.**

Dawn was one of three people who agreed to be filmed by QED on my Eight Week Happiness Programme for the BBC documentary 'How to be Happy'. On our first meeting, she told me how she had moved house some thirteen times in recent years in search of happiness. 'I first moved to get as far away from my family as I could,' she said. 'I hoped that if I put some physical distance between me and my pain I would be free again, but wherever I moved to my pain came with me.'

Dawn had decided to take the Eight Week Happiness Programme because, in her words, 'Everywhere I moved to I was really happy, at first. But then the novelty would go, and the happiness soon wore off. The only problem with each new place was that I kept turning up there! I wasn't happy with me. I can see now that until I am happy with me, nowhere will be good enough.'

I explained to Dawn during our times together that,

> *healing is not about changing your address;*
> *healing is about changing your mind about*
> *yourself, i.e. giving up your self-judgements.*

A beautiful mansion adorned with priceless antiques may well inspire happiness initially, but this change of address cannot compensate completely for a lack of inner peace. It is certainly true that an environment may encourage peace of mind, but no environment can give you peace of mind[3].

Why is this? The answer lies in the understanding that *perception is projection*. How you see anything external to you is exactly how you see yourself. Each judgement about yourself muddies the lens of your perception so that everything you see is stained with that judgement. It was the philosopher, Immanuel Kant, who wrote,

> *'We see things not as they are, but as we are'.*

For as long as you judge yourself 'not good enough', then no mansion, no garden, no luxury yacht and no paradise five-star hotel will be totally satisfactory. At first, all may appear well, but that is because you are in wonder and you have forgotten to judge yourself. Once you are settled and all becomes familiar, then the self-judgements will darken the lens of your perceptions once more.

We search the world for a heaven on earth, yet heaven is not a physical place and neither is hell. Heaven and hell are states of mind. Guilt is hell, fear is hell, judgement is hell; heaven is love and Self-acceptance. Heaven and hell are in your mind, and your mind goes with you wherever you go. It was the English poet, John Milton, who wrote, *'The mind is its own place, and in itself, Can make a heaven of hell, a hell of heaven.'*[4]

It is precisely for this reason that the mystics of old kept telling their disciples –

to change the world, first change your mind.

My work with The Happiness Project does focus on one place in particular – not a physical place, but a spiritual place – a place right in the centre of your being. This place is your unconditioned Self. It is where the happiness you long for resides. In *A Course In Miracles* this place is referred to as 'The Changeless Dwelling Place':

There is a place in you where this whole world has been forgotten; where no memory of sin and of illusion lingers still. There is a place in you which time has left, and echoes of eternity are heard. There is a resting place so still no sound except a hymn to Heaven rises up to gladden God the Father and the Son. Where Both abide are They remembered, Both. And where They are is Heaven and is peace.

3. 'Who You Are With'

Part three of the #1 Happiness Principle offers a sobering thought about happiness and relationships, a thought that is expanded upon in Chapter Seven. It states that

> *unless you are happy with yourself you will not be happy with who you are with.*

This is a particularly sobering thought, especially for romantic relationships, not least because often the very reason we look to be with a partner is because we are not happy on our own! We search the world over, desperately looking for a partner who has a better opinion of us than we do. When we eventually find someone, we demand that they love us even if we do not love ourselves, and here we enter a catch 22 because, for as long as we cannot love and accept ourselves, we find it impossible to accept their love for us.

Relationships are deeply personal. They are far more personal than we often realise. The bottom line is,

> *your relationship with your Self sets the tone for every other relationship you have.*

To put it another way, *the way you relate to yourself ultimately determines (1) the way you relate to others; (2) the way others relate to you.* Your relationships with others mirror perfectly your relationship with your Self. In particular, you project your own self-criticisms on to others constantly. Usually, at first, you experience a honeymoon period with new friends, lovers, children and colleagues, where they can do no wrong; eventually, though, any unresolved self-judgements will re-surface and project outwards, causing much mayhem and separation.

When you feel whole and blissfully happy, you forget to judge other people. This is because you are not judging your Self. As soon as you lose sight of your own whole-ness, however, you judge yourself and everyone else. For as long as you believe you are 'not good enough', you will try to improve yourself and everyone else around you. In particular, your lover, your children and your friends will not be safe from you as you make it your mission to 'correct their faults'. How many sons have paid the price for their father's wretched self-esteem? How many partners have been abused because of their lov-er's own self-hatred? How perfect your loved ones are already, and how perfect you are already, if only you could but see.

Deep down, every opinion you have about somebody else is really only a projection of an opinion you have about yourself. Therefore,

eventually everyone must pay for your own self-hatred; either that or you change your mind about yourself.

You may find that every now and then a new person will enter your life who appears to love you even more than you love yourself. It happened to me when I first met Miranda, my wife. Very quickly, it became clear to me that she thought more highly of me than I did of myself. Ironically, it was also clear to me that I thought more highly of her than she did of herself. We tried so hard in those early days to sabotage our relationship and push each other away. The love we experienced was so great it shook our self-doubt and self-hate to the very core. Eventually it all came down to a simple choice – *accept our Self and love each other; hate our Self and separate*[5].

4. 'What You Have'

Part four of the #1 Happiness Principle takes you back again to the idea that *happiness is not in things, happiness is in us*. It states that

unless you are happy with yourself, you will not be happy with what you have.

Nothing is enough as long as you judge your Self to be 'not good enough'. Nothing can make up for a lack of Self-acceptance. The ego, created by a thought of lack, cannot ever be appeased and satisfied, it can only be dropped! You must leave behind your ego-conditioning if you are to return to the happiness of your unconditional Self.

No amount of purchases, products or possessions can give you peace of mind. Once again, they may well encourage you to be happy, but they cannot actually make you happy. Deep down we know this to be true, and yet we still keep trying to find a special 'thing' that will 'make us happy'[6].

The world is seriously into shopping! Shopping is the

number one pastime of the western world. It also appears to be the world's greatest hope for salvation. I love to shop – not quite as much as Miranda – but I do love shopping. I consider Miranda to be an advanced shopper. In fact, I'm sure she won't mind me saying that her capacity to keep on shopping is truly inspirational!

I am an impatient and insecure shopper. When I shop, I have to purchase. Miranda, on the other hand, can shop for hours without having bought a single thing, and she finds that fun. I can't do that. Shopping is wonderful, great fun, and, as Miranda keeps telling me, you can save a lot of money when you shop. What Miranda and I have both worked out, however, is that no amount of shopping can purchase joy. *Joy is not for sale.*

When it comes to true joy, the truth is,

true joy is not about changing your wardrobe;
true joy is about changing your mind, i.e. giving
up your self-judgements.

No single possession in the world can make you peaceful. Peace of mind is something you must choose for your Self. Most of us do not believe this at first. This is why I encourage people to take what I call 'The BMW Test'. Most people long to own a BMW (or a BMW equivalent – a Harley Davidson, a horse, a villa, a Versace tie). My advice is, don't resist! Try it. Go for it! Don't hold back! Do it, so that you can prove to yourself that the world cannot by itself make you happy by itself. Herein lies the key to freedom.

Remember the phrase, '*What profiteth a man if he gaineth the whole world and loses his soul*'[7]. The 'things' of this world are in no way 'bad' or 'wrong' or 'sinful' as some claim, they simply are not enough. Joy is not about accumulation or achievement, it is about acceptance – Self-acceptance. In fact,

> *Joy is Self-acceptance – it is freedom from self-judgement.*

When you accept your Self, you accept joy naturally. Joy is like an inner Light which radiates upon and enlightens everything you see. When you are happy, there is beauty and purpose in everything. You are kind, philosophical and instantly forgiving. When you are miserable however, even your favourite ice cream tastes sour and 'not good enough'.

Joy is miraculous. It can colour everything. What price joy? Sometimes I think what we really need is a different type of credit card – not a card for shopping, but a card which credits us with enough inner joy and inner peace to last an eternity. To be happy, all you really need do is give your Self, your whole Self, credit!

So What's Your Story?

Towards the end of his life, the English philosopher, Aldous Huxley, gave an interview to a young journalist who was keen to extract gems of wisdom from the great man. When asked to sum up his lifetime's work, Huxley paused for a moment, and then smiled. *'It's a bit embarrassing,'* he said, *'to have been concerned with the human problem all one's life and find at the end that one has no more to offer by way of advice than "try to be a little kinder".'*[8]

Your ego and your unconditioned Self both have a story to tell, each very different from one another.

Your ego sees itself in you. It is a thought of limitation and lack, and believes, therefore, that you are in essence, *the Presence of Lack*. The ego is never at peace – it cannot afford to be whilst it believes 'everything good is outside'. It attacks and criticises you in order to motivate and strengthen. It believes judgement buys better protection and better performance. The ego's learned chitter-chatter sounds like the rap of a megalomaniac sports coach who is constantly barking, 'could do better', 'what's wrong with you', 'come on', 'get a grip', 'work', and 'try harder'.

Your unconditioned Self, is a thought of complete wholeness, and believes that you are in essence, *the Presence of Love*. It sees no need for you to improve upon your wholeness; it merely wants to be whole! Quite clearly, then, your unconditional Self sees things very differently to your ego. In fact,

your ego and your spirit have a different view on everything.

If the ego's prayer is always *'Look out!'*, then your spirit's prayer is always *'Look within!'*, for both your ego and your spirit have a different story. Your ego cries *'Look out!'* because it is afraid and because it believes 'everything good is outside'. Your spirit sings *'Look within!'* because It knows you are complete and whole and happy already. These stories could not be more different. Which will you believe?

The ego compares itself to everything, and comes off badly. Having researched the thinking of the ego for many years now, I have come to the conclusion that the ego's disparaging judgements follow four main patterns. Each pattern creates a story of (1) 'I'm not good enough'; (2) 'I'm wrong'; (3) 'I'm bad'; (4) 'I'm nothing'. In truth,

> ***none of the ego's stories about you are the truth,***
> ***but that does not mean to say they do not***
> ***feel true.***

There is no inherent power in any one of these ego story-lines. They have no power at all, other than the strength of your belief. The more powerful your belief, the more powerfully each of these story-lines appears in your life. Indeed, it is possible to become so conditioned by your own story-line that you eventually lose sight of the fact that it is you who are perpetuating this fiction.

Every event in your life can encourage you to feel 'not good enough', 'wrong', 'bad' and 'nothing'. But no event can make you feel that way – only your judgements and fears can do that. Ultimately, then, it is your belief that either strengthens or undoes each of these ego story-lines.

1. 'I'm Not Good Enough'

Clive was a young, single, twenty-nine-year-old bank manager. He was five minutes late for our first appointment.

'I'm so sorry, Mr Holden, it really isn't good enough,' he said. Not being good enough was the story of Clive's life. He was born into a poor family with barely enough to go around. There was never enough clothes, enough food or enough money, but they managed just fine.

Clive's family comprised of a mother, father, older brother and younger sister. Dad was not home enough. He was always working. Clive's older brother, David, sounded like an absolute superstar. The way Clive described David, I was surprised David was not Managing Director of planet Earth by now. Clive always felt he was in David's shadow whilst growing up. Being the middle child, he felt he never really got enough attention.

Clive told me his school years were okay, but nothing special. He got good grades, but not good enough to go to the university he wanted. He had a few good friends. He liked sport, but was never good enough to 'make it my living'. He was quite shy, particularly around girls. Clive played violin for a national youth orchestra. He doesn't play any more. He felt his parents never really gave him enough encouragement for anything.

Clive finally found work at a local bank. He obviously had done very well at his job, judging by the number of rapid promotions he got. Clive doesn't really see it that way, though. To him, he's done all right, but he could do better. Clive is obviously very competitive. He supports the underdog in everything. His confidence is low, but it is improving. 'I'm getting there,' he said. Behind Clive's mild-mannered exterior, there is a perfectionist dictating the play. Clive denies this.

Clive had originally come to see me for some therapy to 'boost my confidence'. I suggested to him that I probably wouldn't be able to do a good enough job unless we took a look at one thought – 'I'm not good enough'. Together, we looked at how this single thought had shaped Clive's personal story, i.e. his history. I explained to Clive that until he was willing to change his mind about himself, his life would always fall short of being 'good enough'.

The inner taunt of 'I'm not good enough' is, if we are honest, a common experience. Both consciously and/or unconsciously we are constantly haunted by doubts and fears that who we are, what we have and what we do is 'not enough'. As a consequence, we wander the globe in search of a treasure called 'enough'. Sometimes we find what looks like 'enough', only to end up disappointed and let down. The fact is, we will always be disappointed until we change our mind about our Self.

> **Nothing is ever enough, if you judge you are not enough.**

How do you know if 'I'm not good enough' is running your personal story? There are many signs, which include:

- You tell yourself, 'I'm not good enough'.
- You demand perfection of yourself, but you think you never achieve it.
- According to you, your best is never quite good enough.
- You believe you never get enough approval or recognition from others.
- You compare yourself unfavourably to everyone who matters to you.

- Envy and jealousy abound.
- Your self-esteem is not high enough.
- Physically, you think you are not tall enough, not short enough, not light enough, not heavy enough, not pretty enough, etc.
- Mentally, you think you are not intelligent enough, creative enough, clever enough.
- Deep down you believe you have no right to your place in the world.
- No personal success is ever enough.
- Your needs, compared to others', are not important enough to be aired.
- You never have enough of anything – enough time, enough money, enough rest.
- You over-achieve in an effort to prove to others and yourself you are good enough.

2. 'I'm Wrong'

I had a client, Susan, who had convinced herself she was 'wrong'. Susan believed, for instance, she was an 'unwanted child'. She also believed she was the wrong sex, because her parents had always wanted a son and never got one. Susan told me she was originally to be called Angela, but her mother judged she was not pretty enough to be an Angel, so she was called Susan instead.

Both her mother and her father were unloving towards Susan. She felt that they made each other unhappy and that they were wrongly suited. Her father was a stern man. He punished her continually for 'getting everything wrong'. Susan described her entire life as a catalogue of mistakes, accidents and disasters, with everything always 'going wrong'.

Now, in her early forties, Susan felt very lonely and depressed. She described herself as a 'misfit'. She never married – 'I never found Mr. Right!' she said. As a young adult she was very rebellious, and she often mixed with the wrong people. Now she keeps herself to herself. Susan always apologised for herself. She had also become very cynical. 'Everything always goes wrong,' she said.

Susan's therapy centred around forgiveness. She was angry at her mother, her father, and, most of all, at herself. This unresolved anger perpetuated her story of 'I'm wrong'. 'I know you have been encouraged to think you are "wrong" and "not enough", but this is not true,' I explained. Over time, Susan began to understand that her belief of 'I'm wrong' was a self-fulfilling prophecy. 'Wrong decisions are made by people who believe in wrong decisions,' I told her. Susan learned to change her mind about herself.

Common signs of the 'I'm wrong' ego story-line include:

- You often tell yourself, 'I'm wrong'.
- You are afraid of getting things wrong.
- You believe things always go wrong, and then they do.
- You feel cursed.
- You feel a misfit.
- You feel an impostor.
- You feel misunderstood and people take what you say 'the wrong way'.
- You feel very uncomfortable when things appear to be going really well.
- You fear everything is your fault.

- You feel like the black sheep – in the wrong family and the wrong place.
- You are alive in the wrong time, and on the wrong planet! Nowhere feels like home.
- Your theme tune is, *If There's a Wrong Way to Do It!*
- You are clumsy and you make a lot of mistakes.
- When things are 'going right' you worry about what can 'go wrong'.
- You over-compensate by insisting you are always right and never wrong.

3. 'I'm Bad'

Our greatest fear is that our core is rotten. The ego, or conditioned self, has learned to believe not only that 'everything good is outside', but also that 'everything bad must be inside'. The fear of 'I'm bad' is a vicious rumour that tries to convince you that not only did Adam eat a bad apple, but that *you are that bad apple*. We prefer not to look within our Self, just in case this rumour holds some truth. Hence, the rumour lives on.

The 'I'm bad' ego story-line can take many twists and turns. It gives rise to much superstition replete with devils, demons and dangerous, angry gods. Bad dreams, bad experiences and bad endings are common, for as long as we believe we may be 'bad' our life must inevitably reflect this. Once again, if we change our minds about ourselves, we will change our life experience.

Common signs of an 'I'm bad' ego story-line include:

- You often tell yourself, 'I'm no good'.

- The best you feel is 'not bad'.
- Your life is constantly in a 'bad patch'.
- People treat you badly.
- You treat yourself even worse.
- You were a naughty child.
- You are a rebel with a 'bad attitude'.
- You have 'bad days' when your mood is very dark.
- You are always in somebody's 'bad books'.
- Someone is always in your 'bad books'.
- You feel guilty about everything.
- You believe you are a sinner.
- You commit crimes and do 'bad things'.
- You have an aversion to any criticism.
- You never commit, because you fear 'bad endings'.
- You believe all good things must come to an end.
- You over-compensate by always having to 'do good' and 'be good', whether you like it or not.

4. 'I'm Nothing'

All of your fears about being 'wrong', 'bad' and 'not good enough' are 'nothing' in that they are not the truth about you. They are a lie. They only feel like 'something' because of the power you give to them. Withdraw this power, and 'nothing' of these fears is left, for they are illusions. The ego is 'nothing', and it is not surprising, therefore, that the ego's greatest fear is 'I'm nothing'.

The 'I'm nothing' ego story-line is based on a fear that if you don't become 'somebody' you will end up a 'nobody'. According to this story-line, there is no unconditioned Self. You have no substance, no spiritual Self. It is because you believe this that when you look for your spiritual Self you find 'nothing'. This is also the reason why when you pray and meditate 'nothing happens' and you 'feel nothing'. As you change your mind, you will change your experience.

Common signs of the 'I'm nothing' ego story-line include:

- You often tell yourself, 'I'm nothing'.
- Whatever you feel, 'It's nothing'.
- You feel like 'a nobody'.
- You fear your life will 'amount to nothing'.
- You feel 'nothing much' happens in your life.
- 'Nothing' ever works out the way you hope it will.
- You often get depressed.
- You often feel over-looked.
- You believe 'nothing and nobody' can ever help you.
- There is no God and there is 'nothing' to believe in.
- You often feel like a doormat.
- You have no time for yourself.
- You dream of being a 'somebody'.
- You over-compensate by always being an exhibition-ist, very public, and always getting noticed.

'I'm wrong', 'I'm bad', 'I'm nothing', and 'I'm not good enough' are four common story-lines that have emerged from the thinking of your ego, or conditioned self. These story-lines, and others, all reflect the ego's fundamental fear of lack, guilt and unworthiness. No matter how strongly you have learned to identify with these story-lines, the fact remains, they are untrue, and *you are not your ego!*

Can You Forgive Yourself?

Forgiveness is the choice for
wholeness.

Many times in your life you may have felt 'not good enough', but it is a mistake to say 'I am not good enough'. Similarly, it is one thing to judge a behaviour as 'not good enough', it is quite another to judge yourself as 'not good enough'. Accordingly, you may think you get things wrong, but it is a mistake to say 'I am wrong'; you may judge a decision as 'bad', but it is a mistake to say 'I am bad'; and although you may appear to have 'nothing', it is a mistake to say 'I am nothing'.

You cannot be a victim and be happy. You cannot judge, criticise and berate your Self and be happy. You may judge that you have made mistakes in your past, but they are not your identity. No matter how many mistakes you think you have made, *you are not your mistakes*. To be happy, you have to know this is true.

To be truly happy, you must be willing to give up the story of your ego. In other words, you have to be willing to give up your identity with the self 'that has been wronged', 'that did not get the love', 'that doesn't feel good enough', 'that grew up poor', 'that was once abused', 'that is unlucky', 'that always has to fight', 'that was unpopular', 'that was bullied', 'that failed at something', 'that is a slow learner', 'that nothing good ever happens to', 'that gets everything wrong', 'that is shy', 'that was once rejected', etc. These experiences do not define who you really are.

The process for undoing your self-judgement, self-doubt and self-hatred (i.e. your ego conditioning) is *forgiveness*. Most often, when we talk about forgiveness we talk about 'doing' something to someone else. The forgiveness I am speaking of is quite different and much more personal[9]. For me, true forgiveness is a self-healing process which starts with you and gradually extends to everyone else. In essence,

true forgiveness is a willingness to change your mind about your Self.

Forgiveness is the process of giving up your limited self-concept for your whole Self. The willingness to forgive yourself is really the willingness to replace thoughts of fear with thoughts of love, thoughts of condemnation with thoughts of kindness, thoughts of doubt with thoughts of trust. Forgiveness is transformational – it gives you wholeness in exchange for all your learned fears. The unconditioned Self is remembered as you forgive yourself for all your fearful self-doubts and self-judgements.

What will you value more – the story of your ego, or the story of your unconditioned Self? Forgiveness is like a cosmic eraser that rubs out the pencil marks the ego has drawn upon your mind. Forgiveness works in the present. It teaches you (1) you are not the pain of your past; (2) the pain of your past is over *now*. Ultimately, *forgiveness undoes illusions of weakness and limitation; through forgiveness you become whole and joyous once more.*

With forgiveness, you choose to forget your conditioning and remember the truth about your unconditioned Self.

Forgiveness leads to enlightenment, i.e. reclaiming your inner Light.

Who is the 'Light of the World' if it is not you? Through forgiveness, you wipe away your fears, you undo your doubts, and you wash away all darkness to reveal the Light of your unconditioned Self once more. *Forgiveness gives you back your freedom.*

The following process is a typical example of a forgiveness meditation used at The Happiness Project. Take a moment to be still and to sit with this process as you read it either out loud or quietly within your mind. This process will allow you to relax, release and let go of your fears. It offers you a chance to forgive yourself for the times you have attacked, criticised and judged your Self.

Breathe freely, and allow each inhalation and exhalation to be easy, effortless and natural. As you read, take a moment to pause and to breathe fully after each sentence.

> *'I forgive myself for all the times I have been so hard on myself.'*
> *'I forgive myself for all the times I have condemned myself.'*
> *'I forgive myself for all the times I have been cruel and unkind to myself in any way.'*
> *'I forgive myself for all the times I have criticised and betrayed myself.'*

102

'I forgive myself for all the times I have told myself "I'm not good enough".'
'I forgive myself for all the times I have told myself "I'm wrong".'
'I forgive myself for all the times I have told myself "I'm bad".'
'I forgive myself for all the times I have told myself "I'm nothing".'

'I forgive myself for being afraid.'
'I forgive myself for feeling unworthy.'
'I forgive myself for all my judgements.'
'I forgive myself for all my mistakes.'

'Through forgiveness, I am ready to remember the truth about my Self, no matter how beautiful it is.'
'Through forgiveness, I am ready to remember the truth about my Self, no matter how wonderful it is.'
'Through forgiveness, I am ready to love and trust again.'
'Through forgiveness, I am ready to trust in love again.'

'I am willing, now, to accept I am not my fears.'
'I am willing, now, to accept I am not unworthy.'
'I am willing, now, to accept I am not guilty.'
'I am willing, now, to accept I am free.'

'Through forgiveness, I am free to enjoy love.'
'Through forgiveness, I am free to enjoy peace.'
'Through forgiveness, I am free to enjoy happiness.'
'Through forgiveness, I am free to enjoy my Self.'

'I am willing, now, to forgive and be free.'
'I am willing, now, to forgive and be happy.'
'I am willing, now, to forgive and be free.'
'I am willing, now, to forgive and be happy.'

CHAPTER FOUR

꧁꧂

Practising Acceptance

꧁꧂

In the early days of The Laughter Clinic I designed a wealth of exercises and techniques called 'creative growth games' which helped to cultivate a greater awareness and acceptance of joy and happiness[1]. Many of these games were made up quite spontaneously and are still used to this day in The Happiness Project. The following story involves three of these games.

One afternoon at The Laughter Clinic I gave the participants a creative growth game for homework called *Happy Days*. The challenge of *Happy Days* is to dedicate one day a month to your own personal nourishment, well-being and happiness. When asked for further information, I suggested that people might want to use this time to be kind to themselves, to rest, to have an adventure, to try something new, or simply to practise gratitude. Everyone loved the idea and there was a sense of real excitement as people went home.

One month later, I asked the group to share their experiences of *Happy Days*. A rather awkward silence followed. It turned out that not one of thirty people had given themselves a *Happy Day*. A 'lack of time' seemed to be the chief obstacle. A whole day of happiness on top of a career, housework, the children, grocery shopping and gardening was asking a little too much.

Not to be deterred, I came up with another exercise for homework called *Happy Hour*. 'Once a week, I would like you to take one hour – a *Happy Hour* – to indulge yourself with love, treats and kindness. I want you to feed your spiritual bank-account,' I said. The next week, I suggested we begin with a round up of *Happy Hours*. More silence. No one had done the exercise. Once again 'lack of time' was sited, and also 'too much to do', 'the children', 'I forgot' and 'I was too tired to do anything'.

'I have a new exercise for you,' I said. 'It's called *An Ecstatic 60 Seconds*! The challenge of this game is to give yourself one minute a day to stop everything and simply *be happy*.' 'What can you do in just one minute?' someone asked. 'You can smell a flower, smile for no reason, say "Thank you" for something, breathe in peace, recite a favourite prayer, say an affirmation like "I accept happiness easily, effortlessly and naturally", massage your head, whatever you like,' I suggested.

One week later, and, maybe you have guessed, I learned that not one single person had been able to enjoy *An Ecstatic 60 Seconds* for each of the seven days since we last met. Some had managed one or two brief bouts of joy, but that was all. When I asked why this was, many of the participants tried to convince me that *An Ecstatic 60 Seconds* is not always practical, and that some days are quite clearly better suited than others.

This series of events was a turning point for me in my work. It showed me in no uncertain terms that

lack of time is never a real obstacle to happiness.

Life has certainly speeded up. That I acknowledge. Do you remember, for instance, how as a young teenager the summer holidays felt like an eternity? Those six weeks or so of holidays were an absolute lifetime! And do you remember how, when you were four or five years old, every day was like an eternity? Something obviously happens to us when we hit twenty-one – it's as if life goes on fast-forward, and all of a sudden the months go by like the weeks used to, and the weeks go by like the days used to.

For many of us, life is faster than ever, we are busier than ever, and we work longer hours than ever. We live our life on the run, juggling duties, meeting responsibilities, always queuing for something, paying the bills, catching up on our 'to do' lists, etc. We are in a race against time. Time is precious, and so we 'buy time', 'steal time' and 'make time', but still 'time flies'. No matter what we do, it appears we are simply too busy to be happy.

The question is, though, how much time does it really take to *be happy*? Happiness is of the moment – it is timeless – and, therefore, we each of us surely have time enough to be happy? I suggest that

it takes as much time to be happy as it does to be depressed or resentful.

Happiness requires no extra time. In fact, it requires no

time. As I have already stated, *happiness waits on welcome, not on time.* The exercise *An Ecstatic 60 Seconds* proved to me beyond doubt that 'lack of time' is not an authentic obstacle to happiness. 'Lack of time' is a smoke-screen – it hides the real obstacle, the only obstacle – to accepting happiness *now*.

Happiness and Self-Acceptance

A little bit of pleasure every now and then, an occasional sixty seconds of joy, is for most of us quite acceptable and much appreciated. After all, it more than makes up for the work, the toil, the suffering and the sacrifice that went before. We are comfortable with life's little pleasures; we are less comfortable, however, with prolonged happiness, full blown joy, and everlasting bliss.

Ask yourself, 'how much happiness can I really handle?' One hour perhaps? A week, a month, a year, a lifetime? For how long can you live with happiness and joy before you begin to question and doubt what is happening? For how long can you wholly accept being peaceful before you become restless and anxious? For how long can you unconditionally enjoy someone's love and attention before you grow uncomfortable? For how long can you accept and trust the feeling of complete freedom, before you decide it must end?

The real issue is not time; it is acceptance, and, in particular, Self-acceptance. Happiness and Self-acceptance go hand in hand. *In fact, your level of Self-acceptance determines your level of happiness.* The more Self-acceptance you have, the more happiness you will allow yourself to accept, receive and enjoy. In other words,

you enjoy as much happiness as you believe you are worthy of.

Happiness is natural, easy and effortless to you when your Self-acceptance is high, but happiness is blasphemous to you when your Self-acceptance is low. When you feel low, you dream of being happy, but you also secretly fear that maybe you are not worthy of happiness, and so you question, doubt, resist, test, defend against, overlook and push away invitations to be happy.

To withhold Self-acceptance is to judge you are not worthy of happiness. You cannot, however, have low Self-acceptance *and* happiness. To persist with a judgement of unworthiness and also accept happiness is too much of a contradiction – a contradiction that will leave you feeling guilty. How can you accept happiness and also believe you do not deserve it?

You attract what you believe you deserve. Thus, not only do you enjoy as much happiness as you believe you are worthy of, but

you suffer as much pain as you believe you are worthy of.

Self-acceptance (i.e. Self-worth) is the key to both happiness and unhappiness. If you can accept yourself as whole, worthy and well, then happiness is natural and acceptable to you. If, however, you judge yourself as 'not good enough', then you are not good enough for happiness. Indeed, for as long as you judge you are 'not good enough' you must always throw happiness off for fear of guilt.

Happiness and the Guilt Thing

The most popularly attended workshop at The Happiness Project is called *How To Be So Happy You Almost Feel Guilty, But Not Quite!* This should come as no surprise to you, for the greatest obstacle to accepting happiness is our guilt, and we have plenty of it.

What is guilt? Well, simply put, *guilt is the belief that you do not deserve happiness*. It is the belief that you are 'not good enough', 'wrong', 'bad' and 'nothing'. This belief is learned. It is not natural to your unconditioned Self. It is a thought of lack, and all thoughts of lack belong to the ego, that part of you that hopes for happiness but ultimately has learned to believe you are not really worthy of it.

We long for happiness, but we also judge we are far too guilty to accept it. We like the idea of happiness. It feels good. But we also fear that maybe it is selfish, wrong, inappropriate, and that it comes with a hidden cost. We have learned to believe that happiness demands a payback – some suffering, labour or sacrifice, perhaps. Guilt is not just about happiness, however. Have you noticed, for instance, how

that which you most desire is what you feel most guilty about!

The ego feels guilty about happiness because it feels guilty about everything, particularly nice things. Take pleasure, for instance. Pleasure is happiness of the body, it is enjoyment of the senses. Pleasure is about beautiful colours, rich aromas, wonderful music, a healing touch and exotic tastes. We have also learned to believe, however, that pleasure is of the devil[2].

Somehow we have learned to believe that pleasure is 'so good it's a sin'. We fear that too much pleasure can kill off all morals, subvert all virtues and ruin all values. All by itself, pleasure can, apparently, lead to hedonism, laziness, selfishness, anarchy, war, damnation, the end of the world and the downfall of the monarchy!

Sex is pleasure. The idea that sex is natural, good fun and healthy sounds really great, very logical, objective and mature, but most of us still feel 'guilty as hell' talking about 'you know what'. Personally, I still remember vividly how all through my teenage years I felt absolute angst about the 'nudge-nudge, wink-wink' issue. In particular, I remember the agony of visiting the chemist to buy condoms. My planning was military. I used to think days ahead. Most often I would pick a chemist out of town, where nobody knew me. Also, the cashier could not look like my mum, my dad, or my biology teacher. Attractive women cashiers were also completely out of the question!

I eventually lost count of how many times I visited the chemist to buy condoms, only to leave with yet another tube of toothpaste. Please do not judge me too harshly. Remember, I am English, and my conditioning has been most thorough. Indeed, to the rest of the world the idea that the English actually reproduce sexually is completely unbelievable! Our secrecy betrays our shame.

Sex, 'in the biblical sense', was apparently what got us all into trouble in the first place, with Adam and Eve. If Adam hadn't got all hot and bothered about Eve, maybe we would still be whole and worthy of happiness? Religion and mythology teaches us to be guilty about sex. For young boys, this guilt is forever reinforced, particularly at bath time when parents impart such wisdom as, 'Play with it and it will fall off' and 'Do that again and you will go blind'. Young girls go through something similar I am told.

We have learned to feel guilty about everything we like. Food is 'naughty, but nice'. Money is the 'root of all evil'. Peace and rest is dangerous, for 'the devil makes use of idle hands'. Laughter 'will end in tears'. Success will ruin you. Indeed, our learned response to success and happiness has many parallels. For instance, have you ever experienced 'fraud guilt', the belief that your success is really a mistake and you do not deserve it?

The real test is to find something you are not guilty about. Guilt is so widespread, however, that I would have to say,

> ### *guilt is not so much an emotion – it is more a way of life.*

Guilt is a way of life built upon a conditioned belief of *unworthiness*[3]. For as long as you judge yourself to be *unworthy*, you will never be able to freely accept happiness. You will attempt to bargain, barter, pay for and exchange happiness for something less pleasant, but even then, without Self-acceptance, happiness will feel uncomfortable.

Self-acceptance and happiness are both impossible whilst you believe in guilt, i.e. that you do not deserve happiness. If you replace the phrase 'Self-acceptance and happiness' with 'Self-acceptance *is* happiness', then maybe you will see more clearly how important it is to let go of guilt. Ultimately, letting go of guilt is undoing the ego.

Undoing Your Ego

Our world is littered with man-made myths, superstitions and stories of creation which tell tall tales of our descent from heaven, our fall from grace, and our separation from God. According to these myths, Creation did not really begin with Light, but with *guilt* and *unworthiness*.

The mythologies of Egypt, Greece, Rome, Scandinavia, the Celtic Lands and *The Bible*, are full of fearful stories – ego nightmares – of drunken, sex-crazed, violent gods full of anger and disdain for their creations. The story of Adam and Eve and their rejection from Eden is well known, for instance. Another story, from Egypt, tells how humans were first born as fish inside the tear of an angry and disillusioned god; the tear dropped to earth and formed the oceans[4].

The Christian tradition reflects a confusion that exists in many other major religious and philosophical traditions. On the one hand, there are Christians who believe in a God of Love and who believe in man's *original blessing*, i.e. that you and I are, in essence, whole, worthy and well[5]. On the other hand, there are Christians who ask God to bless bombs, who fear God's vengeance, and who believe in *original sin*, i.e. that you and I are guilty.

The Catholic Church is known as 'The Guilty Church'. I well remember one ex-client of mine, a Catholic, who once told me, 'I know I am guilty – I just don't know what I'm guilty of'. Guilt is not exclusive, however, to Catholics contrary to what some Catholics might think. The Jewish faith is riddled with guilt. The Hindu's have their 'karma'. The Muslims are constantly atoning. Guilt is quite clearly non-denominational!

I remember giving a talk called *How To Be So Happy You Almost Feel Guilty, But Not Quite!* to a group of orthodox Christians. We met in a village hall, in the middle of the countryside, on a dark, wet and windy winter evening. In summing up the great teachings of Jesus Christ I reminded my audience how Jesus himself said, *'These things have I spoken unto you, that my joy might remain in you, and that your joy might be complete'*[6]. I also mentioned how *The Bible* speaks of the 'joy of thy Lord', of 'joy [as] the fruit of the spirit' and of heaven as 'a kingdom of joy'.

My audience appeared to enjoy these references, and the young priest who had invited me especially enjoyed them. The old priest looked quite stern, however. I went on to remind my audience that Jesus also said, *'You are the Light of the World'*[7] and *'Ye are Gods'*[8]. I talked of original blessing and of the idea that heaven and Eden are really the unconditioned Self in all of us. The audience looked to the old priest for guidance.

Next, I suggested that the best way to accept the joy of God is to stop defining yourself as a 'sinner' and accept your role as the 'Light of the World'. At this point, *all hell let loose.* 'It is because I am a sinner, that I know I will one day be happy with God,' said the old priest. I replied, 'It is because I know you are not a sinner that you can be happy with God right now.' The applause was somewhat muted at the end of my talk!

From an early age, then, we are encouraged to think that our essence is not love, but guilt. We are taught strange ideas such as:

> Guilt is natural.
> Guilt is good.
> It is bad to feel not guilty.
> Without guilt, anarchy rules.
> Guilt makes you act 'good'.
> Guilt shows you care.
> Guilt shows you are sorry.
> Guilt stops you sinning.

Of course, the reason we sin such a lot, i.e. act up and play 'bad', is because we feel so guilty in the first place. Guilt begets guilt.

> ### Guilt cannot take you to love, peace or happiness.

In our childhood our parents sang hymns of guilt to us, such as 'You should be ashamed of yourself', 'We are very disappointed in you', and 'How could you do this to us'. Other great hymns of guilt include, 'You just don't care', 'How selfish can you get', 'You'll be the death of me' and 'You'll send me to my grave'.

Children are quick learners. We made up some good hymns of guilt too, such as 'My friend's father always lets him', 'Why can't we have one too', 'We never go anywhere' and 'Please, just this once'. Love gives way to guilt.

At school we are told by our teachers, 'What would your mummy say?'; at church we are reprimanded with 'What would God think?'; at Christmas time we are interrogated with 'Have you really been a good boy *all* year?'; at work, our boss gives us another 'Whatever you do, don't screw up' pep-talk; and back in the apparent safety of our own home, our lover tells us, 'You never take me out' and 'You don't love me'.

You can begin to undo your ego and let go of your conditioning right now if you can accept and adhere to a most fundamental key to happiness –

> *you cannot teach anyone they are guilty, if you*
> *are to be free of guilt yourself.*

It is important to understand that, on the level of consciousness, thoughts are never given away, they are always shared. Therefore, if you teach someone they should be guilty, you are simultaneously teaching yourself that you should be guilty too. Also, when you judge someone as *unworthy* of happiness, you are in that very same instant telling yourself you are also *unworthy*.

The reverse of this principle is that every time you affirm another person's goodness, their inner light, their original blessing, their innocence, you are affirming these qualities for yourself also. The truth is, either we are all free or none of us are. You cannot buy your freedom at anyone else's expense. Happiness would have you commit to the idea that you are, in essence, not guilty and neither is anyone else.

You Do Not Deserve Happiness

The following story is one I often tell at The Happiness Project:

There once was a monk who travelled from village to village, smiling. His name was Ananda, which translated means 'joy' or 'bliss'. He had no home, no money and no possessions to speak of. He wore a saffron robe, some beads, and a wonderful smile which he gave away to everyone he met. So warm, so loving and so infectious was his smile, everyone would smile in his presence.

One day the monk met a boy, also called Ananda. The boy walked beside the monk along a winding path. He asked the monk, 'Are you a holy man?' The monk smiled, 'I am as holy as you are.' The boy smiled. 'Why do you not own anything?' he asked. 'My smile is my own,' the monk replied. 'But what about money, a home, a horse?' asked the boy. 'The world cannot give me my smile – my smile is between me and God,' said the monk.

The boy and the monk walked along in silence. Eventually the boy asked, 'Who are you, monk?' 'I am the smile that went around the world,' explained

117

the monk, 'and my gospel is a gospel of smiles.' 'Do you always smile?' asked the boy. 'Yes, even when I am asleep,' laughed the monk. 'How do you manage to smile always?' asked the boy. 'Smiling is easy because I believe in happiness and I also believe in you,' replied the monk. Now the monk and the boy were both smiling.

This story illustrates two very important points. Firstly, if you are to be happy you must accept your holiness, or, if you like, your *wholeness*. In other words,

if you are to accept happiness, you must believe in your Self!

To be happy, you must be willing to accept that you are created perfectly whole, and that you are not, therefore, fundamentally guilty, lacking or unworthy. You may make mistakes, but you are not a sinner. As you learn to love and forgive yourself for your fearful beliefs and self-judgements, you automatically connect consciously once more to the everlasting joy of your unconditioned Self.

Secondly,

If you are to be happy, you must believe in happiness.

The monk, Ananda, could afford to smile all day long because he believed happiness is natural to him *and to everyone else*. He saw happiness as a natural experience, not a peak experience. For Ananda, there was no mountain to climb, no sacrifice to make, no work to do in order to be happy. He simply chose to be happy. He had no 'happychondria' and he was also perfectly Self-accepting.

Again and again I have witnessed how our fearful limiting beliefs about happiness deny us our natural right to happiness, and also cause us so much extra suffering. The most damaging erroneous belief about happiness is, of course, the belief that *happiness is somewhere else*, i.e. it is not with you. After that, the next most painful and limiting belief about happiness is that *happiness has to be deserved*.

The belief that *happiness has to be deserved* has led to centuries of pain, guilt and deception. So firmly have we clung to this single, illusory belief that we have almost forgotten the real truth about happiness. So busy are we trying to deserve happiness, we no longer have much time for ideas such as, happiness is natural, happiness is a birthright, happiness is free, happiness is a choice, happiness is within, happiness is *being*. The moment you believe happiness has to be deserved you must toil forevermore.

One of my clients, Jenny, once illustrated perfectly how many of us feel about happiness. 'Everything feels so pointless,' she told me. 'How do you mean?' I asked. Jenny sighed, 'Well, no matter how hard I try to be happy, I get absolutely nowhere. I feel so frustrated, Robert, because I have done so much hard work on myself.' 'You sound angry,' I said. 'No. I'm depressed and angry!' We both smiled, and then Jenny began to cry. 'I feel so doomed,' she said. 'I feel as if I'm being punished.' I asked Jenny, 'Do you believe you deserve to be happy?' 'Probably not,' she replied.

Ask yourself now, *do I deserve to be happy*? Be careful how you answer this question, however, for there is a catch. If you answer 'no', then no matter what you do, you will, like Jenny, not accept much happiness. If you answer 'yes', then you are subscribing to the idea that happiness must be deserved and you will therefore have to fulfil all sorts of criteria (set by you) before you can be happy. Both 'no' and 'yes' are dishonest answers. The point is,

you do not deserve happiness!

This is not a message of gloom, it is a message of hope! One of the greatest single steps you can take to happiness *now* is to let go of the belief that happiness has to be deserved. *You do not deserve happiness, you choose happiness.* Happiness is natural. It is freely available to all. It is unconditional. And when you are unconditional about happiness, then happiness merely happens! Happiness happens, if you let it.

The belief that happiness has to be deserved has no power, other than the power you give to it. The problem is, you have learned to give it a lot of power. This single thought not only reinforces your belief in guilt and unworthiness, it also contributes to almost every other major fearful belief about happiness. It contributes, in particular, to the work ethic, the suffering ethic, and the martyr ethic – three ethics heavily endorsed by our society.

From an early age we are all spoon-fed beliefs about how important it is to work for happiness, suffer for happiness and sacrifice for happiness. Generation after generation, this fearful and thoughtless conditioning is handed down in much the same way that physical weaknesses and ailments are handed down through the genes. The good news, however, is that,

it takes only one loving belief to undo an entire belief system based on fear.

Changing your fearful beliefs about happiness, particularly

the belief that happiness has to be deserved, requires absolutely no labour, suffering or sacrifice on your behalf. It merely takes willingness, (1) the willingness to see that you are not unworthy and guilty; (2) the willingness to let go of your conditioned beliefs about happiness; (3) the willingness to accept that happiness is natural to your unconditioned Self. Willingness is the key.

Healing the Work Ethic

According to the work ethic, happiness is not natural – happiness is a pay-packet you earn for putting in the hours.

The work ethic is one of the most dominant ethics of the western world[9]. When I refer to the work ethic here, I am not talking about the *joy of work*; I am talking about the compulsive *need to work*. Work and more work is the key to happiness, according to the work ethic. And if that doesn't work, try even more work. The work ethic supports the pursuit of happiness, and it states quite categorically, *happiness will not happen unless you work for it*.

There are, in particular, four erroneous, and fearful beliefs about happiness that help make up the work ethic:

Happiness has to be deserved.
Happiness has to be worked for.
Happiness has to be earned.
Happiness has to be paid for.

The work ethic is all about labour – birth is labour, life is labour, love is labour, happiness is labour, work is labour, death is rest. We labour, not for the joy of it, but because we have learned to believe we must. The purpose of the work ethic is to work hard so as to atone for your guilt and unworthiness and thereby 'deserve happiness' once more.

'Workaholism' is endemic, and for many of us our life is governed entirely by work. Once upon a time, we worked to live; now, we live to work. Any 'life' we do have is merely recovery from work. We work, recover from work, and then work again. We go to the office to work. After work, we bring some work home with us. For rest, we go to the gym for a work-out. Totally exhausted, we go to therapy to work through our problems – 'I've done a lot of work on myself,' we say. After all that, there's the house-work! Finally, we go to bed, too tired to be happy, but our mind is still working and we cannot sleep. No problem. Insomnia is a wonderful chance to get more work done!

The work ethic is motivated by the belief that anything worthwhile requires great work, effort and labour. According to the work ethic – creativity is not inspiration, it's perspiration; love is a labour, not a joy; success is a fight, it never comes easily; health is about a 'no pain, no gain' attitude; salvation is hardest of all, it is a wrestling match with the angels, just ask Jacob. Nothing comes easily according to the work ethic.

Has it ever occurred to you that

you are trying too hard to be happy?

The Vietnamese Buddhist, Thich Nhat Hanh, offers a beautiful teaching to the world through his ministry of peace and Self-acceptance. He encourages us continually to give up *trying to be happy* and simply *be happy*. He writes:

Do we need to make a special effort to enjoy the beauty of the blue sky? Do we have to practise to be able to enjoy it? No, we just enjoy it. Each second, each minute of our lives can be like this. Wherever we are, any time, we have the capacity to enjoy the sunshine, the presence of each other, even the sensation of our breathing. We don't need to go to China to enjoy the blue sky. We don't have to travel into the future to enjoy our breathing. We can be in touch with these things right now.[10]

We are too busy working to be happy, to actually *be* happy. In the last ten years, the average working week has increased by over ten hours to nearly fifty hours a week; the lunch break faces extinction; six out of ten men and four out of ten women work on Saturdays; Sundays are also a workday for many. To cap it all, when we dare leave the office at 5pm, there is always one sad, brainless colleague who shouts out, 'Part timer' or 'Only doing a half day?' Guilt ensues[11].

As a society we spend more and more time as a *human doing* and less and less as a *human being*. Indeed, the work ethic despises rest and play. We hardly ever go out to play any more; instead we go for cardiovascular workouts, business lunches and corporate away days. According to the work ethic, rest is 'downtime' – nothing useful is happening. Too much rest and you lose your edge!

If you are resting, you are not achieving. This is a worry because

the work ethic thinks of happiness as an achievement and not as a natural way of being.

The thinking that promotes the work ethic fails to appreciate the idea that happiness is free. According to the work ethic, life is about achievement and so too is happiness. The work ethic is ego-driven, for it is only the ego that believes your Self-worth is zero without achievement. We suffer, therefore, from an *achiever fever*, which is essentially the desire to achieve *anything* so that we can feel good about ourselves and thereby deserve happiness.

Let me be clear – work itself is not the problem. On the contrary, work can be a marvellous opportunity to serve, to develop skills, to be creative, to meet people, to travel and to grow. What I am really referring to is the addiction to work, and, in particular, *an addiction to the belief that you have to work, earn, deserve and pay for happiness.*

How do you know if you are 'suffering' from the belief that you have to work for happiness? Here are some tell-tale signs:

- You believe happiness is not natural; it has to be deserved.
- You believe people must earn happiness; it is not freely given.
- You believe that all happiness has a price.
- Your life is a never-ending 'to do' list.
- Your reward for completing a 'to do' list is to make another 'to do' list.
- You are lost without something to do. Without achievement, you are nothing.
- You can't relax. In fact, you believe relaxation 'makes you' feel guilty.
- People who only do one thing at a time are, in your opinion, under-achievers.
- You think exhaustion is a weakness and a failure.

124

- You feel far too guilty to take all of your holiday leave from work.
- You feel you must keep busy, you must fill every moment, and there is always more you could be doing.
- You suffer from 'hurry sickness' – there is never enough time for you to do everything.
- What you achieve is never good enough.
- Your friends don't ask 'How are you?' they ask 'Are you keeping busy?'
- At the end of a day of work you do not get on with your life, you merely recover from work.
- You would like to lie in on Sunday mornings, but you get too restless.
- You only take time off work to be ill, and even then you manage to get a bit of work done.
- You feel guilty if you have too much fun.
- You are suspicious of good times, success and things that flow easily.
- You have no friends, only work colleagues.
- You have 'really great friends' who you never get to see.
- Time with the family is, strictly speaking, time away from work.
- You promise your children more time, soon, one day, maybe next time.

A few years ago, a good friend of mine, Graham Taylor-Chilton, suggested we play a game of golf together. 'It will have to be during the week,' he said. I had been working hard, too hard, and I needed a rest. I was a non-confessed workaholic, and so I did the 'sensible' and 'mature' thing and turned him down once, twice, three times. The harder

I worked, the more exhausted I became, and the less I achieved. Finally, common sense (i.e. my wife!) prevailed. I agreed to play.

I remember how, on the drive over to the golf course, I felt so guilty about taking time off in the middle of the week. I got stuck in traffic, I got lost, I arrived late, I was edgy all day, the weather wasn't great; I kept thinking about work; and I played lousily. 'What a waste of time,' I thought. Now I felt even more guilty.

When I got home I told Miranda about my day. 'Something's not right,' I said to her. 'I am probably the hardest working person I know, so how come I give myself such a hard time for taking some time out?' The guilt had to be faced. Together with Miranda, I decided the best way to face the guilt was to arrange another round of golf with Graham for the most guilt-inducing time possible – Monday morning! I did it. And with the help of my friends, I continue to do it.

We work to pay off our guilt. The moment we stop working, we feel our guilt. So we start working again. The work ethic is a symbol not only of our guilt but also of our confusion. In particular,

the work ethic confuses willingness with hard work

Happiness only requires willingness, not hard work. In particular, it requires us to be willing to slow down, loaf, laze, relax and *be happy*[12]. Just as the work ethic is about guilt, true willingness is about Self-acceptance, i.e. the acceptance that (1) you are entitled to joy; (2) joy is your unconditional Self.

Healing the Suffering Ethic

My father brought my brother David and I up on suffering stories. Time and time again he took great pride in recounting how difficult and tough life was for him when he was as young as we were. He would repeat the same stories over and over again, and each time the suffering became more and more exaggerated!

Our father's face would light up when he told us his tales of hardship. In fact, the harder the suffering, the warmer his nostalgia would glow. The 'School Story', as it was affectionately known in our family, finally went something like this:

> *We were so poor, we had to walk to school every single day. We couldn't afford a car; we couldn't even afford bus fare. I had to walk six miles there and back, come rain or shine. I had only one pair of shoes, with no soles. I had only one set of school clothes in seven years, and even they were handdowns.*
>
> *I never missed a day of school, ever. Even when I had a temperature of 108, I'd still go. You had to go or you were flogged. At school, we always behaved ourselves. If you didn't behave you were punished and beaten. We also remembered everything our teachers told us or we had our knuckles rapped.*
>
> *With not a penny to our name, I had to share books, pens, pencils, ink even. Books were a luxury in my day. We worked in the cold – central heating hadn't even been invented. Food was one meal a day. And*

at Christmas we were lucky if we got an orange and some nuts – there were no computer games in my day.

Other great lines I remember were, *'we had to clean the house twice for a penny'* and *'anything less than a "B+" and we had to mow the sports field for a week'*. Strange as it may sound, both David and I would say that some of the happiest moments of our childhood were spent laughing with Dad as he told us his suffering stories.

The suffering ethic is born of our perceptions of guilt and unworthiness. Like the work ethic, the suffering ethic teaches us that happiness is not free, it has to be deserved. It also teaches us that happiness without suffering has no value and no integrity. This is, of course, absolute nonsense. The unconditional truth is that

you do not have to know suffering to be happy.

And yet, the suffering ethic would try to convince you that suffering is a pre-requisite for happiness. This ethic also insists that you cannot know love until it is lost; you cannot enjoy peace without conflict first; you must fail in order to succeed; you must be weak before you can be strong; and you must fall before you find real faith. The truth is, however, that peace of mind needs no conflict to define it, loves needs no fear to define it, and joy needs no suffering to define it[13].

Many people are heavily invested in suffering because they believe that suffering makes you a great person. Nothing could be further from the truth –

suffering happens, but suffering does not make you a great person.

Suffering does happen, and it is regrettable that it does. We have all of us suffered disappointment, loss, pain, failure, rejection, bereavement, etc. In no way am I trying to belittle this suffering, but what I am saying is that *no amount of suffering adds to your greatness.* Your Self-worth was established in the heavens the moment you were created. Your worth comes, therefore, from who you are, not what you have suffered.

As I have already mentioned, it was at my Stress Busters Clinic that I first noticed how people would pit their illnesses and sufferings against one another in a sad attempt to get more love, more attention, more anything. Often, the first step to healing is to understand that no amount of war-wounds increases your innate worth. In other words,

you have to relinquish your identity as a 'sufferer', a 'victim', or an 'ex-addict' in 'recovery' if you are to be happy.

These days I notice more and more how people introduce themselves with their illnesses. Within the first few minutes of introduction, we often hear something about prozac, insomnia, co-dependence, therapy, road-rage, nicotine patches, emotional hang-ups and just exactly why 'life's a bitch'. Moments after shaking hands, we hear 'I'm a depressive', or 'I'm an agoraphobic', or 'I'm in recovery'. We never call ourselves 'ex-broken-arm patients', but it seems the fashion these days to pronounce, 'I am a sober alcoholic'.

Very recently, I counselled a young woman, Sarah, who had travelled for two days to see me. She is twenty-five years old, tall, willowy, very thin, and for the past ten years she has experienced bulimia. The most poignant moment of our time together came when I asked Sarah a very up-front question, which was 'Would you be able, Sarah, to stop calling yourself a bulimic?' Sarah's whole body shook at the very thought. 'I know you experience bulimia, but can you see that bulimia is not who you are?' I asked.

Sarah responded wonderfully well to this challenge. I somehow knew she would. 'I'm scared,' she said, 'but I can see what you mean. It's just that I don't know who I am or what I am without bulimia.' I reassured Sarah as best as I could. I told her, 'I know you have suffered greatly, but I hope you can see that this suffering does not define you or your Self-worth. Beneath your fears, your tears and your suffering, your happiness still waits for you. Your happiness is perfectly intact, and you are still completely whole. The joy of your unconditioned Self waits on your welcome.' Sarah smiled.

Two weeks after our meeting, I received a letter from Sarah which reads, verbatim:

Dear Robert, Thank You. Thank You. Thank You. You are the first person in ten years who has not treated me as a bulimic. You treated me as a whole person. I found this puzzling at first. I even resented you a little for it. But I am coming around to the idea. For the first time in a long time, I can see myself without bulimia. This thought is scary and exciting. Let's look at that thought next time we meet. I'll call soon. With love and gratitude, Sarah.

The suffering ethic pins its hopes on the idea that suffering is both a suitable atonement for your unworthiness, and an adequate payment for happiness. Like collecting petrol points at your local garage, the great hope is that 'X' amounts of suffering will *earn, pay for, buy* or help you *deserve* 'Y' amounts of happiness. The truth is, though,

no amount of suffering can buy you any amount of happiness.

Happiness cannot be bought because happiness is free. Also, *there is no exchange rate between happiness and suffering*. Suffering cannot be traded in for happiness. Similarly, no amount of pain, hurt, guilt, sacrifice, bad luck, hard work, tragedy, disaster or crucifixion can buy you an ounce of happiness. Happiness is not deserved. Happiness is free – there is no escape from this freedom!

How do you know if you are 'suffering' from the belief that you must suffer to be happy? Here are some tell-tale signs:

- You subscribe to the belief of 'no pain, no gain'.
- You believe nothing valuable can be gained without suffering.
- You mistrust gifts that are not earned by suffering, i.e. 'easy come, easy go'.
- You believe there is no such thing as a free lunch – everything costs.
- You suffer a lot of ill health.
- If there's a hard way to do it, you will find it.
- No one is harder on you than you are.

- You withhold praise because you believe that praise leads to complacency.
- You like to think of yourself as head of the class in the 'School of hard knocks'.
- Comfort, wealth and luxury 'make you' feel uneasy and guilty.
- You are an inverted snob, always attacking people who have a comfortable life.
- Less suffering equals less self-worth.
- You think you are a 'real man' because you continue to suffer.
- Life's a bitch and then you die. Ain't that the truth?
- You convince yourself you are better than anyone who hasn't suffered as much as you.
- You think no one has suffered as much as you have.
- You confuse love with sympathy – suffering gets you sympathy.
- You are 'a drama queen' – if there is no drama you are uneasy.
- Pain is your only learning curve.
- You confuse passion with abuse – all your romantic relationships are a struggle.
- Too much comfort causes too much guilt.
- You hope if you suffer enough God will feel so guilty He will grant leniency.
- You like to strive, but to thrive would increase the guilt factor too much.
- There must always be an enemy somewhere.
- You are always fighting and struggling against someone or something.
- You have a blind spot around easy options – you always make everything difficult.

- You believe you have to fight for what you want, so you get into a lot of fights!
- You like to compare scars.

Another major misperception of the suffering ethic is the idea that *suffering brings enlightenment*. On the contrary, it is not suffering that brings enlightenment,

it is the decision to give up suffering that brings enlightenment

Many of the world's religious and philosophical traditions have tried to promote suffering as a legitimate spiritual path that can buy you something. In particular, the teachings of Christianity have often been distorted to encourage you to suffer for your happiness. Medieval Christianity, in particular, was very severe on happiness, officially denouncing laughter as 'the song of the devil' and attacking happiness as a threat to monastic self-control.

The image of Jesus suffering on the cross is known the world over. Very rarely, however, do you see any pictures of a resurrected Jesus Christ. This obvious imbalance prompted me, a few years ago, to start a new collection – a collection of pictures depicting Jesus laughing, smiling and happy. I have quite a few now.

Whenever I am passing a Christian book shop or church I always ask if there are any pictures of a happy Jesus. Never could I have anticipated the responses I often get. Many times I am greeted with such aghast looks of shock, horror and disdain, it is as if I had just asked, 'Have you any pictures of Jesus picking his nose?' Jesus was joy-full!

Think about it – no one would follow a morbid or miserable Messiah.

Christians often argue for misery. One old argument is that you should be careful not to laugh or smile too much because nowhere in *The Bible* is there any mention of Jesus laughing and smiling. My response to this is that nowhere in *The Bible* is there any mention of Jesus brushing his teeth, buying birthday presents or ordering pizza, but that does not mean we should not do these things. And anyway, there are enough references to joy in *The Bible* to keep everyone happy. In one version of Ecclesiasties, for instance, it is written:

> *'Do not abandon yourself to sorrow, do not torment*
> *yourself with brooding. Gladness of heart is life to a man,*
> *joy is what gives him length of days . . . Beguile your*
> *cares, console your heart, chase sorrow away; for sorrow*
> *has been the ruin of many, and is of no use to anybody.'*

The only value suffering has is that it points out that you are running low on happiness. The function of suffering is, therefore, to remind you to choose happiness, choose love, choose healing, choose forgiveness, choose laughter, and choose freedom. Thus, the most helpful response to suffering is to use suffering as a chance to hit the 're-set' button in your life, and commit once again to what is truly important.

To be happy, you must value joy more than pain. You will also want to remind yourself again and again, *suffering cannot buy me happiness*. Your ego believes that suffering somehow atones for guilt, but, in truth, guilt is not real, it is learned. If you can believe this, for yourself and everyone, you will be free of suffering.

Healing the Martyr Ethic

Happiness is made to be shared.

The martyrdom ethic is built upon a number of erroneous and fearful beliefs about happiness, the major one being that *happiness is selfish*. Another great fear of happiness to the practising martyr is that *my happiness denies others their happiness*. In other words, it appears to the martyr there is not enough happiness to go around. Other fears of happiness for the martyr include, *happiness leads to conceit, my happiness has no value to others*, and *being happy is inconsiderate in a world where there is suffering*.

The fear that *happiness is selfish* is not only untrue, it couldn't be further from the truth. Psychology researchers find time and time again that it is the depressed people, and not the happy people, who are intensely self-focused and self-absorbed. Happy people, by contrast, tend to be outgoing, sociable, generous, loving and kind. They are also more tolerant, forgiving and less judgemental than people who are depressed[14].

The martyrdom ethic confuses genuine happiness with hedonism, trivial pleasure seeking, greed, arrogance, boastfulness, swaggering and pretentiousness. It overlooks the fact that *the basis of true happiness is love.* And like love,

> *the first impulse of true happiness is to share itself; happiness is not selfish.*

I remember reading an interview about a woman who had lived as a hermit for ten years in the wilderness in South

America. At one point in the interview she was asked, 'Were you ever lonely?' 'Yes,' she replied, 'I used to get very lonely, not when I was down, but when I was happy because I had no one to share my happiness with.' True happiness is never selfish.

The history of martyrdom began with good intentions. The original goal of the martyr was to give up the 'ego' so as to remember the 'Spiritual Self'. Spiritual martyrdom was, therefore, originally about giving up illusions of lack, guilt and separateness. It was not about loss, but about wholeness.

Many of the spiritual traditions of the world promote muddled messages about martyrdom. Indeed, ego-martyrdom (as opposed to Spiritual martyrdom) is all about struggle, suffering and sacrifice. For this reason, it is nigh impossible to be a Saint and be happy in the Christian tradition. The great hope of ego-martyrdom is that enough sacrifice will buy happiness. As with the suffering ethic, though, the truth is that

> ### *no amount of sacrifice will buy you any amount of happiness.*

True happiness asks you to sacrifice one idea – the idea that you must sacrifice something real to be happy. True happiness is, therefore, not really about sacrifice; it is about Self-acceptance – the acceptance that you are not guilty and that you are created whole, worthy and well.

I once counselled a lady called Joy who came to see me from London over several weeks. Joy was in her forties, an artist, recently divorced, trying to turn over a new leaf in her life, and, in her own words, 'a depressive'. Joy was brought up Roman Catholic. She had gone to school in a convent where she was taught the 'value' of sacrifice and martyrdom.

'Sacrifice was the primary teaching of the convent,' she told me. 'We were all taught we were sinners and that penance and sacrifice was all we were good for.' 'How did you sacrifice?' I asked. 'We had to take cold showers daily to mortify the flesh; we had to open windows in winter; we had to skip dinners; we had to sleep without pillows; we had to give up anything we enjoyed . . .' The list went on and on. 'And because I wanted to be good, I became the best martyr I could, but it was never, ever enough,' said Joy.

Joy noticed that every time she attempted to be happy, it appeared as if the universe conspired to 'make me miserable'. 'Recently, I tried to go for an aromatherapy massage for the first time in my life,' she told me. 'I felt so guilty, so wrong, but I wanted to do it. But when I got there the aromatherapist was ill and she had gone home. Her colleague told me she has never been ill before.' Joy went on to tell me, 'Last week, I decided to go to an opera as I have never done anything like that. Just as I arrived, there was a bomb scare and the performance was cancelled. Earlier this year, I went on my first holiday for twenty years, and I got ill and spent the fortnight in hospital.'

I put it to Joy that all of these failed attempts at happiness were definitely not God's doing, they were definitely not the universe conspiring against her, and, they were definitely not coincidences. Joy's story was too similar to the martyr's story to be coincidental. 'I know this might be a stretch for you, Joy,' I said, 'but until you give up your belief in the value of martyrdom, I think you will attract even more disappointments like this into your life.' 'You mean they are not coincidences?' she asked. 'No, they are effects – effects created by your ardent belief in your guilt and the need for sacrifice.'

Step by step, we began to challenge all of Joy's learned beliefs about her own *guilt* and *unworthiness*. She had to change her mind about herself before she could change the way her life was going. 'You have learned about lack and sacrifice,' I told her, 'and now we must learn again about wholeness and joy, for Joy is your name is it not?' Joy keeps in touch every now and then and she continues to make good progress.

Most martyrs are 'kill-joys', although they would deny this heavily. Martyrs are so afraid of 'any happiness' that they tend to put the dampers on anyone being 'too happy'. Happiness is a major dilemma to anyone who believes in martyrdom because *you cannot be happy and guilty*. A martyr must decide, therefore, what he or she values most – happiness or guilt?

Martyrdom stems from *guilt* and *unworthiness* and it inevitably ends in *guilt* and *unworthiness*. Most martyrs end up very unhappy because they feel they never get the sympathy they think they deserve. Also, most martyrs end up very manipulative, using their own guilt to levy guilt upon others. Martyrs learn to adjust to disappointment and loss, and although they may dream of joy and happiness they feel very uncomfortable about receiving any. This is because,

to a martyr, to receive is a sign of the devil.

One very common symptom of the martyrdom ethic that you may notice in yourself, is that every time you receive a compliment, a present, or any gift of love, you are tempted to recoil. Learning to accept, receive and say 'Thank you' is quite a skill. The fear of martyrdom is that 'happiness makes you selfish', but, ironically, it is martyrdom that often leads to selfishness because (1) a martyr denies people the chance to give to them; (2) you cannot give freely that which you do not accept freely.

Martyrdom is so wrapped up in illusions of guilt that it overlooks a most important truth –

your happiness is your gift to the world.

Jane was twenty-eight years old, a single parent, who lived in a tower block, supported financially by social welfare. She had diligently followed her 'penance plan' for happiness, and along the way she had lost sight of happiness altogether. She was a classic martyr who had been brought up with the classic martyr teaching of 'a woman's work is never done'. She felt she was a second-class citizen who did not know how to ask for her own needs. 'And when I am with people,' she said, 'I can't just relax; I have to be useful to them, always helping and always trying to please them.'

The turning point for Jane came when I was able to point out to her that every time she abused and neglected herself, her young baby would cry, get ill and be unhappy. Jane saw the link immediately. Within a few days she said to me, 'I get it. I have to be nice to me, because when I am nice to me, my family gets the benefit too.' 'Yes,' I said. 'So happiness isn't selfish. Happiness is okay,' she said.

In truth, your happiness is more than okay. Your happiness is also a great gift. It is a total inspiration, a wonderful example and a great service to the world. Your happiness contributes so much more to the world than your suffering. By choosing to be happy, you are being the 'Light of the World'. At The Happiness Project, we celebrate the idea of happiness as a gift in this statement:

> *It is because the world is so full of suffering,*
> *that your happiness is a gift.*
> *It is because the world is so full of poverty,*
> *that your wealth is a gift.*
> *It is because the world is so unfriendly,*
> *that your smile is a gift.*
> *It is because the world is so full of war,*
> *that your peace of mind is a gift.*
> *It is because the world is in such despair,*
> *that your hope and optimism is a gift.*
> *It is because the world is so afraid,*
> *that your love is a gift.*

CHAPTER FIVE

✧

Living Unconditionally

✧

Happiness is free – there are no
conditions.

One of my clients, Annabel, was much too wrapped up in self-improvement to be happy. Annabel was in her forties, a mother of two, divorced, currently single, a 'fitness fanatic', a 'health food gourmet' and a 'self-improvement nut'. In fact, she once told me she 'lived for self-improvement'. Annabel had even made a career out of self-improvement. She was author of eight self-improvement books, and she had made many appearances on radio and television.

I came to learn that Annabel's description of herself as a 'self-improvement nut' was entirely accurate. Every day began with meditation, affirmations, a health shake for breakfast and a power walk. Each week her basic routine included acupuncture for energy, a deep tissue massage, and on-going therapy. She also read at least two self-improvement books a week. Her best friend was her fitness trainer. And she called herself a 'workshop junkie', because she attended every self-improvement seminar in town.

Such was Annabel's dedication to self-improvement, it clearly came as a shock to her when I suggested that,

to be happy, you have to give up self-improvement.

Annabel's ardent desire for self-improvement was motivated not by joy but by guilt, the belief that she was not already worthy of happiness. I explained to Annabel that until she changed her mind about herself (i.e. gave up her guilt) no amount of self-improvement would bring her any real, lasting peace of mind.

Annabel listened intently. 'I suppose I am living proof that self-improvement cannot make you happy,' she said. I replied, 'I am not asking you to give up trying to improve your life, your career, your health, or your skills, but what I am asking you to see is that true happiness demands no self-improvement, no special conditions, no intelligence test, no pre-entry grades, no financial status, no elaborate sacrifice, no nothing. *Happiness is freely available, always, everywhere to everyone.'*

I told Annabel that her story was very similar to my own. In particular, I shared with her a 'severe case of life' I experienced the day after my thirtieth birthday. This 'severe case of life' proved to be the catalyst for another major turning point in my life, for it was at this time that I finally decided to give up self-improvement once and for all.

My thirtieth birthday 'ended in tears'. The celebrations which I had enjoyed enormously were abruptly and rudely interrupted by a soundtrack in my mind that was playing well-rehearsed anthems and marching songs, like, 'You're still not good enough', 'You're on the wrong track', 'The outlook is bad' and 'You've done nothing with your life'. My ego just had to have its say.

I remember I was halfway through another chorus of 'You've done nothing with your life', when I suddenly stopped the song and yelled out loud, 'Why do I still feel so awful?' As I scanned a period of twelve years, I estimated I had read over five hundred self-improvement books (some of them several times), listened to nearly two hundred self-improvement talks on cassette, attended countless self-improvement workshops, performed thousands of self-improvement affirmations, meditated for up to five hours a day, prayed constantly, etc.

As I continued to tot up all my efforts at self-improvement, it occurred to me that if I had put the same amount of hard work and dedication into something physical like bodybuilding, I would probably be 'Mr Biceps of the Universe' by now! In fact, I reckoned I would be so muscle-clad that I would have to walk through doorways sideways. Why, then, if I had done so much, did I feel there was still so much more to be done?

Tears rolled down my cheeks. I felt utterly broken. I prayed for help. An inner dialogue began almost immediately, and with it a new awareness dawned. I realised, for the first time, that

no amount of self-improvement can make up for
a lack of Self-acceptance.

Happiness does not demand self-improvement; it asks only

for unconditional Self-acceptance, i.e. the willingness to accept that your unconditioned Self is whole, happy and well already. In other words, *whilst self-improvement is the ego's greatest hope for happiness, Self-acceptance is, ultimately, giving up the ego,* i.e. giving up your learned belief in inner lack.

Here, then, is your essential choice – (1) improve your ego; or (2) let go of your ego and accept your Self, your whole, unconditioned Self. From my thirtieth birthday onwards, The Happiness Project offered no more courses on self-improvement. We no longer encourage people to believe that they first have to prove or improve themselves in order to qualify for happy. Instead, we help people to give up self-improvement with a small 's' for a greater practice of Self-acceptance with a capital 'S'.

Self-acceptance is the key to the treasures of the kingdom, the kingdom of your unconditioned Self. I often use the following meditation at The Happiness Project. It reads:

> *Without Self-acceptance, peace is impossible; with Self-acceptance, peace is yours.*
> *Without Self-acceptance, love has to wait; with Self-acceptance, love is made welcome.*
> *Without Self-acceptance, there is no happiness; with Self-acceptance, you know happiness.*
> *Without Self-acceptance, truth hurts; with Self-acceptance, truth heals.*
> *Without Self-acceptance, you can accept no one fully into your life; with Self-acceptance, you can.*
> *Without Self-acceptance, you are always hiding; with Self-acceptance, your spirit is gliding.*

Without Self-acceptance, nothing is enough; with Self-acceptance, you are enough.
Without Self-acceptance, you are not free to grow; with Self-acceptance, your potential is free to flow.
Without Self-acceptance, there is no chance; with Self-acceptance, you are always in with a chance.

Being Happy, Doing Nothing

The following story is really asking you just how lazy you can be before you start to feel guilty:

It was a beautiful, hot, lazy summer day and Billy was fishing by the river. After a while, a stranger in a suit and tie walked by. 'How are you doing?' asked the stranger. 'Being happy, doing nothing,' Billy replied. 'Catch any fish?' asked the stranger. Billy hadn't stopped to count. 'Maybe ten, but I let them all back in again,' said Billy.

'Ten fish! Why, you should have kept them and sold them,' said the stranger. 'Why?' asked Billy. 'You could have made a profit, and then invested that profit in a better rod.' 'Why do I need a better rod?' asked Billy. 'Well, with a better rod you could catch more fish.' 'Why would I want more fish?' asked Billy. 'Well, more fish equals more profit, and with more profit you could have your own fish van,' said the stranger. 'But I like it here, just being happy, doing nothing,' said Billy.

'Okay, but with a great big fish van you could make even more profit,' said the stranger. 'And then what?' asked Billy. 'Hell knows, you could, with enough hard work, end up opening your own fish restaurant one day!' said the stranger. 'And what then?' asked Billy. 'Well, by then you would be so rich you could come fishing here whenever you liked!' said the stranger. 'Aren't I doing that already?' smiled Billy.

The fishing is a symbol for simply *being*[1]. Billy is your unconditioned Self, completely relaxed and *happy being, doing nothing*. The stranger, in suit and tie, is the ego – the little voice that tells you that before you can simply *be happy* you absolutely must, ought and should toil and struggle.

When Self-acceptance gives way to self-improvement, you often end up denying yourself happiness *now* because you believe there are certain conditions which first 'must', 'ought' and 'should' be met first. In this way,

> **you make yourself miserable by your constant demands of 'must', 'ought' and 'should'.**

The unconditioned Self makes no demands for happiness – it is unconditional. The ego-mind, convinced of its own lack, performs once again like a megalomaniac sports coach, shouting out a long list of 'musts', 'oughts' and 'shoulds' that it believes 'must' be met before you can be happy.

For example, the judgement 'I'm not good enough' spawns 'shoulds' like 'I should do more'; the belief that 'I'm bad' fuels 'musts' like 'I must always be good'; the thought that 'I'm wrong' leads to 'oughts' like 'I ought to get everything right'; and a fear that 'I'm nothing' creates 'shoulds' like 'I should do something'. The lists are never-ending.

Cognitive psychology has been particularly effective in identifying the highly irrational and illusory thinking of the ego which makes up the 'musts', 'oughts' and 'shoulds'[2]. Albert Ellis, founder of Rational Emotive Behaviour Therapy, deliberately pokes fun at this ego-thinking by referring to it as 'musterbation'[3]. Laughter is wonderful at helping to dissolve and let go of learned fears.

Common examples of 'musterbation' include:

- 'To be happy, I must be liked by everyone.'
- 'To be happy, I must always be right.'
- 'To be happy, I must always be good.'
- 'To be happy, I must always be in control.'
- 'To be happy, I must be treated fairly by everyone.'
- 'To be happy, I must deserve it.'
- 'To be happy, I must work for it.'
- 'To be happy, I must never get angry.'
- 'To be happy, I must be perfect.'
- 'To be happy, I must always be on time.'
- 'To be happy, I must never let down my guard.'
- 'To be happy, I must hide my feelings.'
- 'To be happy, I must never be vulnerable.'

You may find it helpful to make a list of the 'musts', 'oughts' and 'shoulds' you have invented for yourself. Some of your 'musterbation' may be so set that it has become unconscious and automatic. This is when the 'musts', 'oughts' and 'shoulds' feel more like universal laws than personal illusions. You do yourself a service every time you

uncover, let go of, and smile at your 'oughtism' – remember, happiness is free!

The ego saves most of its judgement, condemnation, 'oughtism' and self-improvement for the body. Every day is a war against cellulite, grey hair, split ends, wrinkles, love handles, sagging breasts, beer bellies, calories and acne. How can you be happy when your elastin is low?! Again and again the ego tries to prop up its fragile happiness with cosmetic surgery, make-up counter attacks, sensuality boosts, face masks and high energy workouts.

The ego's regime includes the following 'oughtism' and 'musterbation':

- 'To be happy, I must weigh less.'
- 'To be happy, I must weigh more.'
- 'To be happy, I should develop more muscle tone.'
- 'To be happy, I should have a smaller stomach.'
- 'To be happy, I ought to exercise more.'
- 'To be happy, I ought not to eat chocolate.'
- 'To be happy, I must get rid of cellulite.'
- 'To be happy, I must get a face-lift.'
- 'To be happy, I must get another one.'
- 'To be happy, I should eat less.'
- 'To be happy, I should eat more.'
- 'To be happy, I ought to have bigger breasts.'
- 'To be happy, I ought to be at least a size 8.'

Over and over you promise yourself that after this last

'must', 'ought' or 'should' you will be completely happy forever. The trouble is, without Self-acceptance, there is no end to self-improvement and to 'oughtism'. The ego is addicted to 'oughtism' because it is also addicted to the idea that happiness requires a perfect condition. Furthermore, the ego, by its very nature, is never ever satisfied. You cannot appease the ego, you can only let go of it.

The choice is, therefore, either you try in vain to first take care of all your 'oughtism' and then be happy, or you just decide to *be happy* anyway! You can do this with Self-acceptance, the acceptance that happiness is free to you always.

Three 'Mirages' of the Ego!

'Joy is not a carrot.'
Linda Carpenter[4]

Think of your ego as the White Rabbit in *Alice in Wonderland*, always late for a very important date, forever dashing, running and chasing after some imaginary carrot. The White Rabbit first makes its entrance by disturbing Alice's peace as she rests by the babbling brook. A lazy, timeless moment is shattered by the White Rabbit's hurry, flurry, panic and pandemonium.

How often do you catch yourself, like the White Rabbit, living life on the hop? How often do you experience peace of mind, or a mind in pieces? 'Faster, faster,' cries the ego, convinced that everything good is outside, and equally convinced that something is missing on the inside. The inner peace of your unconditioned Self holds forever true. It can never be broken, but it can be overlooked.

Until you can accept that true happiness exists within you, you will be forced to hare around, bouncing from place to place, searching the world in vain for some external replica. The ego pins all its hopes for happiness on three very vague goals – the goals of 'more', 'there' and 'next'. Happiness is possible, according to the ego, with 'a little bit more', when we 'get to there' and when we 'take the next step'. The point is, however,

> ### *happiness requires no next step; it is already here!*

Living life in the fast lane, we constantly overlook and fail to appreciate what we already have as we chase after 'more'; we sacrifice what is possible now for what we hope may come 'next'; and we throw away all that is available to us 'here' as we sprint over to 'there'. And yet, without Self-acceptance, the happiness of 'more', 'next' and 'there' fades just like a mirage fades before a thirsty traveller lost in the desert.

1. 'More'

> *Happiness – the more we chase it,*
> *the more it flees.*

The 1980s was the decade of 'more', in which a 'ready, steady spend' society tried to buy happiness once and for all by acquiring more 'stuff'. The world became a giant department store, shopping became the number one national pastime, and rampant materialism offered apparent salvation. Suggestions that the 1990s gave birth to a post-materialistic age are premature, but it is true that more and more people are beginning to realise that

more 'stuff' cannot buy you more happiness.

In recent years, more than five hundred extensive pieces of psychology research have shown quite conclusively that, since the 1950s, (1) we have more things and more wealth than ever before; (2) we are more depressed, more violent, more suicidal and more stressed than ever before[5]. The research indicates that 'more equals less', i.e. as we acquire more we become more demanding and less satisfied.

'More' is the ego's promised land. 'More', or 'The Oliver syndrome', as I affectionately call it, is the ego's hope that 'more stuff' will somehow magic a rabbit out of a hat and you will be happy[6]. The ego is never satisfied, though – how can a thought of lack ever be satisfied? Clearly, we do not need more stuff; we do, however, need more Self-acceptance. We have to learn that although *more stuff can encourage you to be happy, more stuff cannot make you happy*. Zero peace of mind plus lots of 'things' will still leave you wanting more. Self-acceptance is the key. To put it another way,

'more' is never enough until you choose to be happy.

Do you remember how, ten years ago, you promised yourself that you would be happy once you started earning what you do now? Are you happy now? Do you remember how you convinced yourself that your last promotion would make you happy? Are you? And now that you are more successful than, say, five years ago, are you more happy? And isn't it amazing how your most recent successes have seemed to create more work for you and not less?

What are you currently convincing yourself you need more of before you can be happy? What 'more' do you think you need to be good enough, happy and successful? Is it more money? Read the research! Maybe you are after more horse power, one more qualification, more recognition, more wardrobe space, more time, or maybe a home with one more bedroom? Whatever it is, the 'things' of this world are mere toys. They are great fun. Play with them all you like, but do not think for a moment that they are your happiness.

True happiness is unconditional – it requires nothing 'more' than itself to exist. No amount of 'more' can make you 'more happy'. Happiness is not consumed, it is chosen[7].

2. 'Next'

Happiness is present time – it has nothing to do with the future.

At home, I have a very precious clock that was presented to me after I gave a talk at an annual conference for The LIFE Foundation. This clock is a *'now* clock'. It is like any other clock, except that where there are normally the numbers, one through to twelve, there is simply the word 'now', 'now', 'now', 'now'. This clock helps me to keep the time!

The demography of happiness, according to extensive

psychology research, states that your twenties won't make you happy, your thirties won't make you happy, and neither will your forties, fifties, sixties, seventies or 110's! In other words, there is no special time, age, or stage of life that brings with it happiness[8]. In effect,

> ### *happiness has nothing to do with time; it has everything to do with 'now'.*

Contrary to popular belief, time does not heal, time does not fly, time does not do anything. Time has no consciousness. It does nothing for you. The key to happiness *now* is what you choose to do with your time right now. Are you, right now, making the most valuable use of your time? This moment is, after all, the time of your life!

The While Rabbit in *Alice in Wonderland* carries a large clock so as to keep time. In his hurry to get to where he is going to 'next' he repeatedly fails to look at the clock. Not only does he 'lose time', he also loses the moment. How often do you miss out on happiness *now* as you chase the clock? Are you really so sure that 'next' is really any better than 'now'?

Every day I make a point of slowing down my train of thought so as to appreciate the moment. 'Next' can wait for the moment. Now is here and I want to give it my full attention. It's a funny thing, but time and time again I have found that

> ### *the more you give to now, the more you get from now.*

With the help of my *'now* clock' I take time to enjoy the

moment. It does not take much to do this. Sometimes a deep, long, slow exhale is enough. A smile works well. 'Thank you' is prayerful. Wonder and awe also work well. When I am outside and I hear a bird sing, I stop to look for the bird. When I see a beautiful flower, I name the flower, greeting it as I would a dear friend. Happiness makes you eccentric like that!

The ego's goal of 'next' is in keeping with the ego's belief that *happiness is somewhere else*. It is all about living in the *not now*. I often catch myself living in the *not now*. In particular, when I sit down to eat lunch, often my first thought is not for the lunch, but 'what will we eat tonight'. Also, there is a member of my family, who shall remain nameless, who goes on holiday with bags full of holiday brochures to plan her 'next' holiday!

The fantasy of 'next' often prevents you from giving your very best to now. We kid ourselves that happiness will happen and that we will give our very best to the 'next time', the 'next job' and our 'next partner'. The truth is, however, if you do not change first then 'next' will be no different to now. In other words,

time cannot make you happy, your attitude can.

Until you can accept that happiness is about a choice, and not a clock, then what comes 'next' will be no more helpful to you than what is here now. Time is not your answer; consciousness, and the decision *to be*, are your answers. Time will not save you, but changing your mind about yourself can. Slow down a while, cease to hurry for a moment, and let the inner happiness bubble up. In this way, now becomes an ideal preparation for what comes 'next'.

> *'When from our better selves we have too long*
> *Been parted by the hurrying world, and droop,*
> *Sick of its business, of its pleasures tired*
> *How gracious, how benign, is Solitude.'*
> William Wordsworth[9]

3. 'There'

> *Happiness is a way of travelling, and*
> *not a final destination.*

One of the biggest causes of stress in our society is that we have set happiness upon the horizon instead of in our heart. In doing so, we have tried to make happiness into a destination, a place, a point to arrive at and a final sanctuary. All of a sudden, to be happy we have to travel across space and time to get 'there'.

I remember the first time I asked a group of people at the Laughter Clinic, 'What is happiness?' As we looked at each other's answers, mine included, we became aware that almost every answer involved long-haul travel! The answers included, 'Happiness is Miami beach and a Pina Colada', 'Happiness is the stars', 'Happiness is a deserted island in the Indian Ocean', 'Happiness is a carnival in Brazil' and 'Happiness is Hawaii'.

The ego's goal of 'there', or the 'greener grass fixation' as I call it, pins all your hopes of happiness, peace, love and salvation on geography. The point is,

geography can't make you happy.

Geography can certainly help you to be happy, but it cannot make you happy. And there is no amount of geography can make up for a lack of Self-acceptance. Everywhere is hell whilst you feel like hell; but everywhere can also be heavenly when inside you feel whole and well.

New locations can certainly help to inspire new thoughts, new perceptions and new beliefs. There are times, therefore, when it makes sense to change location or change job, for instance, to secure a fresh start. But because the world does no more than mirror your state of mind, 'there' will end up being just like 'here' if there is no Self-acceptance.

Sometimes, as the French novelist, Marcel Proust, once wrote, 'The voyage of discovery lies not in finding new landscapes, but in having new eyes'[10]. To be happy, we must be willing to see things differently and to see ourselves differently. The ego, being a thought of lack, cannot see wholeness. Thus,

the ego has 'been there, done that' and it still ain't happy!

Can you give up the ego? In other words, are you willing to believe and to see that you are whole already, happy already, worthy already. Dare you entertain the possibility that you carry within you all the wonders that you search for outside of yourself? To the ego this sounds blasphemous; but to your unconditioned Self this is merely a natural way of thinking.

Laughing at the Cosmic Joke

What if you stopped searching for happiness?
And what if you then discovered you
were already happy?

Before I reveal the cosmic joke, I would like to share with you a piece of writing called 'Question Time':

'Am I close, God?' pleaded the pilgrim.
'Close?' enquired God. 'What does "close" mean?'
'Close – near to you – towards the front of the
queue – chosen – special,' pleaded the pilgrim.
And God could not understand, and yet God
spoke, 'You are Me – You are as close to God
as You can get.'

'How soon, my Lord?' prayed the monk.
'Soon?' enquired God, 'What does "soon" mean?'
'Soon – quick – fast – how long to go before at
last I am One with you?' prayed the monk.
And God could not understand, and yet God
spoke, 'Nothing can happen sooner or later than
now. Is now soon enough for You?'

'Am I forgiven, Father?' begged the nun.
'I have heard this word many times,' said God,
'What does it mean?'
'Forgiven – loved – paid up – sins forgotten –
apologies accepted – in good standing,' begged
the nun.

God understood none of this, except for love,
and thus, He spoke, 'Love is what You are, and
all I know You by – nothing else is real.'

'Am I deserving?' the disciple asked.
'And what is this word, "deserving"?' enquired
God.
'Deserving – good – worthy – in the money – a
bit of luck my way – well thought of by You,
God,' the disciple explained.
And God was puzzled once again, and yet
God heard Himself say, 'Whatever is worthy
of Me is worthy of You; anything unworthy of
Me is unworthy of You.'

'Will I be saved?' the priest called out.
'Oh dear,' God sighed, 'Here is another word
I understand not.'
'Saved – safe – protected – the lost and found
department – defended,' the priest cried out.
And God replied, 'Save your worries, save
your fears. You are saved because, in truth,
you were never lost – confused, I grant You –
but never lost!'

Beneath all the fearful, guilty and unwise dogmas which so
pollute and stain the spiritual traditions of the world, there
is, at heart, a rich untouched seam of joy, bliss, happiness
and laughter, as typified by stories of the joyful Christ, the
laughing Buddha, the playful Krishna, the singing angels
and others[11]. For us also, beneath our own fear, guilt and
pain, there is, at heart, a rich, untouched spirit of total joy
that is constantly at play. Herein lies the cosmic joke.

Simply stated, the cosmic joke is really a touch of cosmic irony. All the great spiritual teachers, including Buddha, Jesus and Krishna, started out, like you and I, as searchers after happiness, love and God. When the truth was revealed to them, they laughed. They laughed for joy, and with relief, for their searching was finally over. They now understood that what they had searched the world for was within them all along. In other words,

YOU ARE what you seek!

When the Zen Master Po-chang was asked about seeking for the joy of the Buddha, he answered, 'It is much like riding an ox in search of an ox.' The Chinese philosopher, Menicus, from the fourth century B.C., said, 'The tao is near and people seek it far away.' An ancient African proverb on happiness states, 'Why tell animals living in the water to drink?' The eighteenth-century French writer, Voltaire, said, 'Paradise is where *I am*' – *I am* being your unconditioned, universal Self. And, for good measure, the American humourist, Josh Billings, put it like this – 'If you ever find happiness by hunting for it, you will find it, as the old woman did her lost spectacles, safe on her own nose all the time.'[12]

Imagine how funny it would be if you were to overhear the mighty Sun praying for light, the ocean praying for water, the wind praying for a breath of fresh air. Imagine, if you can, a dark sun, a dry ocean, a wind without air, and, for that matter, a universe cramped for space, eternity rushed, infinity feeling slightly hemmed in. And what could be funnier than you and I, made of joy, praying to God for more love and more happiness!

You are what you seek. The cosmic joke challenges you to give up your fears, your guilt, your conditioning and your doubts, and accept the truth about your unconditioned Self. You are not a body, you are not a fearful mind, you are not separate, you are not small – you are the Presence of Love, you are happiness incarnate, and peace of mind is always with you. True Self-acceptance is the realisation that

the soul is joy!

Our greatest fear is that we are, at heart, wrong, bad and not good enough – the devil incarnate. The laughter of the cosmic joke is really relief that this nightmare of mistaken identity and confusion is not the truth. The laughing Buddha laughs because He can afford to. He knows he is safe and that we are all safe. To get the cosmic joke, though, you must be prepared to change your mind about yourself.

Another way of stating the real truth about you, according to the cosmic joke, is to say,

you are truly happy 100% of the time; your only problem is that you are not always aware of this.

Yes! Amazing as it may sound, your happiness is with you 100% of the time. The reason you do not always feel happy is because you let the sunshine of your spirit get eclipsed by clouds of fear, doubt, guilt, illusion and mistaken identity. In truth, you can afford to laugh, however, because no matter what happens to you in the world, your spirit is safe and sound in the heaven of your unconditioned Self. *Happiness cannot leave its source!*

When troubled, therefore, don't pray; 'God, grant me happiness!' 'God send me Your Love!', or 'God, give me peace!' Can you see how each of these prayers pre-supposes and re-affirms that what you want is not already with you? Instead pray, 'God, reveal to me my joy', 'God, heal my fear that Love is not here?', or 'God, teach me to feel again my peace of mind'. Remember,

> *real prayer is not a cosmic DHL delivery service; real prayer is receiving that which is already given.*

The cosmic joke encourages you to laugh out loud at illusions of lack, guilt, and the false conditions and obstacles in the way of your salvation. That is what the poem 'Question Time' is all about. Your inner fears, if not healed, are always projected out onto that which you seek, i.e. God, love and happiness. By letting go of your fears, all projections disappear, and only joy remains.

One of my favourite lines in *A Course In Miracles* is, 'God does not forgive because He has never condemned'. This is a quite brilliant insight. God is unconditional, and so too is love and happiness. Thus, the fears that happiness has to be worked for, suffered for and sacrificed for are truly laughable. Holy laughter pierces through all illusions.

Uncovering the 'Joy' of Happiness

When St. Francis of Assisi was asked by Brother Leo, 'What is perfect joy?', he replied with the following story:

> Imagine that I return to Perugia on the darkest of nights, a night so cold that everything is covered with snow, and the frost in the folds of my habit hits my legs and makes them bleed. Shrouded in snow and shivering with cold, I arrive at the door of the friary, and after calling out for a long time, the brother porter gets up and asks: 'Who is it?'
>
> And I respond: 'It is I, Brother Francis.'
>
> The porter says: 'Be on your way. Now is not the time to arrive at the friary. I will not open the door for you.'
>
> I insist, and he answers: 'Be on your way right now. You are stupid and an idiot. We are already many here and we do not need you.'
>
> I insist once more: 'For the love of God, let me in, just for tonight.'
>
> And he answers: 'Not even to talk. Go to the leper colony that is nearby.'
>
> Well, Brother Leo, if after all this I do not lose patience and remain calm, believe me, that is perfect joy![13]

What St. Francis was trying to teach Brother Leo was that true happiness is unconditional in that it is ultimately unaffected by the world. Joy is, ultimately, not of this world; it is quite clearly very different to worldly pleasure and contentment (see *Table C*). Essentially put, pleasure and contentment are conditional ego-states; joy is unconditional – there is no ego.

Pleasure:
Happiness of the Body

Contentment:
Happiness of the World

Joy:
Happiness of the Spirit

Table C

Pleasure is happiness of the body. It can be thrilling, warm, wet, fuzzy, funny, physical, sexual, exciting, deeply restful and highly arousing. Pleasure is sensual and highly transient in that it quickly comes and goes. Pleasure does not exist on its own – it must always have an external spark or stimulus, such as sound, aroma or touch. Pleasure is also non-universal, i.e. the same stimulus does not elicit the same pleasure in everyone. For instance, I enjoy star-gazing, you may not; I listen to Barry Manilow records, you may not; I like spicy foods, you may not; I appreciate the rich smell of farmyards, you may not; I adore the feel of silk, you may not.

Contentment is happiness of the world. It is about life-satisfaction. Contentment implies a mental judgement, usually favourable, about the 'contents' of the world around you. For instance, 'I am happy because my house no longer leaks', or 'I am happy because my body is the right shape', or 'I am happy because my car is the right shape'.

Contentment always requires a *because*, i.e. a reason. You are happy because you judge that 'This is good', 'This is okay', and 'This is right'. You are happy because the world looks a certain way – it fits your picture. This contentment is very fragile, though, for it hangs on how the world looks. Your contentment is threatened, therefore, each moment the world changes, *and the world is changing each moment!*
 Certainly, circumstances can help you to be happy; but it is a mistake to think you need a precise form or a precise set of circumstances to make you happy.

Joy is happiness of the spirit. It is 'true happiness' in that it always stays true. This is the happiness that goes with you wherever you go. Whereas physical pleasures and worldly contentment are born and then die, joy is eternal and timeless – it is happiness *now*. This joy is inward, it is deeply intimate, a part of the fabric of your soul, and it is the amazing grace of your spirit. As such, it is constant.

This joy is natural. It is 100% unconditional, non-judgemental and free. Wherever you go, there It is. It is not empty, It is full. It is Loving. It has consciousness. You can relate to It. You can ask It for guidance. You can ask It to shine Its Light upon your problems. You can sing to It, pray to It, and dance with It. You can meditate on It. You can draw with It, write with It, and heal with It. You can ask It to bless your relationships, your life, your career, everything. *Let It be!*

Being Unreasonably Happy!

*And all of a sudden I was out
of my mind;
And I lost my head;
And I forgot to remember;
And I could no longer make up
my mind*

*And I was so unreasonable –
Happy, loving, ecstatic, for no
reason at all.
I smiled, I laughed, I loved, I
was generous for no reason
at all.
I sang, I danced, 'Hello,' I
cried.
I was happy – happy for no
reason at all.*

*And I was so thoughtless –
Free to fly without any thought
of fear at all;
Free to go without judgements,
plans or the need to know;
Free to live without any thought
of 'what if', 'watch out', or
'how so?'
I was really not myself.*

*And try as I might,
I still cannot think straight.*

I have still not come to my senses.
Being sensible has lost its appeal.
I live, now, in a world of innocence,
And in no sense at all do I
regret the day
I gave way
And Lived totally out of
control.

Can you remember a time in your life when you were
happy for no reason at all? All of a sudden you were
surprised by joy. It bubbled up as if from nowhere. Your
smile was almost too big for your face, your heart wanted
to leap out of your chest, and your whole body rang like a
bell. 'I'm happy!' you cried. 'I wonder why?' you thought.
'I must know why?' you demanded. And just then, the joy
appeared to die.

Children are often happy without reason – it is a part of
their charm. Often you can catch a child laughing for the
fun of laughing, smiling for the sake of smiling, playing
happily with happiness. It both amuses and saddens me to
think that when a child laughs for no reason at all we think
it wonderful, but when an adult laughs for no reason at all
we immediately fear for his or her health. The point is,

who ever said happiness needs a reason?

The poem above is called 'Thoughtless', and describes
my own experience of what I call 'joy', or 'unreasonable
happiness'. Joy is unreasonable happiness in that it requires
no reason, no stimulus, no special conditions, no controlled
effort and no down-payment. This joy is beyond time,

beyond space and beyond this life we know, and yet it is fully alive, fully present, fully possible *now*. This can only be, however, if we accept that happiness is free.

There is an old joke I picked up at psychology school which goes – if a psychologist came across two doors, one saying 'Heaven' and the other saying 'Lecture on Heaven', the psychologist would walk through the door to the lecture! Honestly, which door would you walk through? Maybe

> ***your greatest downfall is that you believe you have to understand happiness before you can be happy.***

Can you accept happiness unconditionally, without even understanding it? If you can, then happiness is yours unconditionally. Happiness is never grasped, it is simply let loose. In truth, laughter needs no reason. A smile needs no reason. Love needs no reason. Kindness needs no reason. There are gifts for free – life's true treasures. Can you cope with that?

Being Spontaneously Available

> *'The soul should always stand ajar, ready to welcome the ecstatic experience.'*
> Emily Dickinson

My friends Tom and Linda Carpenter have taught me as much about happiness as anyone. They are dedicated teachers of *A Course In Miracles*, who travel the world, quietly sharing their profound messages of love, truth and joy[14]. When they are not travelling they live on a tropical flower farm on the remote Hawaiian island of Kauai.

Tom, Linda, Miranda and I will sit and talk about truth, God and the universe for hours on end[15]. It is our joy to do so. I remember once asking Tom, 'What is happiness?' His answer moved me so deeply it has since become a central principle of my work with The Happiness Project. He said,

> **'Happiness is being spontaneously available to your spirit.'**

Spontaneously available! What a beautiful phrase that is. The moment he said those words it reminded me of a very famous story of a meeting between a Zen Master and a distinguished university professor. The professor, who taught history and philosophy, had requested a meeting with the Zen Master whilst travelling through Japan. The Zen Master agreed to the meeting.

'I have come to learn from you what is truth,' said the professor.

'Would you like some tea?' said the Master, who was smiling from ear to ear.

'Thank you,' said the professor. 'I have little time, but I am keen to learn all that I can.'

The Master began to pour the tea.

'You see,' said the professor, 'my entire life has been a search for truth.'

The Master continued to pour.

'That's plenty of tea, thank you.'

The Master kept pouring.

'Master, the cup is overflowing – no more tea will go in.'

The Master smiled. As he still poured, he said, 'My dear professor, like this cup, you are full of your own beliefs and theories. How can I show you Zen unless you first empty your cup?'

Think of the professor as a symbol of your ego, or conditioned self, full of plans, theories, beliefs and ideas about happiness. The Zen Master is a symbol of the unconditioned Self, entirely empty of hypotheses and schemes. The Zen Master neither searches for happiness nor tries to understand happiness; he simply is happy. He is happy because he is spontaneously available to the joy of his unconditioned Self. *Spontaneous availability is full acceptance.*

Happiness is not an intelligence test. You do not have to understand happiness before you can be happy. Indeed, you cannot understand happiness first. Rather, you must first choose to be happy, and only then will you understand. In other words, you cannot think your way to happiness. Happiness is not a formula of thought. If anything, happiness is the relinquishment of thoughts, theories and theses;

to be happy, you have to give up all concepts of happiness.

This is particularly true if you are currently unhappy, for the thinking that makes you unhappy now cannot make you happy later. You have to be willing, therefore, to be spontaneously available to fresh insight, fresh wisdom and fresh inspiration. The message is, *be fresh!* Now is new. It is not the past. Your mind is full of 'old tea', and so you must first empty the cup, i.e. be willing to let go of limited old fears and ideas.

The mystics of old continually beckoned their students to give up concepts of God, concepts of Love, concepts of Heaven and concepts of Joy. They explained that your thinking is at best like a finger that points to the moon, but it is not the moon. Stop pointing! Stop theorising! Be willing to be available to the joy of your soul. Say, 'I am available'. Affirm, 'I am available'. Sing, 'I am available'. Listen, be open, be clear, be empty. Take a leap! Jump for joy!

To the intellect, just simply choosing to be happy is not enough. It is a silly idea. Sometimes, though, the silly ideas are the best. When I was researching my book, *Laughter, The Best Medicine*, I discovered that the word 'silly' comes from two old European words, 'seely' and 'saelig', both of which mean 'blessed', 'happy' and 'joyful'[16]. When you are silly, you are creative, open, fearless and, above all, you are unconditioned.

When I asked Tom to expand on his idea of spontaneous availability he reminded me of a phrase in *A Course In Miracles* which reads, 'A healed mind does not plan'. He then went on to say,

'Your plan for happiness will not work.'

Tom's teaching of spontaneous availability moved me deeply because I am a 'recovering planner'. Ever since I can remember, I have lived my life to a plan. All through my twenties, in particular, I diligently followed my five year plan, my three year plan, my one year plan, my one month plan, my one week plan, and my daily plan. My whole life was planned out. I was very focused, but I was also rigid, inflexible, unavailable and preoccupied. Have you heard the phrase, 'life is what happens to you whilst you are busy making other plans'?

What Tom infers by 'your plan for happiness will not work', is that happiness requires no plan. If you think happiness needs a plan, then your thinking is off. Happiness need not be planned for, it is here already. Sometimes, though, we are simply too busy planning our future happiness to enjoy happiness *now*. Can you let go of your plans, and accept peace now, love now and joy now? Can you move past your conditioning and accept happiness unconditionally? Can you be spontaneously available?

You Only Live Once . . .

Your whole life is not in front of you –
it is here – NOW!

After years of studying stress, I have concluded that one of the biggest causes of stress is that we wait for happiness to happen. We think happiness is not for now; rather, we see it as a reward we work to, struggle after and suffer for, in the hope that one day it will happen. Following this erroneous train of thought, today becomes a day for well-behaved hardship, noble suffering, mild martyrdom and quiet desperation, and tomorrow, maybe, we might be happy. I believe, however, that

to be happy, you have to lose the 'wait problem'!

Conditions will get no better in the future for as long as you are waiting around to be happy. Indeed, it's only when you stop waiting that conditions begin to improve. I remember how all through my teenage years and early twenties I had this fantasy that life would get better in about eighteen months time or so. I remember how I used to think that I would be less shy, more confident, more successful and probably world famous! I was convinced that something wonderful and special would happen to me.

I had nothing concrete to base these feelings upon; I just hoped that when eighteen months had passed, life would have ironed out its problems for me and I would be a lot happier. What I experienced, however, was that the eighteen months never came any closer – no matter how much time elapsed, the eighteen months always seemed eighteen months away. I finally, painfully, began to realise that, in order to be happy, I had to participate more fully in my life – *now*. In other words,

to be happy, you have to give up 'when' for 'now'!

A good exercise is to take two pieces of paper and write on the top of one, 'I'll be happy when . . .' and on top of the other, 'I'll be happy if . . .' Now complete the list. When do you think you will be happy? 'When' are you hanging on for? And what 'if' has to happen before you choose to be happy? Keep writing and writing, and see how many conditions you have tried to convince yourself you need before you can start smiling.

'You only live once . . .' has a double meaning. It refers to the idea that this moment in time will only ever happen once. Make a point, therefore, of knowing what the date is today, because this date is a one-off. Today will never, ever happen again. Bearing this in mind, how will you choose to live today? Today is not a practice run – the game is on already!

'You only live once . . .' also refers to the 'wait problem' and the fact that we are only ever preparing to be happy instead of being happy. In other words, you only start to really live once . . . work is over, it's Saturday night, the holidays are here, you have some money, you fall in love, you get married, you buy a home, you buy another home, your mortgage is finally paid, your pension plan matures, etc. But even then you still can't be happy, not until the grandchildren get a good education!

What are you waiting for before you give yourself fully to this world? More support, maybe? More confidence? More authority? More opportunity? More qualifications? Can you see that:

> *Whilst you wait, happiness waits.*
> *Whilst you wait, love waits.*
> *Whilst you wait, peace waits.*
> *Whilst you wait, freedom waits.*
> *Whilst you wait, opportunity waits.*
> *Whilst you wait, the world waits.*
> *Whilst you wait, we all wait.*

The 'wait and see' sickness is simply fear. 'What if I stop waiting and go for it, and then I fail?' By waiting, you fail. By giving yourself fully, you will get all you once waited for – all the support, confidence, authority and opportunity. It happens, when you happen.

Happiness happens when you give yourself fully!

Why wait for what is already here?

I experienced very recently one of my most profound psychotherapy sessions ever. Paul is in his forties, a tall man, quite lean, eyes set back in a soft and kind face. He had been on my 'Eight Week Happiness Programme', during which he had shared with all of us the fact that he was recovering from alcoholism. In our one-to-one session, Paul told me how he had tried 'everything' to be happy, but 'nothing' worked. In particular, he described to me how, every time he appeared to take a step closer to happiness, happiness took one step further away. Happiness was always on the horizon, and the horizon was always far away.

'I have given up chasing happiness, and now I am just waiting to be happy,' Paul told me. Without really knowing why at the time, I asked Paul to close his eyes and picture the happiness he spoke of. 'What do you see?' I asked. 'I see a small light in the distance,' replied Paul. 'How small and how far away?' I asked. 'Very small, like a little light at the end of a very long tunnel.' Again, without really knowing why at the time, I asked Paul to imagine that this light was beginning to travel towards him, slowly at first. 'Can you picture that?' I asked. 'Yes,' he said.

As the light travelled towards Paul, I could see that his body began to tremble. 'Take a breath Paul – breathe deeply and slowly. Let the light come even closer.' As he did so, silent tears spilled down both his cheeks. 'How far away is the light?' I asked. 'I don't know – about ten feet maybe.'

Paul wanted to open his eyes. 'Keep your eyes closed, Paul, and let the light approach, and keep breathing,' I whispered.

Inch by inch, in Paul's mind, he allowed the light to come closer, and each time it did, his body trembled more and more, and tears fell to the ground. Eventually, the light was right in front of Paul and covered his whole inner vision. Following my intuition, I then asked Paul to take the light back inside himself. As Paul did this, he sobbed and sobbed – he cried tears which seemed to come up from the very pit of his stomach. At that moment, I don't mind admitting, I cried tears too. We eventually held each other.

I suppose what we had gone through together was a type of time-travel. By bringing the light closer, we were bringing the future closer. We were exchanging 'when' for 'now', 'there' for 'here', 'outer' for 'inner'. Paul's trembling body signalled his resistance to this. His tears, and mine also, were for the grief of denying this inner happiness, and for all the years of looking for happiness in all the wrong places. Without travelling anywhere, Paul's journey was complete.

Paul had, in that moment, accepted happiness unconditionally and the waiting was finally over. A week later, he was still 'over the moon'. Two weeks later, however, Paul found he was pointing at the moon again. The old doubts, fears and conditioning had returned. Before Paul could condemn himself too badly, we embarked upon 'The Journey of Light' exercise again. At the time of writing, we continue to do this meditation together as a way of constantly reminding ourselves that true happiness is here and now.

CHAPTER SIX

✧

Healing Unhappiness

✧

Life is actually bad for your health, or at least that's how it feels sometimes. When we are 'in good heart', life is great, everything is great. We acknowledge life to be a blessing, full of beauty, awe and wonder. We value life and we do everything we can to 'get a life'. But we also have moments when we probably wouldn't recommend life to anyone under any circumstances. *Life feels deadly.*

It seems one moment you can be dancing gracefully, beautifully, with effortless ease, and the next moment you wish someone, somewhere had at least had the decency to tell you your shoe-laces were undone. You know about laughter, but you also know about tears. You have loved much, but you also have your fears. You enjoy highs, you endure lows. You can be warm, you can be cold. Sometimes you are on song, other times you can't even hit a note. Oh, for a drop of hindsight; oh, for a bucketful of foresight!

Life can be testing. The tests are sometimes easy, sometimes difficult; sometimes obvious, sometimes hidden; sometimes multiple choice, sometimes a two-thousand-word essay that has to be handed in *now*! Sometimes you pass the tests, sometimes you have to sit the tests again. And sometimes life is simply too testing. Then the tests really stack up and you fear you might not have what it takes to come through.

My friend and colleague, Alison Atwell, faxed me some time ago a passage by Stuart Wilde, author of *Weight Loss For The Mind*[1]. On top of the fax Alison wrote, 'Is this life or what?!' I met Stuart soon afterwards at a conference and asked him if I could share his words, and he readily agreed. The passage reads:

We have to embrace infinity inside a mortal body.
We have to believe in a god we can't see.
We have to learn to love in a dimension where there
is so much hatred.
We have to see abundance when people constantly
talk of shortages and lack.
We have to discover freedom where control is the
state religion.
We have to develop self-worth while people criticise
and belittle us.
We have to see beauty where there is ugliness.
We have to embrace kindness and positive attitudes
when surrounded by uncertainty.

The passage sums up the challenges of life quite beautifully. It illustrates the maze of mystery, uncertainty, paradox and duality that appears before us on our life's path. The world

is like a chrysalis and we are the butterfly, and somehow
it is up to us to emerge from the world, free again, wholly
joyous, and loving. In spite of it all, we must not stop
loving.

Sh!t Happens!

Sometimes we get frightened. And
sometimes we lose our way.

Unhappiness can be frightening, not least because it feels
so permanent. How ironic it is that when we are happy we
immediately fear it cannot last, but when we are unhappy
we instantly 'know' it will last forever. When depressed,
we rarely think, 'This will be over by lunch time'! Instead,
our perception collapses, our thoughts freeze, and our focus
stays fixed on the pain. Thus, the illusion of unhappiness is
that it feels so final and so forever, when, in truth,

although unhappiness feels so permanent, it is
always transient.

Unhappiness has a way of collapsing time and space. Thus,
when we are unhappy, we not only feel it will last 'always'
and 'forever', we also believe that 'everything' about our
life is 'wrong', 'bad', 'not good enough' and 'nothing'.
We generalise, we 'awfulise', we experience what one of
my clients once called 'humouroids', i.e. *hardening of the*
attitudes which cause piles of problems! Hence, unhappiness

blackens perception and blots the mind with thoughts of despair, hopelessness and more fear.

When unhappy, we lose the art of being specific. One of my clients once illustrated this with great humour. 'I am so dreadfully unhappy,' Mary said. When I asked her why, she folded her arms tight across her chest and said, 'I'm just so afraid.' 'What are you afraid of?' I asked. 'Everything!' she said. 'Can you be specific?' I asked. Mary then smiled, and yelled, 'I am being specific!'

The principle reason unhappiness is so frightening is that

unhappiness is fear!

The story of your unhappiness, i.e. the events, people, reasons and circumstances, may appear different to my story, but the source of our unhappiness is the same. *Every form of unhappiness is a manifestation of fear.* Thus, fear and unhappiness are inextricably linked – they are the same thing. The same is also true of fear and grief, fear and anxiety, fear and depression, and fear and the pain of failure.

Unhappiness is born of fear and it gives birth to fear. When we give our power to unhappiness, we automatically side with fear and we automatically become very afraid of everything. *Fear is afraid of everything because fear can only see itself in everything.* Think for a moment, *what is fear not afraid of?* To make matters even worse, fear's 'solution' to everything is more fear, more panic, more doubt and more defence.

Fear is frightening. It plays tricks with the mind. I once read somewhere that

F.E.A.R. actually stands for *False Evidence Appears Real.*

I have also read that F.E.A.R. stands for *Forgetting Everything is All Right.* And another translation I once read is *F**k Everything And Run!* Whichever one you can relate to, fear is frightening.

Although you have managed to live through every fear, failure, grief and disappointment of the past, there is a part of your mind that always says 'This time it's different'. Welcome to your ego! Your ego, full of fear and doubt, is blind to the strength, power and love of your unconditioned Self. It believes, therefore, that all unhappiness is terminal. Indeed, according to the ego, not only are you about to die – you are going to die alone!

Most frightening of all is the loneliness of unhappiness. We feel so separate, so isolated and so cut off from everything, especially our unconditioned Self, when we are unhappy. Happiness feels a lifetime away, a million miles away, when we are unhappy and afraid. We feel small, weak and vulnerable, and the ego quickly kicks into action, reinforcing the fears with commentary such as 'No one can help', 'Nothing will work', 'It's no use', 'There is no answer' and 'There is no hope'.

Our fears, doubts and loneliness attempt to talk us into even greater unhappiness. It is as if the ego conspires, often in our most private moments, to make us feel as if we are here on the planet to endorse a special type of pain, so deeply personal, awful and unique to us. Surely no one suffers like we do.

The truth is, you can walk up to anyone, on any street, in any city, in any country, in any culture and on any continent, and if you say, 'I am so sorry to hear about your problem', their reply to you will most likely be, 'Who told you!' Unhappiness is not so special! It does not make you unique – lonely, maybe, but not unique. We all know what pain is. We have all 'suffered', and we are all ready to heal. Aren't we?

Give Yourself a Break

Happiness is not just the absence of sadness;
it is also the capacity to love and heal
your sadness.

Joanna's first words to me were, 'I feel totally stupid being here.' She went on to say, 'This is a total failure for me. I should be enjoying my life. I should be happy. I should be care-free. I'm twenty-one for Christ's sake. I'm twenty-one and I'm depressed. I haven't even started to live and I'm depressed already.' We had still barely introduced ourselves when Joanna went on to say, 'I wish I could just pull myself together, but I can't find anything to pull.'

Joanna came for treatment for depression. Several courses of antidepressants had not worked. She was bright, clever, very aware and hyper-critical. According to Joanna, grade seven piano should be grade eight; a 2:1 degree should have been a First; and her golf handicap of eight should be more like four 'if I really tried'. She had a natural flair for fashion design which she gave up because she was 'useless at it'; she sang solo at church and had performed on television, but 'really I'm an awful singer', she said. And so it went on.

I did not treat Joanna for depression. Depression was not her problem; her problem was a constant, learned self-criticism – a self-criticism born from fear of being 'bad', 'wrong', 'nothing' and 'not good enough'[2]. Clearly, no amount of achievement would be good enough for Joanna because deep down she felt guilty and not good enough.

The very first issue Joanna and I addressed was not her criticism of herself or her achievements, but her criticism of her emotions. Joanna was so hard on herself that it was not safe for her to have any emotions. I explained to Joanna a principle of healing which applies to everyone, that

to heal unhappiness, you must make it safe to feel your feelings.

Joanna saved her most severe judgements for her emotions. Every emotion was, in Joanna's mind, completely rubbished as being either 'wrong', 'bad', 'stupid', 'crazy', 'pathetic', 'idiotic' or 'nothing really'. I lost count of the times Joanna said, 'I should be handling this better' and 'I shouldn't feel like this, but . . .' Joanna's excessive judgement about her feelings was really an attempt to control her pain. Alas, she found that *judgement does not control pain; it compounds pain.*

I almost always begin therapy by addressing my client's response to their unhappiness and not the unhappiness itself, for I have come to learn that *it is the response to unhappiness that causes so much pain.* In other words,

unhappiness is painful; but the response to unhappiness is often more painful.

We can be so brutal, so critical, so judgemental and so afraid of our emotions, particular unhappy emotions like grief, anger, sadness and depression. Every time we criticise and judge ourselves for feeling unhappy we are simply adding fuel to the fire. With every self-attacking thought we make, the pain flares up and feels more real. The more we condemn, the more we identify with the pain itself. Soon, pain feels more real than joy.

The first step, then, to healing your unhappiness is a radical one. It is to trust that

unhappiness is not real.

When I say *unhappiness is not real*, what I mean is, *unhappiness is not the truth about you.* The truth is that no matter how much you have learned to identify with your pain, *you are not your illness, and you are not your emotions.* It is a lie, for example, to say, 'I am an anorexic'; you may be experiencing anorexia, but anorexia is not you. The real you has no conditions – it is unconditional. Thus, you are not your anorexia, your alcoholism, your cancer, or any other illness, for these illnesses are experiences and not identities.

Similarly, it is also a lie to say, as Joanna did, 'I am depressed'. Yes, you may be experiencing depression, but you are not depression; you may be experiencing anger, but you are not anger; you may be experiencing grief, but you are not grief; you may be experiencing fear, but you are not fear. Once again, no matter how much you have learned

184

to identify with these feelings they do not, in truth, define you. Emotions are experiences, they are not who you are.

For centuries the Buddhists have taught followers to say, 'I am with anger', as opposed to 'I am angry'; 'I am with sadness', as opposed to 'I am sad'; and 'I am with unhappiness', as opposed to 'I am unhappy'. This practice of naming the emotion you are *with* helps you not to confuse your identity with the emotions you feel. It is also very good for keeping perspective, staying centred, honouring your emotions, practising peaceful acceptance, and healing unhappiness. Try it.

Unhappiness and fear have a way of distorting vision and making *false evidence appear real*. In the Taoist Bible, *Tao Te Ching*, it explains that when you are unhappy and afraid:

> *The way that is bright seems dull;*
> *The way that leads forward seems to lead backward;*
> *The way that is even seems rough;*
> *The highest virtue is like the valley;*
> *The sheerest whiteness seems sullied;*
> *Ample virtue seems defective . . .*[3]

Unhappiness is Self-deception − it is not a truthful state. It has nothing to do with your joyous, loving, unconditioned Self; it is all to do with the ego − the thought in your mind that believes you are small, separate, unworthy, in exile, and with every reason to be afraid. The ego, born of fear, sees no spirit, no happiness and no hope.

Unhappiness and fear feel real, but they are not. They appear to eclipse the joy of your spirit, but they cannot destroy the spirit. Your spirit lives on, always free, loving and happy 100% of the time. Unhappiness happens when you wander away from your true Self and 'lose spirit'; true healing is simply a return to spirit, a return to love, a return to truth, and a return to joy. In truth, then,

pain runs deep, but joy runs deeper.

Whatever pain you may be experiencing right now, it is good to know that your true unconditioned Self is okay and all is well. To realise this, you must first be prepared to give yourself a break – a break from the incessant self-judgement, and a break from identifying with the pain. You are not your pain.

Honesty is the Fast Policy

One day a man went to visit a doctor who was famous for his radical healing cures. 'What is your problem?' asked the doctor. 'I am completely depressed,' said the man. After a brief consultation, the doctor said, 'I will not give you tablets for your depression. The circus is in town this weekend and I want you to go see the great clown, Grimaldi.' The man bowed his head and said, 'My dear doctor, I am Grimaldi.'

Psychology surveys on subjective well-being show conclusively that people tend to exaggerate their public reports of happiness[4]. We will often fake happiness when we are low, such is our shame of unhappiness. We are also keen to keep up appearances, to put on a brave face, a stiff upper lip, a mask and a smile, for, like us, society does not tolerate unhappiness well. As the poem goes, 'Laugh and the world laughs with you; Weep and you weep alone'[5].

'How are you?' we greet our friends. 'Not so bad,' they say. They are telling us nothing. They are neither happy nor sad, good nor bad. When I ask my clients 'How are you?', the answer is often, 'Not so bad', and even, 'Well! Thank you'. They are, apparently, not unhappy, but they have still made an appointment. Similarly, doctors greet their patients, 'How are you?' 'Well!' say the patients. 'Why are you here, then?' asks the doctor.

It is extremely rare for people to admit publicly to being sad, depressed, nervous, angry, jealous or unhappy – the shame of it would be too much. From an early age, we have learned to hide and be dishonest about our emotions, for fear of judgement and guilt. Common 'you should be ashamed of yourself' messages include:

- 'Big boys don't cry.'
- 'Take that look off your face.'
- 'I'll give you anger.'
- 'How dare you . . .'
- 'Don't be a cry-baby.'
- 'What a song and dance!'
- 'You'll be smiling on the other side of your face in a minute.'
- 'Pull yourself together.'
- 'Who do you think you are?'
- 'Get a grip.'
- 'Stop crying.'
- 'Stop laughing.'
- 'There will be tears before bedtime.'

We have learned to be secretive. We hide our feelings. We suppress our emotions. Suppression, denial, rationalisation and other defences all seem to work well at first, but they soon fail, for what felt like peace was only avoidance. We cry alone and in private. Eventually, when the pain of suppression and shame begins to scream unbearably, we jettison our pride and we visit self-help groups with names like *Depressives Anonymous* – the shame and the secrecy continues.

Being secretive about your emotions does not heal your pain, it exacerbates it. In fact, I would say that

90% of any pain comes from trying to keep the pain secret.

You cannot keep a secret and let it go. By being dishonest about your pain, you stay in pain. Dishonesty may appear to help you get through your day, but it will always leave you in pain at night. Healing is a process of truth, and you cannot get to truth via dishonesty. Dishonesty is, at best, a control tactic; it is not a medicine. It cannot give you peace.

To heal, you must be prepared to accept that *you are not wrong for feeling unhappy or being unwell.* You must surrender the temptation to use your unhappiness and illness as a verdict or as evidence to prove you are guilty and 'not good enough'. *Your disease is not the truth about you.* It is not you, it is merely an experience.

Again and again, I have to remind my clients that being unhappy is not a capital punishment. I tell them,

unhappiness is not a sin!

For as long as you continue to judge yourself for feeling unhappy or being unwell, you will feel shame. After judgement and shame, there comes punishment (see *Figure 3*). At the precise moment you most need love and care, you administer a course of personal abuse and neglect. By refusing to love and be kind to yourself, you are punishing yourself, playing out your guilt, atoning for your weakness and 'getting what you deserve'.

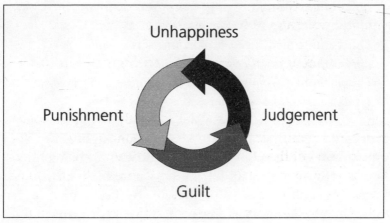

Unhappiness

Punishment

Judgement

Guilt

Figure 3

You cannot heal in secret. You must be prepared to tell the whole truth to someone, to God, to the Holy Spirit, to a healing agency. When it comes to healing, honesty is the fast policy. Secrecy only adds to your pain, for

secrecy feeds shame!

Where there is shame, there will be pain, and for as long as you believe you are guilty, you will continue to attract unhappiness. In fact, *you will experience as much unhappiness as you believe you deserve.* Honesty lets the truth out, and truth eventually dispels all shame. This is important because a belief in unworthiness creates a world of experience entirely different and separate from that created by a belief of true Self-acceptance. For instance:

Unworthiness attracts pain; worthiness is peace.
Unworthiness casts doubt; worthiness is certainty.
Unworthiness projects guilt; worthiness is freedom.
Unworthiness spreads fear; worthiness is loving.
Unworthiness fuels anger; worthiness is a smile.
Unworthiness is suffering; worthiness is rest.
Unworthiness demands sacrifice; worthiness is whole.
Unworthiness always falters; worthiness is true.

Honesty is the first freedom! It is the key to healing. Your ego cannot afford to be honest, but you can. By being honest about your most private self-judgements, the pain you feel begins to melt almost immediately; by being open about your shame, the agony is shared and quickly begins to fade; and by being truthful about your fears, their tight, fixed grip instantly begins to loosen. By being honest, you discover you are no longer alone, and help is now at hand.

Letting Down Your Defences

My encounter with Donald was to affect me profoundly. Donald was a short man with a small body, but his spirit was gigantic! In his late sixties, his face was covered in character lines. He had one eye, a full smile, a bushy black moustache and rosy cheeks. He always sat with his shoulders hunched, leaning fully forward towards me. It was on about our third session together that he said to me, 'Robert, I think my real problem is I have forgotten how to be honest with myself.'

'I can smile for you, Robert,' Donald said, 'but my smiles are fake. I can laugh for you, Robert, but I no longer know what it *feels* like to laugh. In fact, I can't feel anything very much.' Donald went on to tell me that the last time he had cried was as a young boy, and how he was permanently haunted and taunted by self-criticism and self-doubt. 'I want my real smile back,' said Donald. Perhaps his request becomes all the more poignant for you when I tell you that Donald is a professional clown.

Donald had got straight to the heart of the matter when he told me, 'I have forgotten how to be honest with myself.' So afraid was Donald of his unhappiness, he had decided to put up a barrier to defend himself from the pain. The barrier had seemed to work at first, dulling the pain quite well, but he soon discovered that by cutting himself off from his pain he had also, inadvertently, cut himself off from his joy.

Donald had discovered that defences are dishonest. He had hoped his defences might somehow lessen the pain, but instead they only added to it. He felt cut up and cut off from his feelings. He also discovered that you cannot be selectively honest about feelings, i.e. honest about joy, but dishonest about anger, or honest about anger, but dishonest about jealousy. In our discussions together we arrived at the conclusion that

what you defend against you attract!

All too often the language of medicine and healing is a language of war. We talk about 'tackling health issues', 'defeating depression', 'banishing the blues', 'killing cancer', 'overcoming anxiety', 'beating period pain', 'winning the fight against AIDS', etc. I also contributed to this war-like language with my clinic, 'Stress Busters'. Healing is not a war, it is a peace process. It is not about resistance, it is about acceptance. Acceptance is the key to peace, love and healing.

A feeling has only one ambition in life, and that is to be felt! Emotions want *motion*. Every time you resist and defend against an emotion, the pain will persist for longer. You must be prepared to honour every feeling you experience, be it anger, jealousy, depression, sadness or hate. Honouring the feeling is the same as being honest about and accepting the feeling. *Ultimately you accept the feeling, not because it is real, but because Love is real.* In other words, pain is always only a visitor. It is transient. It always ends. Meanwhile, your unconditioned Self remains intact, forever loving, truly whole and free of pain. Thus,

acceptance is a set-up for love.

Defensiveness will not heal, love will; condemnation will not heal, kindness will; judgement will not heal, forgiveness will; fighting will not heal, peace will; resistance will not heal, acceptance will. At The Happiness Project I often share what I call 'The Declaration of Acceptance'. It reads:

Without acceptance, anger will enrage you.
Without acceptance, guilt will shame you.
Without acceptance, judgement will condemn you.
Without acceptance, anxiety will torment you.
Without acceptance, sadness will depress you.
Without acceptance, fear will terrify you.
Without acceptance, pain will hurt you.
Without acceptance, loneliness will isolate you.
Without acceptance, love cannot love you.

Donald played with the idea of acceptance. 'Fighting it has got me nowhere,' he said. As Donald became more and more defenceless, he discovered a new strength and a new freedom. At first he talked about his unhappiness without really feeling it, but one day the tears finally came. The day Donald cried was the day he began to smile again and really feel it. Donald's courage was exceptional. He was an inspiration to me. We would often hug and hold each other, crying and laughing. Together we gave each other the courage to accept, love and let go of our pain.

Suppression, repression, denial, intellectualisation, rationalisation, avoidance, lying, and every other type of defence, is not the easy option it might first appear to be. Like a bad drug habit, defences keep asking more and more of you. It takes a lot of conscious and unconscious effort to keep the lid on unhappiness. Defensiveness is exhausting.

Medical drugs, if wrongly prescribed, can be another form of defensiveness that actually hinders the healing process. All too often in modern medicine, drugs are used incorrectly to suppress feelings. I think of unhappiness as a piece of information – it is like a red light on your car dashboard telling you to attend to your engine. Well, to follow this analogy, taking heavy sedative drugs inappropriately is a bit like taking the fuse out of the car dashboard so that the light no longer shows. No light does not mean no problem.

Fortunately, more and more doctors are learning to prescribe their drugs more wisely. In particular, they are learning not to use drugs to simply 'shut their patient's feelings up'. Sedation is not the same as healing. This short-term 'solution' is a false economy that eventually leads to more pain, not less. For too long, the medical profession has pondered, *drugs or therapy*[6]. Sometimes both are necessary. Whatever is the most loving option is best.

Soon after Donald stopped coming to see me, I received a letter from him in which he had included a passage written by the German poet, Hermann Hesse. It reads:

Suffering only hurts because you fear it.
Suffering only hurts because you complain
about it.
It pursues you because you flee from it.
You must not flee, you must not complain,
you must not fear. You must love.
You know all this yourself, you know quite
well, deep within you, that there is a single
magic, a single power, a single salvation,
and a single happiness, and that is
called loving.
Well then, love your suffering. Do not

194

resist it, do not flee from it.
Taste how sweet it is in its essence, give
yourself to it, do not meet it with aversion.
It is only your aversion that hurts,
nothing else.[7]

Asking For Help

'Ask, believe, receive!'

There is a story of a school teacher who one day told her class of young children the story of Moses. The children listened attentively. After she finished, she asked, 'Why do you think Moses wandered lost in the desert for forty years?' There was a rather long hush. Suddenly, a boy shot up his arm; obviously inspired by a genuine flash of insight: 'Maybe Miss, Moses was afraid to ask for directions!'

Healing is restoration. It is about clearing away the rubble of your conditioned mind to reveal once more the wholeness of your unconditioned Self. As with true happiness, this restoration does not require excessive labour, huge sacrifice, endless struggle, heavy suffering or any large down-payments. Healing asks nothing of you other than your willingness to accept healing.

The willingness to accept healing is the key to restoration, and part of that willingness also includes being willing to ask for help. For, in truth,

you cannot be healed alone!

Too many times we try to heal alone. We somehow have it wired up in our mind that, *asking for help is a failure*. We are either too proud or too guilty to ask for help. Selfishly, we deny people the opportunity to love and care for us because we feel too clumsy, too embarrassed, too undeserving, too selfish, too superior, or too much of a nuisance.

During my years with the Stress Busters Clinic, I found that most of my clients had suffered alone with their stress for an average of between two and ten years before they first asked for help. On a similar note, my friend Michael, an Anglican vicar, once told me, 'People love God so much they don't worry Him with their own problems!' Healing and freedom must mean more to you than pride and guilt if you are to be happy.

It is a classic symptom of stress to *discount solutions before you try them*. This is the 'Yes, but' disease. Therefore, if it is not your pride and guilt that is getting in the way of your asking for help, maybe it is your cynicism. Cynicism is like a mental cancer. It attempts to kill all hope, light, adventure, growth and healing. Cynicism is a decision to be a victim. Apart from being unhelpful, cynicism is also never justified, never real, never true and never accurate.

Cynicism delays healing in a number of ways – (1) we do not ask because we already 'know' that 'it' won't work; (2) we do not ask because we believe that 'I can't be helped'; (3) we do ask for help, but we fully expect to get no answer – this suits our cynicism perfectly, because as long as we get no answer we can hold on to our imagined guilt and still play victim.

In *The Bible* it is written, 'Ask, and it will be given you.'[8] What a deal! Don't you think, however, that it sounds almost too good to be true? It looks a little like a free lunch. Where's the hidden extras, I wonder? What's the flip-side to all this? Check the small print. Easy come, easy go! Many times in my past I have waved my fist in the air, feeling angry, abandoned and aggrieved, quoting *The Bible* to God – 'I'm still asking, where's Your answer?'

I have come to learn from my own experience that when it comes to asking for help,

you cannot hold on to pride, guilt, cynicism, and be healed!

When you ask for help you will receive the answer you believe you deserve. This is the key to asking. Thus, the sentence 'Ask, and it will be given you', maybe makes more sense if you say, 'Ask, *believe* and it will be given you'. You cannot be proud and open, guilty and open, cynical and open. For as long as you want to stay proud, guilty or cynical you close the door on any real answer to your request for help.

When you ask 'for help' you have to be open and spontaneously available 'to help'. Therefore, before you ask for help, it is important to put aside all pride, guilt and cynicism. In other words, you have to surrender illusions for truth, past for present, resentment for hope. Ask – believe – receive! To heal and be happy

you must be willing to ask, **and** *be willing to receive.*

I am currently practising to be a better asker. For too long in my life I have suffered from a condition I call B.M.S. – *By Myself Syndrome*, the main symptom of which is being too afraid to ask for help. For example, in a busy shopping centre I will spend forty minutes (not quite forty years!) looking for a shop, when I could easily ask one of a thousand people for directions. In a music store, I will search over and over for a particular album before thinking to ask for help from someone who is paid to help people who ask for help.

I am told that *fear of asking* is unique to men! I believe, however, that both men and women know what it is to play martyr, to refuse help, to try to go it alone. Too often healing is delayed because we try to mend ourselves before, and not after, we have asked for help from friends, family, counsellors, God and the Holy Spirit. We heal by being willing to ask and willing to receive.

Stick To Your Strengths

*If you are unhappy, maybe it is because
you have abandoned your greatest
sources of strength.*

My mother, Sally, recently experienced what could be called 'a severe case of life'. What started out as a routine treatment for a bout of depression became a close encounter with death after she was prescribed a combined course of sedatives, tranquillisers, antidepressants and other drugs that almost killed her. Three different times my brother David, Miranda and I said our 'goodbyes' to Mother, believing she might die that night.

About six months into my mother's nightmare, I became completely exhausted. Travelling hundreds of miles to the clinic, often late into the night, four times a week, had taken its toll. The endless, fruitless attempts to open communication with clinic administrators and doctors did not help either. And then there was also the fear and worry for my mother.

Fear is exhausting. Having no time for rest is also exhausting. But even worse was the fact that somehow, in the middle of this crisis, I had managed to abandon my true sources of strength when I most needed them. Bit by bit, without me even noticing, I had cut myself off from all that nourishes and sustains me.

My sources of strength include morning meditation, prayer, God, my family, my friends, the gymnasium, a healthy diet and evening meditation. Well, my healthy diet collapsed immediately. Night after night I dined alone in my car driving to the clinic, eating vegetables (crisps, actually!), fruit and nut (chocolate bars!) and drinking diet sodas. My morning meditation, which usually lasts an hour, somehow became fifteen, ten, five minutes long. Prayers were said on the run. Friends understood why I didn't ring back. Miranda and I, completely exhausted, 'vegged out' on videos. The idea of visiting the gym exhausted me even more. And I usually only remembered about my evening meditation the morning after!

'Time is the problem,' I kept telling myself. The reason I had no time, however, was that I had strayed from my sources of strength. There is never enough time if you have no energy. How ironic, then, that when I most needed my sources of strength I completely deserted them. I remember promising myself constantly that once my mother was better, *only then* would I start meditating, exercising, talking to God, and eating healthily again.

I was in a rut, and

the strange thing about a rut is that you never consciously fall into one!

I bet you have never thought to yourself, 'Here is a rut, I'll fall into this one', or 'That looks like a nice rut, I'll give it a go'. No! The psychology of ruts is more subtle and deceptive than that. Ruts are periods of Self-deception. They can last three months or three lifetimes. They are times when you forget to be true to your strengths.

The question is, are you clear what your greatest sources of strength are? Can you name them immediately? Or, do you need more time to think? Has it ever occurred to you that maybe you are unhappy or unwell because you are not clear what your greatest sources of true strength are? Or maybe you are suffering because you are being egotistical in trying to rely solely on your own strength?

Whatever your sources of true strength I guarantee you that, like me, you will be tempted to abandon them the next time you are stressed and unhappy. It is indeed a great irony that when we are under pressure or in pain we move away from, rather than towards, our sources of strength. Just like the story of Peter and Jesus, when Peter distanced himself from Jesus three times, we do exactly the same with our own sources of strength when we are in crisis.

Some strengths, particularly external ones like friends and family, come and go, live and die, for such is the nature of life in this world. The eternal spirit of your unconditioned Self is, however, always strong and true. You could say, then, that *happiness is remembering not to lose spirit.*

Beneath the pain that feels so very real, your spirit is still at play, blissfully free and unaffected by the dramas of the world. Stay close, surrender, be open and let the strength and spirit of your unconditioned Self guide you, inspire you and heal you.

Do Not Control Your Own Healing

Be responsible: give up control!

The following story offers an excellent illustration of the dangers of trying to control your own healing process.

There once was a man who was trapped on the roof of his house while dangerous flood waters were rising up all around him. Clinging to the chimney, he feared for his life. Never before had he felt such a desire to live. He called for help, 'Dear God, I want to live. Please help!' Instantly God replied, 'I will help you, my Son.'

Shortly thereafter, a neighbour came by in a canoe: 'Hop in old boy,' cried the neighbour. 'Thanks anyway, but God is on His way,' cried the man.

Time passed, and the flood waters still continued to rise. A complete stranger passed by in a motor boat and this good Samaritan offered the man a lift. 'Thanks anyway, but God is on His way,' cried the man.

Soon the man was standing on top of his chimney, the waters still rising. Out of nowhere, a helicopter arrived with rope. 'Thanks anyway, but God is on His way,' cried the man.

The man eventually drowned. Before Heaven he angrily confronted God, 'Why didn't You help me?' he cried. 'I would have thought You of all people would have kept Your word?'

'Well, I tried,' said God, 'I came in a canoe, a motor boat and a helicopter, but each time you turned me away.'

The man in this story is a symbol of the ego which always wants to be in control of everything, including its own demise. The man asked for help, but he did not receive. Three offers of help were made, but three times the man gave up his chance for safety because he had already determined in his mind what his rescue should look like.

The willingness to accept healing requires you to give up all temptation to control what you think your healing 'must', 'ought' and 'should' look like. The bottom line is,

you cannot control your own healing.

The temptation to play doctor and control your own healing can inhibit essential healing agencies like trust, openness, surrender, spontaneous availability, possibility thinking and relaxation. Control is often motivated by fear, and it is fear that often prevents acceptance and willingness. Hence, healing happens when you give up control, not when you keep control.

Everything and anything can help you to heal once you

are willing to accept healing unconditionally. Give up your prejudices, therefore. Listen with an open mind to every offer of help that comes your way. Do not discount solutions before you try them. Antidepressants have their place. Complementary medicine can work. Counselling and psychotherapy have value. The doctor may listen to you more than you think. Forgiveness may be the answer.

Willingness is like the electricity that makes all your household appliances work. Without electricity your new phone, your forty-two programme washing machine, your super-dooper computer and your television set are all useless. Similarly, without willingness, no healing treatment will work. Hence, the willingness to accept healing for yourself must come first. After willingness, anything and everything can work, especially if you give up control of the process.

Staying Open For Miracles

There is an ancient story from India about a Prince who was out hunting one day when he was shot in the heart by an arrow soaked in poison. The arrow appeared to come out of nowhere. Physicians arrived immediately, but before they could begin to administer their medicines, the Prince ordered, 'First, tell me what is the poison on this arrow.'

After the poison was identified, the physicians were about to begin their treatment when the Prince ordered, 'First, tell me what type of material this arrow is made of.' After he was told, he then demanded to know who might have made the arrow. All the while, the poison on the arrow tip was spreading through the Prince's body.

The Prince began to weaken, but so enraged was he at being shot he said to his doctors, 'Before you begin, I must first know who shot me. You must bring him to me so that I can ask him who he was sent by.' The Prince then requested that his spiritual advisor be called. 'I need to know why this has happened,' he demanded. Eventually, the Prince died with the arrow still in his heart.

In this story, the Prince is a symbol of the ego. He is not ready or willing to accept healing. First, he wants to understand everything, and then he will let his physicians heal him. His stubborn insistence on understanding everything is eventually what kills him.

It is a common mistake to think that healing requires understanding. It does not. Whilst understanding can certainly be helpful, it is not a necessary pre-requisite for healing. All too often the healing process is blocked, delayed and complicated by an insistence (by both client and counsellor) to get to the root of all understanding first. Too much analysis, dissection, breakdown, separation and logic can close you down rather than open you up. Thus,

being open to healing is more important than
trying to understand healing.

This is true for both client and therapist. When I first became interested in healing, I travelled to meet with many of the

204

world's greatest healers. Over and over, I would ask them how healing works, and invariably they taught me that trying to understand logically how healing works can often block it. The key, they said, is to get your ego out of the way. Your job, then, is simply to be open to the miracle of healing. First, be open, and then you will understand.

Healing is all about miracles, i.e. seeing things differently. If you are unhappy or unwell you are being asked to give up your current frame of mind so as to picture things differently. Healing is about giving up the thinking that led you to feeling unhappy or unwell, and being open to seeing differently, thinking differently, believing differently, expressing yourself differently and acting differently.

One of the most important principles of healing at The Happiness Project is the idea that

there is no such thing as a 'negative emotion'.

For as long as you believe something is 'negative' – such as anger, jealousy, unhappiness, depression and other 'negative emotions' – you will not gain anything positive or helpful from these experiences. To heal you must be open to dropping your prejudices, your conditioning and your judgements, so as to see the Light.

Being open to miracles means being open to everything, including your pain, your fear and your guilt. When you are truly open and unconditional you see that nothing is implicitly 'bad', 'wrong' or 'negative'. Everything, handled in a healthy way, can contribute to the value and enrichment of your own life.

Remember Joanna, the twenty-one-year-old girl suffering from depression who I mentioned at the beginning of this

chapter? Well, after about three months of seeing Joanna,
I gave her an assignment for homework. The assignment
was, 'What is the wisest thing you have ever learned
handling your emotions?' Her answer was quite beautiful.
It read:

*I have never ever had time for my emotions before now. I used
to think emotions are a total weakness. The truth probably
is I've been too scared to look at them. But the thing I have
learned most recently is that perhaps my feelings aren't
out to get me! Feelings are not punishments. Feelings are
information. It is as if every feeling I have is trying to tell
me something.*

*I never thought I'd believe this, but I actually feel grateful
for my depression. My depression has been a gift. I am ready
to build a new life now.*

Joanna is thrilled to know that her words are included in
this book. We have talked together many times about the
'gift of her depression'. We both understand that, in truth,
depression is not the real gift; the real gift was Joanna's
courage to face her depression openly, with honesty and
love. Joanna's willingness to heal ensured that condemnation and fear eventually gave way to openness and
forgiveness. A miracle had happened.

Commit To Happiness NOW!

Do not wait until all your unhappiness is over before you commit to happiness. Commit to happiness *now*!

If, right now, you feel unhappy, pray out loud, 'I commit to happiness'. If, right now, you are experiencing conflict, affirm, 'I commit to peace'. If, right now, you feel depressed, sing 'I commit to joy'. If, right now, you are experiencing resentment, state, 'I commit to freedom'. If, right now, you feel grief, declare, 'I commit to healing'. If, right now, you are experiencing anger, assert, 'I commit to love'.

There is no better time to commit to happiness than when you are unhappy. Committing to happiness is, however, the very last thing you feel like doing when you are down to your last nerve, your muscles are set rigid and your head is auditioning for a part in 'High Anxiety'! Nevertheless,

> *unhappiness undoes itself when you commit to happiness 'now'.*

I am not asking you to deny that you feel unhappy. Pretending not to feel what you are feeling is not honest, truthful or helpful. What I am suggesting is that you feel what you feel *and choose to commit to happiness*[9]. It is your commitment to freedom that will unlock the prison door. So:

> *When in fear, feel fear, and commit to love.*
> *When in tears, cry tears, and commit to healing.*
> *When unhappy, honour it, and commit to joy.*
> *When in conflict, own it, and commit to peace.*
> *When in pain, express it, and commit to freedom.*

When angry, feel it, and commit to harmony.
When resentful, be honest, and commit to forgiveness.
When hurting, nurse yourself, and commit to laughter.
When down and out, rest up, and commit to success.

When you have committed to happiness, what then? The answer is, *nothing*. Perhaps the hardest lesson for us to learn in our own healing is that,

there is nothing for you to do, other than to accept healing for yourself.

Healing is not a task. It is not work. Remember, healing does not require labour, suffering, struggle or any other great effort; it merely requires your willingness. Believe, above all, that your willingness is enough. Follow your willingness, let your willingness bless you, and let your willingness bring healing to you.

Love is the Answer

Judgement is the source of all sorrow.

Depression is a call for love. Fear is a call for love. Anger is a call for love. Grief is a call for love. Jealousy is a call for love. Guilt is a call for love. All unhappiness is a call for love[10]. This becomes clear the moment you are willing to stop judging yourself and your unhappiness. Healing is all about a decision either to

love or judge?

Unhappiness is energy plus judgement. Can you see that all unhappiness stems from a judgement of 'This is bad' and 'This is wrong'? Nothing, of itself, can make you unhappy, but the belief that what you are witnessing must be 'bad' and 'wrong' will certainly encourage grief. Redundancy, for instance, need not be 'bad' or 'wrong', but if you insist it must be so then you will suffer great unhappiness. Look at your judgements!

There once was a man who never once lost his smile. One day he was fired from his job. 'This is bad news,' said his colleagues. The man smiled: 'It is,' he said. Within a week he found a job that paid double his previous wage. 'This is good news,' said his friends. The man smiled: 'It is,' he said.

On the first day of his new job, the man who never once lost his smile spoke up to disagree with his new boss. 'This is bad news,' said his new colleagues. The man smiled: 'It is,' he said. The next day, his new boss commended the man for being honest and forthright with his opinions. 'This is good news,' said his colleagues. The man smiled: 'It is,' he said.

A month later, the man who never once lost his smile was badly injured in a terrible car crash. He was hospitalised for six months as a result. 'What bad news,' his friends said. 'It is,' he said, still managing to smile. The man received a five figure compensation payment for his injury. 'What great news,' his friends said. The man smiled: 'It is,' he said.

A year later, the man who never once lost his smile

lost all his money as the stock exchange collapsed. 'Bad luck,' said his friends. 'It is,' he said, and still he smiled. Soon after, he was made redundant again. 'Bad times,' commiserated his friends. 'It is,' said the man who had now lost everything, except his smile.

His friends, amazed the man was still able to smile, asked, 'How can you still smile when things are so "bad"?' The man replied, 'I see nothing "bad".' His friends countered, 'But when we say "How bad" you say "It is" and you agree.' 'No,' said the man, 'When you say "How bad" or "How good" I cannot agree with you because in my mind there is no "bad" or "good". I simply say "It is", and in doing so I am practising acceptance and freedom from judgement. It is because I do not get caught up in judgement that I can always afford to keep my smile.'

The problem with judgement is that there is no *is*! Nothing *is* because everything has to be 'good' or 'bad' and 'right' or 'wrong'. In other words, there is no acceptance. Everything you see you judge. Seeing is judgement. Thinking is judgement. You see nothing as it *is*; you only see your judgement of it. It is this lack of acceptance and openness that causes you so much pain.

Judgement is not natural, it is learned. Judgement is an attribute of the ego, and the ego is always on guard and ready to dispense its judgements. Whilst you continue to judge, there is no acceptance, no peace and no rest. Because you were once afraid, you taught yourself to judge, but now you find judgement only increases fear. Similarly, because you once lacked trust, you taught yourself to judge, but now you find judgement diminishes any chance of trust.

If you judge something as 'bad', you must inevitably feel 'bad'; if, you judge something as 'good', you will feel 'good'. This is solid emotional mathematics. True freedom, however, comes from the willingness to give up judgement for love. This is particularly true when it comes to your judgements about emotions. When you are willing to give up judging your emotions, you are left with acceptance, and when you have acceptance you also have love. Can you see that:

Fear, without judgement, is Love.
Anger, without judgement, is Love.
Guilt, without judgement, is Love.
Depression, without judgement, is Love.
Jealousy, without judgement, is Love.
Hate, without judgement, is Love.
Anxiety, without judgement, is Love.
Sadness, without judgement, is Love.
Pain, without judgement, is Love.
Love, without judgement, is Love.

Wisdom is not judgement; wisdom is the relinquishment of judgement. Can you see that whenever you judge anyone or anything it is *you* who experiences the effect of the judgement? This is what is meant by the phrase, *'Judge not that ye may not be judged'*. You may be angry at your mother, but it is your nervous system that feels the anger. You may be upset at your partner, but it is your mind that is unsettled. Judgement condemns and punishes everyone, including 'ye' who judges.

Giving up judgement is only difficult because you still believe judgement will somehow give you peace. To give up judgement, you must first realise that judgement cannot and will not give you peace. In other words,

> ### *judgement will not make you safe, it will only make you afraid.*

Secondly, to give up judgement you have only to understand that you do not know enough about anything to make an accurate judgement. In other words, all your judgements are half-baked opinions and not whole truths. In the manual of *A Course In Miracles*, there are some wonderful words which read:

> *It is necessary for the teacher of God to realise, not that he should not judge, but that he cannot. In giving up judgement, he is merely giving up what he did not have. He gives up an illusion; or better, he has an illusion of giving up. He has actually merely become more honest. Recognising that judgement was always impossible for him, he no longer attempts it. This is no sacrifice. On the contrary, he puts himself in a position where judgement* through him *rather than by* him *can occur. And this judgement is neither 'good' nor 'bad.' It is the only judgement there is, and it is only one: 'God's Son is guiltless, and sin does not exist'.*

Thirdly, in order to give up judgement you can begin by not judging yourself for your judgements! I was recently interviewed for a magazine in which I was asked, 'Are you judgemental?' The most honest reply I could give was, 'I am as judgemental as I have ever been. However, I have learned not to judge myself for my judgements. I have also learned to take my judgements less seriously. Most judgements are fears, and I am determined not to live my life by fear.'

Finally, judgement and love are opposites. By making a commitment to love and by cultivating a more loving outlook, judgement will automatically fall away. Love begets love, judgement begets judgement. The truth is,

you cannot judge and love!

The experience of your entire life boils down, then, to a simple decision – do you love, or do you judge? Which do you value the most? You so hoped that judgement would give you strength and peace, but there is no strength and peace in a mind that constantly judges. Love is strong. It is strong because it is free of fear and judgement. Love will give you all the peace you long for.

CHAPTER SEVEN

⌇

Lots of Love!

⌇

Where there is love,
pain breathes,
tears smile,
hurt softens,
guilt loses its edge,
judgement forgets to judge,
fear is no longer afraid,
separation is over.

Where there is love,
You are there.

One day a young boy who had wandered away from
the crowd came across an old yogi, dressed in gold,
who was dancing and laughing all by himself in the
middle of an open field. It was raining. There was no
music and there were no other people, but still the yogi

danced for joy. The young boy was transfixed by the eccentric looking yogi. After a while, the boy shouted out, 'Why do you dance alone?' Without missing a step, the yogi replied, 'What makes you think I am alone!' The yogi continued to dance and to laugh. The young boy soon joined in.

The wise mystics of old continually referred to this world as a place of illusion. They also said the greatest illusion of all is that you and I appear to be totally separate from each other. This sense of separation increases and heightens each time you are afraid, hurt, unhappy or in pain. If, however, you have truly loved, *for only a single moment even*, then you too have felt the all-encompassing sense of wholeness and oneness of love that defies the information of your physical senses.

Love is bigger than anything. It is bigger than your body, your mind, your self, your fears, your guilt, your ego and your loneliness. Love is union. When you love you join, you connect, you feel as one. With true love there is no separation, no little 'me', no more than or less than, no distance, no lack, no limits. Love is wholeness and love is healing, for

happiness starts with love, and sadness ends with love.

Love is also bigger than romance! Therefore, the love I speak of is not reserved for one special person and denied to all the rest. This is not true love. True love is the intention to make love the basis not only of your marriage but also all your friendships, all your work and all your life. Love is precious, not because it exists between two people, but because it is a part of all of us.

Love is Heaven!

Fear is hell!

Picture the following scene:

I am in a hospital in the middle of England. It is late afternoon. I have just finished facilitating a one-day workshop on the connection between health and happiness to senior doctors, nurses, occupational therapists and administrators at the hospital. I have said my goodbyes and I am now walking through a series of very long, dark, empty and cold corridors, searching desperately for 'Exit' signs as I go. I am lost.

As I enter another long corridor, I see someone up ahead walking towards me. It is then that I embark upon a distinctly schizophrenic conversation in my own mind:

Voice 1: 'Here comes someone.'
Voice 2: 'It's a stranger.'
Voice 1: 'I'll ask him for directions.'
Voice 2: 'You don't know him.'

Voice 1: 'I'm lost – I need help.'
Voice 2: 'No you don't. Keep quiet.'
Voice 1: 'I'll say "Hello".'
Voice 2: 'Are you mad?'

Brief pause.

Voice 1: 'He looks friendly enough.'
Voice 2: 'He's wearing a white coat – he's probably a doctor.'
Voice 1: 'Good. I'll ask for directions.'
Voice 2: 'It's unprofessional to ask for directions.'
Voice 1: 'No it isn't.'
Voice 2: 'Keep your head down, and avoid eye-contact. Make it look like you're not lost.'
Voice 1: 'Asking for help will save time.'
Voice 2: 'You are mad.'

Brief pause.

Voice 1: 'I'll smile, say "Hello", and ask for directions.'
Voice 2: 'He'll think you're a patient.'
Voice 1: 'No he won't.'
Voice 2: 'He doesn't look friendly.'
Voice 1: 'I'll be friendly, and then he will be too.'
Voice 2: 'You have no idea what you're talking about.'

Is this madness I wonder? I think so! And I invite you to laugh at my madness, for laughter is the most healthy response to this nonsense. However, before you sign any petitions to have my licence to practise revoked, look at your own thinking for a moment and check to see if you have not already had an inner dialogue like this today. I do mean 'today'.

Voice 1 is the 'voice of love'; and Voice 2 is the 'voice of fear'. The voice of love is natural, innocent, wholly present and unconditional. This voice is, according to the voice of fear, too friendly, too trusting, too loving, too open, too naïve, too optimistic, and too happy. In every situation, no matter how mundane or insignificant, your fear will always try and talk you out of love.

In any given moment of your life you are either moving closer to heaven or closer to hell. In other words, you are either being loving or fearful. Love is heaven, fear is hell. When you are truly loving, you feel like heaven; but when you are afraid and cynical you feel hellish.

> In h.e.a.v.e.n. all the letters stand together:
> Happiness next to Eternity; Abundance,
> Vision and Ease joined to Now, as one.

> In h.e.l.l. all the letters stand alone: the
> Horrific Effect of not enough Love and
> Laughter, waiting to be undone.

Love and fear are more than mere emotions. They are two distinct frames of mind, two contrasting philosophies, two opposite intentions, each capable of creating a world of experience both entirely separate from one another. Love and fear are two different stories. Every day you walk out of the front door of your home, either into a world of love or a world of fear depending on which story you most believe in. You choose the story.

At The Happiness Project, I often quote a passage from *A Course In Miracles* which reads:

'Whenever you are not wholly joyous, it is because you have reacted with a lack of love to one of God's creations.'

When we love, all is well. When we use fear to get love we end up feeling lonely, abandoned, guilty, cut off and afraid. Where there once was love, there is now fear, hastily built defences, walls of projection, a desire for absolute independence, a need for tight control, a lack of trust, paranoia, a fear of intimacy and a fear of rejection. When you go with fear, love is no longer realistic, heaven is a myth, and happiness is but a dream.

Fear preys, Love prays! All the while, fear shouts, 'Look out!', love sings, 'Look within'. Fear screams, 'Close your heart and be safe', love asks, 'Keep your heart open and be strong'. Fear says, 'Take what you can', love says, 'Give what you want'. Fear wants you to 'Defend yourself', love wants you to 'Stay open'. Fear advises, 'Be afraid!', love advises, 'Be loving!'. Fear preys, 'love is weak', love prays, 'love is God'. Love and fear each has a different opinion about everything and everyone.

Let Love Be Your God

If you dedicate your life to love
you will be happy.

My father died when I was twenty-five years old. Whenever anyone you love dies it can change your life forever.

It was a dark night. No moon. Heavy cloud. Horizontal rain was lashing against the windscreen of my car. I had driven nearly two hundred miles and it must have been nearly midnight by the time I reached the hospital. My brother, David, was already there, and he was the first to tell me that our father had died. He put his arms around me and said, 'Dad's dead. He's in peace now. There is nothing left for us to do here. Let's go home.'

As we drove home, I remember feeling sadness and joy. The sadness was for me, for I would never see my father in his physical body ever again. The joy was for my father. I somehow hoped death would be a fresh start for him. My father had left home when I was fifteen years old in pursuit of alcoholism. For years he lived rough on the streets, in hedges, under Waterloo Bridge. David and I worked half of any week to try to get him proper care. To me, my father was never an alcoholic though; he was a warm, loving, beautiful man who had simply lost hope.

Back at home, David, my mother and I talked long into the early hours of the morning. *We had to because death feels so unreal.* I think I am speaking for most people when I say that, when somebody dies you just don't get it! For days, weeks and months after my father's death we still kept expecting him to walk into the room at any moment just like before. Until the actual funeral, death feels completely unreal; after the funeral, death just feels very unreal!

David and Mum finally went to bed. I stayed up. My mind was wide awake. Over and over I kept on thinking just one thought – 'What's real?' In my mind I surveyed the world for something real, something reliable, something everlasting that does not die. Like a mantra, I kept on asking 'What's real?' I got my answer pretty much straight away, but I did not take it seriously until I realised it wouldn't go away. Every time I asked 'What's real?', the answer was

'Love is real!'

It was shortly after my father's funeral that, for the first time ever, I consciously dedicated my life to love. I wanted to do this so that I could live my life as a mark of respect to my father, and to everyone else I have known who has died. I was grieving, and deep down I wanted there to be a point to it all. Again and again, the only thing that felt at all real about life and death, was love. I realised that *love inspires everything that is whole*, that *love animates life*, and that, after death even, *only love remains*. It took my father's death to show me that *we live for love*, and that

love is the whole point of everything!

We are each of us so impressive, so attractive and so inspirational when we dare to open our hearts to love. It is as if we radiate when we love. Think of a time when you have been truly loving. Bring those feelings forward to now. Can you remember how you walked, how you talked and how you held yourself? Do you remember the light in your eyes, and the light in other people's eyes? And do you remember how much energy you had? Generous, creative, abundant, open, defenceless – the whole world was aroused by you!

It is as if you fulfil the purpose of your being each time you choose love. What higher purpose to life is there other than love? Can you think of a better reason to be alive other than love? Invent other reasons if you will, like victory, fame, wealth, success, happiness even, but can you see how these lesser gods are but a pale reflection, a mere consolation prize, for the only real god, which is love?

There were many times, soon after my father's death, when I felt like giving up on love. It felt so tempting to give in, to give up, to become cynical, to cut off, and to die also. Cynicism was my protest march. Love was my acceptance speech. Daily, I began to call upon the power of love to inspire and guide me – with clients, seminars, talks, telephone calls, meetings, fun, play, family, rest, everything.

Love's power is unconditional – it is unconditionally wise and unconditionally available. People sometimes forget that they can pray to love for help, strength, guidance and surrender. I often share in my workshops one of my prayers called 'Let Love Be Your God'. It reads simply:

> *Love, and let*
> *Love be your*
> *God.*
>
> *Pray to Love.*
> *Worship Love.*
> *Sing to Love.*
> *Meditate on Love.*
>
> *Walk with Love.*
> *Talk with Love.*
> *Look with Love.*
> *Listen with Love.*
>
> *Dedicate your*
> *Life to Love.*
> *Dedicate your*
> *Relationships to Love.*

Dedicate your
Work to Love.

Love, and let
Love be your
God.

Love And Be Happy!

To be happy, love must mean
more to you than anything.

I was once reliably informed by one of my clients that the only place where happiness comes before love is in the English dictionary! In real life, love comes first. Happiness is an attribute of love. One might even say, *love is happiness.* If your current plan for happiness does not put love first, do not think for a second you will be truly happy. To be happy you cannot get around love, you can only go through it.

The fundamental principle upon which I base my entire life and work is very simple. It is, *love and be happy.* These four words are my Bible of Happiness. I honestly believe that these words, plus the willingness to live by them, are enough to help build a life of unimaginable joy, healing, intimacy, wholeness and creativity. Love is the material that happiness is made from. Thus,

your intention to love, no matter what, is the
absolute key to happiness.

Think about it. Try, if you can, to hate someone and be happy. Try to resent somebody and be joyous. Try to be angry at someone and be peaceful. Try to judge someone and feel free. Try to control someone and not feel controlled. Try to be fully independent and intimate. Try to cheat somebody and feel safe. It can't happen, because what you do to another you are doing to yourself. *Love works!*

Fear begets fear. Make no mistake about this. Fear can only offer itself to you. So often we try to convince ourselves that 'the means justifies the ends' and that 'the destination will make up for the journey', but we know this is not true. The destination is the journey, and fear cannot lead you to love. Fear leads to fear. Similarly, guilt leads to guilt, judgement leads to judgement, punishment leads to punishment. Love, on the other hand, leads to love. And love also leads to happiness.

Affirm, therefore, your intention to love. Make it your prayer, your mantra, your meditation, your morning ritual and your evening ritual. Put love first – above everything. You will find that as you strengthen your intention to love, so automatically will the temptation weaken to replace love with lesser gods like control and fear. If you are prepared to stick with love for long enough, you will discover for yourself that

love is the key to real abundance.

First, love! *Love and enjoy everything!* If you are waiting to be happy before you start being loving then you will find you are in for a very long wait. Similarly, if you are waiting to be successful before you are truly loving and generous then you will be greatly disappointed and frustrated. There is no such thing as happiness without love first, success without love first, health without love first, peace of mind without love first, freedom without love first. First, love!

> **Love,**
> **And you will enjoy abundance;**
> **Love,**
> **And you will enjoy success.**
> **Love,**
> **And you will enjoy peace;**
> **Love,**
> **And you will enjoy happiness.**
> **Love,**
> **Place love above everything.**
> **Love,**
> **And you will enjoy everything.**

Love is your best bet for happiness. That being so, I am often asked, 'How do I know if I am being truly loving or not?' Well, one acid test for checking to see if you are being true to love is – *if you are being genuinely loving you will feel happy*. Conversely,

> *if you are not happy, you know you are not being loving.*

Love and be happy is the key. Therefore, to say that love is your best bet for happiness is not strictly true. The whole truth must be, *love is your only bet for happiness*. Happiness cannot ever happen without love.

Love Never Leaves You

'You are never not full of love.'

Your unconditional Self is always loving, unlike your ego which has learned always to be afraid. Like happiness, love is natural to you. It is constant. Certainly, there are times in life when love can appear to be overwhelmed by fear and hurt – for all the world it can feel like love is lost – but, in truth, love does not die, love does not fade, love does not change. Love is forever. Love is never destroyed, it is only ever eclipsed.

Love is the essence of your unconditioned Self, and love does not leave its source. *Love never leaves you*. If you were to take away your possessions, your history, your wealth, your conditioning, your pain and your glory, you would be left with nothing – nothing but love. Love remains. Love is the inner god of your unconditioned Self. *Table D* gives you two profiles, one for your loving unconditioned Self, the other for your fearful conditioned self.

By dedicating your life to love, you are attempting to change your mind about yourself. In truth, you are full of love, and yet you have learned to believe that there is little or no love within you. The moment you scared yourself into thinking that love was outside you, and not within, was the moment your ego made love special, limited, scarce, weak, rare, and, above all, elusive.

Loving relationships are born of Self-acceptance, i.e. (1) I accept I have love to give; (2) I accept the love of others; (3) I accept love lives within. Without Self-acceptance, truly loving relationships are impossible. Peace, joy and union

Unconditioned Self	conditioned self
whole	split
oneness	separate
love	fear
joy	pleasure/pain
knowing	searching
trust	doubt
abundance	lack
acceptance	judgemental
free	defensive
infinite	small
eternal	temporal

Table D

with others happens only as you heal the conflict in your own mind. Self-acceptance is essential, therefore, because

you cannot be loving and guilty!

The greatest contribution you can make to any relationship is to love and accept yourself. For as long as you insist on believing that deep down you are unworthy of love and not good enough, all of your loving relationships will eventually deteriorate into a fearful contract of needs. Thus, you will find you are constantly having to change your friends and your lovers so as to give love another go.

Relationships are the experience of personal beliefs projected. In other words, *you get the relationship you think you deserve*. If, for instance, you judge you are worthy of a little bit of love, you will experience relationships which have only a little bit of love. If, however, you judge you are entirely worthy of love, you will experience relationships where love continually renews itself.

If you are willing, even just a little bit, to entertain the possibility that you are whole, worthy and well, you allow for the possibility of experiencing wholeness and joy in each of your relationships. As your belief in your own wholeness strengthens, so too will your experience of whole, healthy, loving relationships strengthen. In other words, by giving up guilt, you make yourself more available to love.

The Law of Projection insists that

what you believe about yourself you will project onto your relationships

Therefore, if you judge yourself to be 'not good enough', you will always find, eventually, that your partner and your friends are 'not as good as you first hoped'. Also, for as long as you believe that something is missing in you, you will experience something missing in your relationships. Similarly, if you judge yourself as 'bad', 'wrong' or 'nothing', then your relationships will turn sour, go wrong, and amount to nothing, unless, that is, you are prepared to change your mind about yourself.

The love that inspires a relationship never leaves, but it can be overlooked. There is never 'no love', but there is often pain, conflict, separation, abuse, anger and a need for revenge that can appear to eclipse love's presence. If you are experiencing any pain in your relationships, the key to healing and happiness is to realise that,

the source of the problem is not the relationship; it is projection.

Unfortunately, none of us can keep our damning self-judgements and guilt to ourselves. We always attract people (consciously and unconsciously) into our lives who we can share (i.e. project onto) our suffering and conflict with. When the pain and abuse is too much, you are not bound to stick around in a relationship, but it is a good idea to address why you might attract such abuse. This is vital for the health of all your relationships now and in the future.

It is always tempting to lay blame for all your relationship problems on 'the other person'. If healing, and not revenge, is your true intention, then you will want to ask yourself: (1) What have I projected onto this situation?; (2) What is my part in this conflict?; (3) Why have I attracted this person into my life?; (4) What can I do to be loving here and now? Blame is dishonest – no one is completely responsible for your pain.

When a relationship appears to be full of pain it is because your relationship is full of projections. Sometimes we are scared to take responsibility for our projections because we fear, 'If I take more responsibility, I will feel more guilty.' You take responsibility for your part, not to step into more guilt, but to take the first step into undoing your guilt. Honesty is not about condemnation; it is about a willingness to be free, loving and true. By being honest about your fears, your projections and 'your part' in any conflict, you instantly create a possibility for more honest, loving relationships.

In your quest for happiness you can never escape the fact that *you can only love another person as much as you are willing to love yourself.* There is no way around this. To be even more blatant, I could say, *unless you are willing to be loving to yourself, you cannot be loving.*

So many relationships run into trouble because we expect our partners and our friends to give us something we are not willing to give ourselves, i.e. love and acceptance. The fact is, however,

no one can love you more than you are prepared to love yourself and get away with it!

The bottom line is, you will not let anyone love you if you are not willing to love you. When anyone turns up in your life wanting to love you more than you love yourself, you may well be amused and excited at first, but your lack of Self-acceptance will eventually try to talk you out of love. Too much love and not enough Self-acceptance leads to too much guilt. Eventually, you must either change your mind about yourself (i.e. drop the guilt), or you must change the personnel.

You will also find that *when people do love you, you won't allow yourself to see it unless you love you!* Have you ever been in a situation where your partner or a friend showers you with bouquets of 'I love you', 'You're wonderful', 'You're beautiful', 'You're amazing', and all the while you are thinking, 'He/she doesn't really love me'? Or maybe you have experienced it the other way round, where no matter how much you tried to love someone, they wouldn't, couldn't, dare not let you.

Projection is powerful. Whenever you are upset because you judge your partner or friends do not love you enough, you can be sure that what you are really witnessing is the projection of *your own reluctance to love yourself enough*. Similarly, if you feel you are not getting enough recognition from someone, you are really witnessing the projection of *you not giving enough recognition to yourself*. The more you love yourself, the more you are able to recognise how loved you are.

It is uncanny, but completely true, how over and over again, you find that

people will treat you the way you treat you.

What you do to yourself, others will do to you also. In other words, no one can do anything to you that you are not already doing to yourself. Similarly, no one can make you feel anything you do not choose to feel yourself. There is absolutely no way around this. *Your relationships mirror your judgements.* Hence, you will find that if you reject yourself, others will too; if you condemn yourself, others will too; if you distance yourself, others will too; if you judge yourself, others will too; and if you overlook and undervalue yourself, others will too. Projection is the Law of 'Others Will Too'.

If you want peace, first make peace with yourself; if you want love, first practise love on yourself; if you want kindness, first be gentle on yourself; if you want acknowledgement, first pay respect to yourself; and if you want faithfulness, first be true to yourself. Put another way:

Love thyself, so that you can love another.
Love thyself, so that you cannot project fear.
Love thyself, so as to let others love you.
Love thyself, so as to let people near.

The gift of relationships is that together we can encourage one another to believe once more in our innate wholeness. Although no one can make you happy, everyone can encourage you to be happy. The intention to love can work miracles. Through relationships we learn to practise forgiveness, i.e. we make the choice for wholeness. As we forgive ourselves and one another for our fears and doubts, we strengthen our resolve to trust once more in the love that created us.

Unless you can accept your wholeness, all your loving relationships will become needy relationships. All pain in relationships has something to do with perceptions of personal lack, i.e. needs. Without Self-acceptance, you will always end up resenting and abusing any person whom you demand must meet your needs. This is true whether they meet these needs or not.

Wholeness has no needs. With wholeness, relationships are joyful, not needy. By being willing to love yourself, to accept your own wholeness, you open yourself up to a wholly different experience of loving relationships.

Love Has Never Hurt You

One of the happiest days of my life was my wedding day. Miranda and I were married in my grandmother's English country garden, with acres of rich, green lawn rolling down to a beautiful river below. We were blessed and honoured to have Edward Carpenter, now ex-Dean of Westminster, and his wife Lillian Carpenter, begin our wedding ceremony.

What followed was a profusion of Bach, harp, prayer, flowers, friendship and champagne. The whole event was a celebration of love – universal love.

There are so many wonderful memories of that day, but one very amusing one that Miranda and I often recall happened during the receiving line, when the guests lined up to give us their congratulations. One by one, we received congratulations plus advice, like, 'Enjoy today – it doesn't get better than this', and 'Make the most of this – this is as good as it gets'. Other pieces of advice included:

- 'It takes more than love, you know.'
- 'Enjoy love while you are young.'
- 'You can't just rely on love – you have to work at it too.'
- 'You're young, and I know you think love lasts forever, but . . .'
- 'Love is hard.'
- 'Love is never easy.'
- 'Love is not without its pain.'
- 'The first year is the hardest. Survive that and you'll be okay.'
- 'Remember, don't live in each other's pockets. Have lots of time apart.'
- 'You've done it – you're trapped now!'
- 'Be realistic – it won't always be this wonderful.'
- 'Don't let love stop you having fun!'

On and on it went. It was as if, one by one, each person had plucked a thought of fear out of my mind and Miranda's mind and said it out loud to us. Now, to be fair, there were a hundred times more wonderful thoughts of love and of hope for love! However, what we witnessed were two distinct attitudes to love – one attitude very limited and fearful, the other very abundant and hopeful.

Your ego can only judge anything, including love, as it judges itself. So, to the ego, love is limited. Conversely, your unconditioned Self, being completely whole, accepts love is whole. Once again, the ego and the spirit have a completely different point of view, as shown in *Table E.*

Perhaps the greatest misperception of love is that *love hurts*[1]. Of course, nothing could be further from the truth. Any one thing can only give of itself, and in the case of love, love can only give love. What hurts is not love itself, but your misperceptions of love, your fear of love, your giving up on love, and, in particular, your resistance to love. In fact, it is true to say that

most of all it is your resistance to love that hurts you so.

Miranda and I chose six readings for our wedding service, one of which is a famous passage by Emmett Fox. It reads:

There is no difficulty that enough love
will not conquer;
no disease that enough love will not
heal;
no door that enough love will not open.
It makes no difference how deeply
seated may be the trouble; how
hopeless the outlook; how muddled the tangle;
how great the mistake.

*A sufficient realisation of love will
dissolve it all. If only you could
love enough you would be the
happiest and most powerful
being in the world.*[2]

The problem is not that love does not work; the problem is
that we do not trust that love will work. When loving feels
difficult we are easily discouraged, and we often give up on
love too soon. Ironically, the moment you turn away from
love is when you begin to feel let down by love. This, once

Love is . . .	
conditioned self	Unconditioned Self
limited	infinite
weak	powerful
dangerous	safe
not enough	everything
frightening	comforting
special	universal
hard	kind
blind	true
painful	healing
a trap	freedom
a dream	real
death	life

Table E

again, is projection. We then search for love-substitutes, most of which lead to loss, pain, sacrifice, fear and illusions of separateness.

We have become too accustomed to looking at love through the limited, fearful eyes of the ego instead of through the wholly joyous vision of our unconditioned Self. It is important, therefore, that when you are tempted to limit the power of love, or when you are finding it difficult to love, you call for help from your unconditional Self, from love itself, and from your God.

One prayer I once wrote for myself is called 'Consciousness of Love'. It reads:

Beloved Creator,
Consciousness of Love.
Open me up to the Love that I am.
Let the Love that I am light up my
relationship with You, with _____,
with everyone.
Let the Love that I am sing constant
hymns of divinity to all of me, that
I might remember You in everyone.
Let the Love that I am relax me,
inspire me, help me to be, that this
world may enjoy the best of me.
Let the Love that I am hold me,
guide me, casting out fear, healing
all pain, that I, the One and the
many, may feel Your beloved peace
once again. So be it.

By being willing to heal your misperceptions and fears of

love you are not only healing your relationship with love, but you are also healing your relationship with yourself and with everyone else as well.

Always Communicate Your Love!

*Love is the most fun you can
have with anyone.*

The following story serves as a reminder of how important it is to communicate from the heart at all times.

A husband and wife, both in their late seventies, decided that, after fifty-five years of marriage, it was high time they got a divorce. When their counsellor asked them why, the wife issued a catalogue of reasons. 'He never asks if I'm happy,' said the wife. 'I assumed you were,' said the husband. 'He never says he loves me,' said the wife. 'I thought you knew I loved you,' said the husband.

The wife continued, 'He never says I'm beautiful.' The husband replied, 'I look at you every day and admire your beauty.' 'We rarely talk,' said the wife. 'I know you like to read a lot,' said the husband. 'I read because we don't talk,' said the wife. There was a pause. 'And we never go out,' said the wife. 'I thought you liked to stay in,' said the husband. 'I only stay in because I'm waiting to go out,' said the wife.

The counsellor continued to take notes. 'He's also very mean to me,' said the wife. 'In what way?' asked the counsellor. 'Well, at breakfast, three times a week for fifty-five years, he always serves me the crust of the loaf, and I hate the bread-crust!' The husband was distraught, 'I give you the crust, my dear, because that is my favourite part of the loaf.'

Did you know that the word 'assume' can make an 'ass' out of 'u' and 'me'?

I once gave a workshop to a group of nurses at a Royal Hospital in the middle of England. The workshop was about the value of love and laughter in the healing process. The morning had been truly joyful, creative and great fun. One hour after lunch, everyone in the room was in tears, experiencing profound grief. There were no handkerchiefs, so I placed an order for kitchen towels!

The trigger for all the tears began with a comment I made about how important it is for personal health and healthy relationships that we express openly the love we feel. 'Love should not be suppressed and hidden,' I suggested. I talked, in particular, of my father's death and how, although I knew he was certain of my love for him, I still wished I had told him 'I love you' more often.

I went on to say that after my father's death, I undertook emotional surgery to remove my stiff upper lip and to heal my British conservative conditioning. From now on, I was going to express my love for everyone I knew. My mother and David got it first! Then my close friends. And then everyone else. 'What could be more sad,' I said, 'than not having the courage to tell someone you love them?' It was at this point that I noticed the tears start to roll.

One by one, the health professionals shared their stories. One young nurse shared her grief that none of her family had ever said they loved each other. Everyone in the room, without exception, could relate to her grief. Another nurse said, 'My parents never directly praise, show affection, or say "I love you" to my face; but my sisters tell me that as soon as I walk out of the room my parents don't stop talking about how proud they are of me.' We all smiled, for we recognised the pattern. 'I just wish we could be more honest,' said the nurse.

How many loving relationships have appeared to die because no one could quite bring themselves to say 'I love you'? It is indeed a common fear that as soon as you pronounce your love for someone out loud, fate must immediately issue a penalty calling for punishment, rejection or some other payment. This fear is not natural. It can only be your learned guilt and unworthiness that breeds such fearful superstition. Out of fear, you decide to hide your love and play it safe. Yet

> **by playing it safe you lose what you are trying to keep.**

Talk joy! Talk love! Talk happiness! In my book, *Living Wonderfully*, I wrote that, 'for every one word of joy in the English language there are over forty words for misery'. Too many relationships crumble simply because there is not enough talk and focus on joy, love and happiness. If it is a truly loving relationship you are committed to, then expressing your love will strengthen the love and not weaken it.

When counselling couples, I often ask each person to

draw their own individual picture of happiness. It becomes clear when both pictures are being compared that, although both people want happiness for themselves and for each other, they have hardly ever taken the time to talk openly, honestly and directly about happiness. There is nothing stopping you asking your partner or your friends, 'What is happiness?', 'How can we be happier?', 'Do you feel loved by me?', 'How can I love and support you better?'

You Have To Jump For JOY!

*Do you want to be independent
or happy?*

The 'Me Generation' is our society's most recent experiment in a catalogue of ill-fated attempts at the pursuit of happiness. It is about individualism, ego, separating out, making it on your own, setting your boundaries, doing your own thing, being unattached, being free of commitment and being fully independent[3]. The point is, however, you are not independent! Independence is a complete and utter illusion, for you are inextricably connected to the whole of everything.

In therapy circles and popular psychology, much is made of healing 'co-dependence', the addiction to apparent external sources of love. This is good work, except when it leads to more boundaries, more defensiveness, more separation and unhealthy independence. Perhaps what we most need now is a movement for 'recovering independence addicts' – a movement which helps people give up lack and separation for wholeness.

Independence is nonsense – any environmentalist, biologist, quantum physicist, poet, spiritual master or young baby will tell you so. The English poet and cleric, John Donne, put it well in 'Iland Verse':

No man is an Iland, entire of itself;
every man is a peece of the Continent,
a part of the maine; if a Clod bee washed
away by the sea, Europe is the lesse, as
well as if a Promonterie were, as well as
if a Mannor of thy friends or thine own
were; any man's death diminishes me,
because I am involved in Mankind; and
therefore never send to know for whom
the bell tolls; it tolls for thee.[4]

Independence is a defence, a defence against fear, against hurt and against commitment to love. How can you be independent and intimate? How can you be independent and receive? How can you be independent and experience the joy of sharing yourself wholly with another person?

Independence as a defence tends to stem from two fundamental fears in relationship, (1) the fear of rejection; (2) the fear of intimacy. Both of these fears are learned. They are not natural. They have each become, however, heavily ingrained in our way of thinking. In a nutshell, then,

every relationship must face the fear of intimacy
and the fear of rejection.

Fear of intimacy and fear of rejection are all about imagined needs that arise from a perceived lack of wholeness. In other words, both the fear of intimacy and the fear of rejection stem from learned guilt and unworthiness. Thus, you are afraid that if you are intimate with anyone they will eventually judge you as severely as you judge yourself. And you fear rejection by others because you have already judged yourself to be unacceptable and you don't want to be reminded of the pain.

Where there is fear of intimacy and rejection, you may notice some of the following behaviours:

- You try to reject others before they reject you.
- You never commit fully, preferring to keep your options open.
- You are shy.
- It may look like you commit fully, but you know you never do.
- You have many, many acquaintances, but no one knows you really well.
- You find yourself needlessly upsetting, quarrelling with and annoying your loved ones.
- When it gets really good, you test it and sabotage it.
- You give people your time, your money, your mask, but never You.
- You are afraid that what you give you will lose.
- You 'wait and see' if the relationship 'is going to go somewhere' before you hop on.
- You take a long time to get to know people and you always begin by putting firm boundaries in place.
- You prefer the focus to be on others, and never on you.

- There is no one you share all of your parts and all of your Self with.

For years I prided myself on being 'completely independent'. I was the proverbial 'one-man show' who would make room for a little bit of love every now and then – just enough to convince me I wasn't as miserable and as lonely as I felt. Independent people tend to keep busy to prevent themselves from recognising their pain. Independence looks like safety, but the safety is sterile. Even now, I am aware that when I am hurt or in pain my temptation is to pull away fast and be independent again. The fact is, though,

intimacy heals!

When loving is difficult, the key is to move in closer – nose to nose. The more you move away, the easier it is to project, numb out, separate, be safe and sterile, be superior and lonely. If your intention is to love, no matter what, then you will want to get close, let down the defences, and be open. This can be difficult, for love brings up fear. But the more willing you are to put love first, the less difficult this becomes[5].

One key is to *share the feelings; don't shoot the feelings*. In other words, you must commit to the truth that (1) there are no enemies, (2) your feelings must not be used as weapons. A relationship that is truly dedicated to love can afford to drop guilt, defence, attack and the desire for separation. To experience joy again, you must jump for joy. To do this, joy must mean more to you than vengeance.

Lose Control

Do you want to be happy or in control?

Love does not control. Control is not love, control is fear. You do not attempt to control a relationship because of joy, but because of fear. Control is meant to bring certainty and safety, but this so-called safety is so sterile it soon smells of fear and death, and not love and life. Control is also meant to secure no losses, but whatever you try to control you will ultimately end up losing.

Love and joy require freedom, not control. This is difficult to understand for those of us who have been brought up in and conditioned by a culture which demands that you try to control life. The ego always seeks to control everything, the unconditioned Self seeks to set everything free. Love and joy cannot be organised, controlled and dictated to; it can only be accepted, shared and allowed to be.

One day a young apprentice devil came running to the chief devil and said, 'Chief devil, sir, something awful is happening to planet Earth!' The chief devil frowned and growled, 'What is happening?' The young devil, very afraid, stuttered, 'There's a bloke called Jesus, and he's teaching everyone to love one another. He's also telling them that God is Love and not fear.'

The chief devil was busy writing his book, *The Joy of Politics*. He told the young devil to keep an eye on things for him and report back later. The young devil soon returned looking even more worried than before. 'Chief devil, sir,' said the young devil, 'Now

Jesus is encouraging people to give up fear, hate and resentment, and to start practising forgiveness.'

The chief devil was still busy writing. He was half-way through a chapter on 'Bureaucracy'. He frowned and growled at the young devil, 'Go away and watch for me.' It was not long before the young devil returned again, looking totally terrified. 'It's got worse, chief devil, sir. Now Jesus is talking about joy and that the Kingdom of Heaven is within.'

The chief devil put down his pen. He had just finished the final chapter on 'Control'. He frowned and growled at the young devil, 'Why do you worry so! As soon as Jesus dies we will enlist people to organise, control and make rigid his teachings. We will create another religion! And soon the love Jesus speaks of will be lost in dogma.'

It was the poet William Blake who wrote:

> *He who binds to himself a joy*
> *Does the winged life destroy;*
> *But he who kisses the joy as it flies*
> *Lives in eternity's sunrise.*[6]

I remember how, soon after I fell in love with Miranda, I became terribly afraid. At first we experienced what I call the *wonder period*. We were open, honest, loving, defenceless and entirely grateful to be together. We both forgot to be guilty and unworthy of love. Gradually, however, I began to fear and doubt that the love might not last, and so I added some control and defensiveness for good measure – a pre-emptive strike!

For about the first two years of my relationship with Miranda I can honestly say that I prayed *every day*, first thing on waking, *'Dear God, I give You my relationship with Miranda. I give You my desire to control this relationship. Let Love be my guide. So be it.'* I still repeat the prayer every now and then, for the truth is,

you cannot be in control and happy!

Control is not only about the fear of loss. Although it may not look obvious, another reason for trying to control your relationships is because on one level you are afraid of too much love. The ego objects to too much love, because more love means, ultimately, less fear, less judgement, less defensiveness and less separation. Where there is only love, the ego is out of a job. So, either the ego re-asserts itself, or you change your mind about yourself – you love yourself and you accept your wholeness.

If you could accept that you are whole already, you would no longer fear loss or love. Fear leads to control, and control equals trouble. Have you noticed, for instance, that you experience the most pain with people whom you most try to control? Also, have you noticed that the more you control your partner, the less attractive they become? Furthermore, have you noticed how resentful and bitter you become whenever someone tries to control you? Like a butterfly caught in the clutches of a sticky hand, love's beauty is lost without the freedom to fly. The bottom line is,

you cannot love what you control.

Apologise Quickly!

Do you want to be proud or happy?

Every relationship, be it romance or friendship, begins with a honeymoon phase, or *wonder period*. The new person in your life can do absolutely no wrong. You are loving, accepting and completely forgiving of the fact that this new person worships football, works late, has emotions, lives with mother, is set in their ways, only likes fast food, forgets to flush, keeps stray animals, eats crisps in bed, and regularly gets spinach stuck in their teeth. It's easy to love in the *wonder period* because you are in the present time.

After a while, relationships move into the second phase, which I refer to as the *now that you're mine phase*, or, the *familiar period*. In this phase, the new people in your life become familiar to you, and they begin to 'sound familiar', to 'remind you of . . .', and to 'behave in the same way as . . .'. The ego is always looking for patterns to defend against, and now the emphasis shifts from present to past, imagination to memory, hope to doubt, love to fear, freedom to control. You remember how, in the past, you appeared to lose out in love, and so you become afraid and attempt to top up love with a little more control.

Next, love gives way to a power-struggle for control, dominance, sitting in the driving seat, feeling superior and being right. This is the *control period*. Now, love is no longer natural. Instead, it becomes a learning curve. You will inevitably make mistakes when you engage in a power-struggle. You will mess up, act bad, get things wrong, fight, attack, defend yourself, get hurt, get petty, lose it and *feel guilty*. Neither you or your partner or friend will want to enforce the guilt, however, if your relationship is consciously dedicated to love and truth.

There will be many opportunities for you to make an apology during the power-struggle. Unfortunately, the goal of being happy often gives way to the goal of being right during the *control period*. In other words, being right means more to you than being happy. You have to ask yourself,

do I want to be right or happy?

The more you want to be right, the less happy you will be. You will become more and more defensive, stubborn, resentful, bitter, petty, suspicious, vicious and small. Love is big, pride is small! Welcome to the *coma period*. This is where you look like you are still together, but you are not. The battle to be right appears to have worn you both down. You are tired, closed down, exhausted and numb. One of you will have to put down your weapons of guilt before you can both awaken again to the love that is still beneath the battleground of fear.

The *awakening period* usually begins with an apology or forgiveness. You will want to apologise if love means more to you than guilt, pain, mistakes and the past. You will want to ask for forgiveness and give forgiveness if love is more valuable to you than fear and resentment. If you are really smart, you will no longer try to be right, you will simply try to be loving.

I promise you this – nowhere on your grave or in your obituary will it be written, 'He was always right!', or 'She never, ever had to say sorry!' Hopefully, words like 'loving', 'kind' and 'forgiving' will be mentioned over and over.

Also, I promise you that some of life's sweetest moments are those that follow an honest, heartfelt apology!

Forgive Fast And Be Happy NOW!

Do you want to be superior or happy?

I often ask participants on my workshops to be still for a moment and become aware of what holding a resentment feels like both physically and emotionally. We then list these feelings to estimate the cost of resentment. The cost includes 'anger like black rain', 'constant fear and an inability to relax', 'feeling like a victim', 'physical pain', 'a heavy heart', 'empty superiority', 'no air and no breath', 'a preoccupation with the past', 'vengeful hate', 'a cold heart', 'no joy and no love', and 'a feeling like you are slowly dying'.

The most chilling and accurate description I have ever read of the unforgiving mind appears in *A Course In Miracles*. It reads:

> *The unforgiving mind is full of fear, and offers love no room to be itself; no place where it can spread its wings in peace and soar above the turmoil of the world. The unforgiving mind is sad, without the hope of respite and release from pain. It suffers and abides in misery, peering about in darkness, seeing not, yet certain of the danger lurking there.*
>
> *The unforgiving mind is torn with doubt, confused about itself and all it sees; afraid and angry, weak and blustering, afraid to go ahead, afraid to stay, afraid to waken or to go to*

sleep, afraid of every sound, yet more afraid of stillness; terri-
fied of darkness, yet more terrified at the approach of light.

Resentment costs too much. Make no mistake, it is you who
has to pay the bill for the resentment you hold on to. It
is your nervous system, your lungs, your muscles, your
heart, your perception and your mind that deteriorates and
decays during every moment you try to defend yourself
with hate.

Resentment is an investment in hate – it believes hate will
give you something that love cannot. Resentment is learned.
It is not natural. It is the ego that believes resentment, hate,
punishment and attack will protect you and preserve you.
According to what you have learned, you are apparently
safe with hate in your heart – safer than if you were to love
or to forgive.

The problem with resentment is that *you cannot be resentful*
and happy. There is an old saying, *'If your heart has room for*
one enemy, it is not a safe place for a friend'. You cannot hate
and be happy. You cannot hate and love. You cannot hate
and win. You cannot hate and be free. You cannot hate
and be present. You cannot hate and have a future. The
bottom line is

you cannot carry resentment and peace of mind
at the same time.

For as long as you still value resentment, forgiveness will
have no appeal. Forgiveness only has appeal for people who
are interested in freedom, love, peace of mind and joy.

Your ego and your spirit have two completely different
opinions about forgiveness. The ego, convinced of your

own smallness and weakness, advises you that you cannot afford to forgive. Guilt, fear, defensiveness and attack are the ego's answer. Forgiveness is, ultimately, the betrayal of the ego and all it stands for. Forgiveness is the choice for wholeness.

True forgiveness is not about condoning, agreeing to forget, or sacrifice. True forgiveness is not about stuffing your emotions or keeping quiet about your resentments. True forgiveness is not about doing the right thing. Neither is it about being a doormat or about blaming yourself. No! The truth is,

> *true forgiveness is the willingness to believe (1)*
> *(1) you are whole; (2) no one can threaten or*
> *take away your wholeness.*

Forgiveness becomes easier when love means more to you than anything else. Also, it helps when you see the cost of resentment for what it really is. See *Table F* for the contrast between the forgiving mind of the unconditioned Self and the unforgiving mind of the ego.

True forgiveness is an act of Self-love and Self-acceptance. When you forgive, you put away toys of guilt and embrace love once more.

Forgiveness heals pain. Pain is a fearful nightmare that leads you to believe you are weak, small, isolated, vulnerable and alone. Pain feels real. Pain feels like it will last forever. And yet, if when you are in pain you can muster even a little willingness to forgive, you will begin to see differently. In truth,

> *forgiveness is a decision to see the 'whole truth'.*

Unforgiving Mind	Forgiving Mind
Judges you are weak and un-whole	Loves you without judgement
Sees you are separate and vulnerable	Love sees no separation
Believes you are guilty and unworthy	Loves you wholly, unconditionally
Projects fear	Extends love
Encourages you to defend yourself	Encourages you to be loving
Attracts attack and abuse	Love attracts love
Uses hate, fear and resentment to keep you safe	Calls upon love to free you of pain
Preoccupied with the past	Continually lets go into 'now'
Mistrusts happiness	Accepts happiness

Table F

The willingness to forgive is really the willingness to see that 'I am not my pain', 'I am not my mistakes', 'I am not my past'. Forgiveness acknowledges that 'This pain is not who I am'. As you pray to your whole Self, to God, or to any symbol of wholeness, your perceptions will change as you begin to see again that 'I am whole.

I am safe. I am not a body. I am free. I am the Presence of Love'.

Forgiveness is a miracle – the greatest of all miracles. Every instant of forgiveness is a vote for greater peace, strength, love, freedom and joy. When you forgive you are truly changing your mind about yourself. You are giving up your fearful, learned self-image for the loving, powerful, whole and original Self that you are. Forgiveness elects love to rule. Happiness flourishes where there is love. Whenever you feel low, you may like to affirm:

I feel tender, but I pick forgiveness now.
I feel afraid, but I choose love now.
I feel hurt, but I want healing now.
I feel angry, but I affirm peace now.
I feel sad, but I wish for happiness now.

I let go, now, of my fear of forgiveness.
I declare today a day of Amnesty in which
I gratefully volunteer to give up all my
resentments and grievances. One by one,
I give away every fear, scar, guilt and hatred,
for I will not keep what, in truth, does not
belong to me.

I choose wholeness now. I will no longer teach
myself or anyone else that we are guilty. We are
free. We are free. I pray for peace, and I
will sprinkle kindness, radiate love and
scatter joy wherever I go. And may
God help me to handle well all of
the happiness that must inevitably
follow! So be it.

CHAPTER EIGHT

❦

Travelling Light

❦

O Travelling Light, wrapped up in darkness,
still clinging to fear, convinced of your guilt,
still dreaming of death. Wake up! Wake
up to happiness 'now'!

Take your mind back to first thing this morning. Would you describe the way you woke up today as a beautiful performance, or, more simply, a performance! Was it peaceful, or were you in pieces? Did you rise and shine, or rise and whine? Did you wake up fresh, or on auto? Do you ever find that the effort of waking actually exhausts you for the rest of the day?

How did you greet this new day? Are you, for instance, the sort of person who wakes up in the morning and says, 'Good morning, God', or swears, 'Good God, morning!'? Maybe you like to start the day with a smile, to get it over with. How do you prepare for each new day?

255

Try to recall specific decisions you made during the very first hour of today. Your first decision may have been to hit the 'Snooze' button on your alarm clock. What then? A fast coffee, maybe? Hit the shower. A cigarette. A search for socks. New underwear. Yesterday's underwear. Hurry the children along. Make-up. Breakfast on the run. Catch the news headlines. Hunt for your wallet. The 'find the keys' game. Walk the dog. A quick jog.

Most early morning decisions are about showers, make-up, clothes, children, food, time and transport. They are 'doing decisions', as opposed to 'being decisions'. What I am most interested in is not your 'to do' list, but your 'to be' list. In other words, did you make any conscious decisions about how you wanted 'to be' today? To put it another way,

what sort of a day did you decide to have today?

Percentage wise, how much time did you spend preparing your body for today, i.e. washing, feeding and clothing, as opposed to preparing your mind for today? What was the split? Body 95%; mind 5%, perhaps? Body 25%; mind 75%, perhaps? Generally speaking, how do you like to prepare yourself mentally and spiritually for each new day of your life?

Your first hour on waking is like the rudder of a ship, in that it serves to steer a course for the rest of your day. More specifically, it is during this time that you make up your mind exactly what sort of a day you will have. In other words, you set your intention for the day, unconsciously and consciously. So, once again, think back to first thing this morning and ask yourself, how did you decide to be today? What sort of a day have you already decided to have?

Decision is power! Decision, above circumstance, is the key to happiness *now*. Know, therefore, that your decision counts. You really can decide what sort of a day to have today. In fact, you already have. Nothing, absolutely nothing, can happen without your decision.

Happiness cannot happen without your
decision to be happy.
Love cannot grow without your
decision to be loving.
Peace cannot blossom without your
decision to be peaceful.
Freedom cannot bloom without your
decision to be free.
Miracles cannot flower without your
decision to be open.
Bliss cannot flourish without your
decision to be guiltless.
Heaven cannot bear its fruits without
your decision to receive.

Everything ultimately rests on your decision, including pain, fear, suffering and death. Your mind is like a TV set with a hundred different channels, and it is you who decides which channel you tune in to. You can choose, for instance, the Victim Channel or the Freedom Channel; the Resentment Channel or the Forgiveness Channel; the 'X' rated Guilt Channel or the Happiness Channel; the Yesterday Repeat Channel or the Now Channel; the Ego Channel or the Spirit Channel. You can flick onto whichever show you want to see today. Intention is your remote control.

Sometimes you may find that you have decided consciously to have a happy day, but still your experience is one of misery. This is a common experience. What has happened here is that, consciously you have decided for happiness, but unconsciously you have still decided for misery. Often, unconscious conditioning has the casting vote. What really helps is forgiveness, the choice for wholeness, and the decision to let go of *all of your guilt and unworthiness*. Whatever happens, keep deciding for joy.

Meditation, prayer, silence, stillness, mantra, yoga and reading inspirational texts, for instance, can all be helpful in aiding you to set your intention for the day. There is no strict formula, technique, dogma or ritual that must be followed. Ultimately, intention is a single thought which, when valued above all else, can illuminate your entire day.

The key to happiness *now* is to see that *intention creates outcomes*. In other words,

> *your intention determines everything. It is a great 'power'!*

Every morning I sit upon my *flying carpet* – a beautiful silk carpet Miranda and I bought on our travels through India. Whilst sitting, I set my intention for the day through prayer and meditation. Sometimes I recite set prayers and sometimes I pray spontaneous prayers. I follow whatever feels natural. One of my favourite personal prayers is my 'Peace Prayer'. It reads:

Peace be to my mind.
Peace be to my thinking.
Peace be to my body.
Peace be to my senses.
Peace be to me now.
Peace be to me always.
Peace be to me here.
Peace be to me everywhere.
Peace be to me with you.
Peace be to me with everyone.
Peace be to One and All.

This prayer quite clearly sets an intention for peace. Other times, I might pray, 'Dear God, what would You have my intention be today?' Again, there is no set formula. At all times, what I am aiming for is to take guidance from my unconditional Self. Now is new. Today is new. Above all, then, I want to be open and spontaneously available to all that *is* and all that *I am*. This is my intention.

Be Wholehearted!

A monk asked Chao-chou,
'If a poor man comes, what should one give him?'
'He lacks nothing,' answered the Master.
Zen Mondo

When Miranda and I first arrived in India with our friends

Nick, Ben and Therese, we each felt that we had somehow been flung from Earth's orbit during our flight and had landed on another planet. Everything was completely different to what we had ever known – everything!

The entire trip was a mixed bag of shock, surprise, wonder, awe, Delhi belly, poverty, peace, ashrams, hotels, adventure, despair, and also magnificent beauty. The geography and landscape of India is truly beautiful, but nothing was more beautiful to us than the moments when we were greeted by the local people.

Greeting is a sacred art in India. For many Indians, greeting the day and greeting one another are both cherished events that are performed mindfully with great care and positive intent. When an Indian greets you, therefore, they actually *stop to be with you*. They clasp their hands together, they smile, they stare deep into your eyes, and they sing, '*Namaste!*', which means, 'I bow to the Light in You'. This is somewhat of a contrast to, '*Hello darling*', '*All right mate*', '*Yo, dude!*', '*Hey, man!*' and '*How the hell are you?*'

Since our trip to India, I have collected greetings like '*Namaste!*' from all over the world. In Central Africa, for instance, there is a greeting where one person says to another, 'I am here to be seen', the reply to which is, 'I see you'. In the Far East, there is an old Gnostic greeting that still survives which, translated, means 'I am the Light in You'. These greetings are really blessings. They are blessings of love, and they help set a definite intention and purpose for time spent together.

The beauty of these sacred greetings is that they bless both the receiver and the giver. They are also wonderful affirmations and teachings of our innate wholeness and oneness with each other. This is helpful because I believe that *the true function of friendship is to remind each other of our wholeness.* In this way, the function of friendship and the function of therapy and medicine are the same.

These sacred greetings celebrate the gift of friendship. They also remind you that *every* person who stands before you is a teacher. If there is one certainty in life you really can rely upon, it is that

if a person is in your life it is because you have a gift for each other.

Yes! The people you know – *not hope to know* – are the ones who have a gift for you, a gift waiting to be received right now. With each person you are close to, ask yourself, 'What is their gift to me?' and also, 'What is my gift to them?' Don't just ask these questions of the people you find easy to love, ask them of the people who are more challenging!

Make it your intention, today, all day, to be present and willing to learn, receive and give fully to the people you meet. It is impossible to over-estimate the value of the person standing before you. Look carefully. All too often we have, in the past, overlooked the person in front of us because we were too busy searching for a 'more' suitable person, over 'there', coming 'next'.

Above all, the real reason why greetings are so important is that you never meet just any-*body*; you always meet your Self. In *A Course In Miracles* it is written:

When you meet anyone, remember it is a holy encounter.
As you see him you will see yourself.

As you treat him you will treat yourself.
As you think of him you will think of yourself.
Never forget this, for in him you will find
yourself or lose yourself.[1]

So much of our pain stems from our persistent attempts
to cheat what many ancient philosophers have called The
Golden Rule, which is, *do unto others as you would have done
unto you*. Another version of The Golden Rule is, *do unto
others as though you were the others*, and another *be careful what
you do unto others because you are the others!* The point is,

you cannot be happy and cheat The Golden Rule!

What you throw at another person hits you! Therefore, you
cannot throw hate at someone and feel peace. You cannot
throw guilt at someone and experience freedom. You cannot
throw anger at someone and enjoy love. You cannot throw
any attack at someone and be safe.

The Golden Rule also works the other way. For instance,
as long as you judge yourself to be 'not good enough', you
will invariably end up judging those people most familiar
to you as being 'not good enough'. *This is the ego's blessing.*
Nothing astounds the ego more than when a friend you
know does something wonderful, wise and world-class.
'They can't be great because I know them,' says our ego!
Whenever you greet someone, therefore, be clear where you
are coming from, – ego or spirit.

Your greeting is both an affirmation and a teaching of
'who I *am*'. *What you teach yourself, you teach others also.*

So what are you, today? Are you guilty, unworthy and a victim, or will you be your loving, free and wholly joyous unconditional Self? Where are you coming from? You decide. A fine way to begin each day is to ask yourself,

what would I have my teaching be today?

Whatever your decision, let your greetings be a demonstration of your teaching. By the way, the power of your greeting is not necessarily in the words you use, but in the consciousness with which you speak the words. In this way, a simple greeting can become a wonderful tool of teaching, inspiration and healing. Indeed, a simple 'Hello!' is often enough to shift a perception of fear to love, lack to wholeness, isolation to unity.

Recent social research tells us that 70% of people do not know the name of their own next door neighbours. 70%! We live on top of each other, and yet we feel increasingly isolated[2]. I remember as a young child, when times were very hard, we lived in a high-rise tower block with eighty other families. Here we literally did live on top of each other. I remember, in particular, how we got to know the footsteps that belonged to 14a, 14b, 14c, but never the faces and the names. We were all so close, and yet so separate.

I believe it is time you and I resurrected the art of greeting. Remember today, you are in great company wherever you go. Look for it, and you will see it!

Be What You Want!

You will never become happy – you
can only be happy.

There is an old Sufi story of a conversation that once took place between Mulla Nasrudin and a good friend of his.

'I'm getting married on the morrow, Mulla,' pronounced his friend, smiling wide from ear to ear. Mulla Nasrudin was quiet and thoughtful. 'Isn't marriage wonderful, Mulla! It is quite the best! Have you ever considered getting married, Mulla?'

Mulla Nasrudin sighed, 'In my youth I thought of nothing else. In fact, I so wanted to find the perfect wife I travelled the world searching for her. In Damascus, I met a woman who was beautiful, spiritual and loving, but, alas, she had no worldly knowledge. In Isphahan, I met a woman who was beautiful, loving and worldly, but, alas, she was not interested in the spiritual life.'

'Where did you travel to next, Mulla?' asked his friend. 'I forget where, but I met a woman who was truly spiritual, loving and worldly, but, alas, she was not beautiful. Finally, I went to Cairo and there, after much searching, I found the perfect wife. She was everything I had wanted her to be. She was perfect,' sighed Mulla Nasrudin.

'If she was so perfect, why did you not marry her, Mulla?' asked his friend. 'Alas,' said Mulla Nasrudin, shaking his head, 'she was, unfortunately, looking for the perfect husband!'

Often, what we demand of others we are not willing *to be* ourselves. In particular, we spend too much time looking for the right person instead of *being* the right person. The story of Mulla Nasrudin and his friend illustrates well how *you have to be what you want*. Indeed, one of the most hopeful and helpful teachings of my work through The Happiness Project is –

you can be what you want!

Did anyone tell you when you were growing up, *you can be what you want*? Hopefully, if you were fortunate, there was at least one person in your life who encouraged you to dream, to dare and to be. The words, *you can be what you want*, sound so positive, hopeful and affirming. They are also a statement of truth, for they illustrate a very important principle of *being*. This principle is outlined in a poem of affirmation I wrote called 'You Can Be What You Want!'. It reads:

If you would want love, be loving.
If you would want care, be caring.
You can be what you want.

If you would want joy, be joyful.
If you would want peace, be peaceful.
You can be what you want.

If you would want happiness, be happy.
If you would want kindness, be kindly.
You can be what you want.

If you would want forgiveness, be forgiving.
If you would want acceptance, be accepting.
You can be what you want.

Being is proactive. It is literally *being what you want.* It is also about *being first,* for example, if you want honesty, be honest first; if you want loyalty, be loyal first; if you want trust, be trusting first; if you want enthusiasm, be enthusiastic first; if you want courage, be courageous first; if you want inspiration, be a Light first! *Be what you want,* and stick to it! Your courage will be rewarded[3].

If you are not *being,* you are either waiting or searching. Many times I have said through my work at The Happiness Project –

there is a world of difference between searching for happiness and choosing to be happy.

Between searching and choosing, two worlds are born. Searching for happiness gives birth to an experience of fear, lack and guilt. You only search for that which you fear you do not have, or for that which you are not yet willing to accept you have already. Searching is Self-denial. With Self-acceptance, searching is over. Now you can choose to *be what you want to be.* Now you discover the *power of Being.*

In life there are, broadly speaking, three routes marked 'Happiness', but only one of these routes can take you all the way. The three routes are, (1) the 'Doing Route'; (2) the 'Having Route'; and (3) the 'Being Route'.

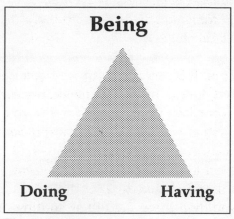

Figure 4

The 'Doing Route' is based on the great hope that enough accomplishment, production and good deeds will make you happy. The key word is 'achievement'. The 'Having Route' is based on the great hope that what you buy, collect and own will make you happy. The key word is 'accumulation'. In truth, neither of these routes can make you happy, but both routes can encourage you *to be happy*. The secret is – you cannot 'do happy' and you cannot 'have happy', but you can 'be happy'!

Being is the key to happiness. The 'Being Route' is all about the courage to be what you want. The key word is 'acceptance'. The inspirational psychologist, Carl Rogers, made a study of both *acceptance* and *being* for much of his life. He understood that the power of 'being' is real, more real than any amount of 'doing' and 'having'. He once wrote:

The individual moves towards 'being', knowingly and acceptingly, the process he inwardly and actually is. He moves away from being what he is not, from being a façade. He is not trying to be more than he is, with the attendant feelings of guilt or self-deprecation. He is increasingly listening to the deepest recesses of his physiological and emotional being, and finds himself increasingly willing to be, with greater accuracy and depth, that Self which he most truly is.[4]

Your ego, born of lack, has a 'do or die' mentality. It would encourage you first 'to do' and then 'to have' so as 'to be'. For example: *do* a good job, *have* a big income, so as to *be* happy. Your unconditioned Self would have you know, first *be* and then you can *do* what you like and you can *have* what you like. *Be first!* It was the great Russian novelist, Leo Tolstoy, who wrote, *'If you want to be happy, be'*[5]. To be is to accept and live from your original wholeness. *To be* is wisdom.

Give What You Want!

Giving is a gain, not a loss.
Give generously!

One of the healing processes I most enjoy using during my workshops is called 'Complimentary Medicine Therapy'. This process acknowledges the enormous healing potential of kind, loving and encouraging words of compliment.

These are three stages to 'Complimentary Medicine Therapy'. You might want to try each stage for yourself. The first stage is to write down five compliments you would most like to receive from anybody. These compliments may highlight a particular quality, talent, skill or value that is dear to you. Once written, I ask participants to repeat these compliments out loud to themselves. Why? Because

> *often what you want to hear from others is*
> *what you are currently not saying to yourself.*

Other people can compliment you a thousand times over, but you will only truly hear (i.e. receive) as many compliments from others as you are willing to give yourself. Thus, giving to yourself can help you to receive from others. Keep your list of compliments on hand. Read them not just once, but three times a day, for seven days minimum.

The second stage of 'Complimentary Medicine Therapy' is to think of someone in your life who is perhaps overdue a sincere compliment from you. The name or face of this person will appear almost instantly. Think carefully now what it is you would most like to compliment them for. Why do this? First, because being loving is fulfilling your purpose; second, it's great fun; and third,

> *whatever you compliment in another person you*
> *are strengthening in yourself also.*

Compliments are affirmations. Like sacred greetings, they bless both the receiver and the giver. A good way to strengthen any joyful quality in yourself is to first spot it in others. What you spot in others, you give life to in yourself. The Buddhists refer to this practice as, *sympathetic joy*. The ego, born of lack, cannot afford to be this generous, but you can! Remember, giving is a gain, not a loss.

The third stage is to think of a person whom you feel is overdue in giving you a loving compliment. Once again, the name or face of this person will appear almost instantly. Think for a moment, what would you most like them to say to you? Next, make contact with this person and give to them the compliment you would most like to receive from them. Give what you want. Why? Because

> ### *often what you are not getting may be what you are withholding.*

Other people are you. They are your mirrors. And just as it would be entirely unreasonable to stand before a mirror and demand to see something you are not presenting, so too, is it unreasonable to expect from someone something you are not willing to give. Many people have experienced great breakthroughs in their relationships (with both the living and dead) during this third stage.

Loving is easy when we perceive we are being loved. It can be very tempting, however, to withdraw our love whenever we feel mistreated, attacked or let down in some way. Similarly, even though we may want to be loving, it can be difficult, when someone we know is being dishonest, disloyal or petty, not to fall into playing the same game. We protest – we offer an attack for an attack. And yet

> ### *the moment you withdraw love from any one*

*person, you withdraw yourself also from the
experience of love.*

The moment you withdraw love, it is you who suffers. You
are, in truth, the Presence of Love, and it is impossible for
you to be authentic and free and not loving. You must be
very clear on the consequences of withholding. For instance,
withhold love, fear takes hold; withhold kindness, love
goes cold; withhold forgiveness, resentment chokes you;
withhold acceptance, peace alludes you; withhold trust,
betrayal is certain; withhold yourself, and you will end up
by yourself. To put it another way:

*Withhold love from your brother, and you deprive
yourself of the feeling of Love's Presence.
Withhold kindness from another, and you will no
longer fully enjoy Kindness's sweet essence.
Withhold acceptance from someone, and your
rampant judgement will deny you any peace.
Withhold forgiveness from anyone, and you die
of the resentments you refuse to release.
Withhold your smile from me, and you will feel
my tears upon your own face.
Withhold your gentle gaze from me, and you
will overlook your own good grace.*

Only your ego can be attacked. Indeed, it must be attacked
because it is always attacking. The ego is always 'on the
take', continually making up for its perceived lack. The ego
cannot be generous in giving, for it believes *giving equals
loss*. There is, however, a place in you which is whole, safe
and beyond any threat. This is your unconditioned Self.

Your unconditioned Self understands that giving is a multiplication and not a subtraction. What you give, multiplies. Also, it doesn't think in terms of 'giving and receiving', but that 'giving is receiving'. Giving, from your wholeness, is the key to abundance. When you give unconditionally, *the only cost of giving is receiving*. Therefore, look around today, and give what you want!

Today is your gift to the world.
Give what appears to be missing.
Give what you appear not to be
getting.
Give what you think you have
been searching for.
Give what you believe you are
waiting for.
Give generously, without thought
of loss and sacrifice.
Give openly, that you may receive
what you want.
Give freely, that you may find
what you are after.
Give fully, that your waiting may
be over.
Above all, give what you want.

Remember What's Important!

Real goals are not about the future; they are
about your life right here and '"now"'!

'I know who you are! You're the happiness doctor,' said
the taxi driver. I smiled politely. 'I've been called a few
things in my time,' I said, 'but that is one of the better
ones. Thank you.' I was on my way to a television studio,
and Simon, the taxi driver, had come to pick me up from
the train station. The conversation we were about to have
proved most illuminating.

'Come sit in the front with me, mate,' said Simon in
his strong cockney London accent. No sooner had I put
my seat-belt on, when Simon said, 'I've discovered the
secret to happiness you know.' 'Really?' I said, trying
not to sound too surprised. 'Yeah, I've got the secret,'
he said. Call me psychic, but I somehow knew I would
not have to ask Simon for his secret! 'I'll tell you my
secret if you like,' said Simon. 'Yes please,' I nodded.
Simon paused a moment, and then he said, 'Triple bypass
surgery!' 'What?' 'The secret to happiness is triple bypass
surgery!'

'That's a new one on me, Simon,' I said. 'Let me tell you
mate, my life was a bloody mess before my triple bypass
surgery. Can you believe I owned this car, fifteen others,
two Rolls Royce motors and loads more before my heart
attack. There I was, on the operating table, when I rang
up my business partner and I sold the whole bloody lot
to him. I said "Good riddance". Now I own nothing. But
thanks to triple bypass surgery, I'm a happy man!

'Ever since triple bypass surgery,' continued Simon, 'I've seen more blue sky, more sunshine, more beauty, more green fields, more friends, more West Ham, more everything.' Now I was really excited, 'Are you a West Ham fan?' I asked. 'All my life,' he said. 'Me too,' I said. Now we were real friends! 'Anyway,' Simon continued, 'I see everything differently now.' Just as he said those words, a driver from behind gave a prolonged blast on his horn at us. Without missing a beat, Simon said, 'Take that bloke behind us. Before triple bypass surgery I would have thought this geezer was giving me grief, but now, thanks to triple bypass surgery, I realise he is actually honking his horn to applaud my beautiful driving skills through the busy streets of London!' I tightened my seat-belt.

Simon continued, 'You can put this in your next book if you like, but before triple bypass surgery all I ever thought about was the future. I worked so hard I lost my way. I was away from home eighteen hours a day. I used to have to remind my wife who I was. I've got two beautiful daughters, grown up now, and they've both got two children. I'm a grandad! But I never saw my children grow up. I was too busy. I lost my way. I really lost my way.'

'So what's the real secret to happiness?' I asked. 'One thing,' said Simon. 'Wake up every day and ask yourself, "What's important?" Never ever forget what's important. My only goal every day is to know what's important and then take care of it. Life's too short otherwise.' Simon paused a moment, and I took my chance, 'So, what's important, Simon.' Simon smiled. He then went all quiet, and began to look quite shy. He then leaned over towards me and said in a softer, more hushed voice, 'Don't think me funny for saying this, will you?' 'No,' I said. 'Well, it's love, isn't it? Love's what's important.'

For me, conversations don't get much better than the one Simon and I had. I did most of the listening, and I was happy to do so. Simon was a wise man. He reminded me that

> ### *the key to happiness is to remember what's important to you.*

During my days with my Stress Busters Clinic, I had noticed that people get ill and unhappy because (1) they forget what's important; or (2) they know what is important but they put their time, energy and attention elsewhere. We mean to take care of the important business of our life, but all too often the small details crowd in and cover over the big picture. We get busy, preoccupied, waylaid and forgetful. Like a traveller without stars or compass, we eventually lose our way.

The Happiness Project focuses a lot on goal-setting with a difference. The difference is that we attend to what I call *Present Time Goals*. Most goals are all about your tomorrows, your future, and how great you hope your life will one day be. Real goal-setting is all about the present moment. It is about here and now. Your most powerful goals, therefore, are not about future happiness, they are about happiness *now*!

Happiness *now!* is about *Present Time Goals.*

It was the Swiss psychologist, Carl Jung, who wrote, 'Most

of the people I see suffer not from physical illness, but from spiritual aimlessness. They have lost their aim. They have lost sight of who they really are and what is really valuable'[6]. One key to happiness, then, is not to wait until you need triple bypass surgery before you remember what's important. Let joy be your learning curve, not only pain.

Therapy is about remembering what is important and discarding the rest. One simple exercise I use you may want to try. First, write down ten things you love to do. Some people have so lost their way that they cannot think of ten. Now, write down next to these ten things the date you last did each one. After that, write down the names of the ten most important people in your life, and then place next to each name a date when you last spent 'real time' together. Look carefully and see if you are attending to what is really important and valuable to you – *now*!

Today is your whole life, and your only real goal is to live well today. Remember, therefore, what is important. The formula for *Present Time Goals* goes like this:

If health is important to you, ask yourself,
how can I be truly healthy today?
If balance is important to you, ask yourself,
what are my real priorities today?
If love is important to you, ask yourself,
how will I show my love today?
If service is important to you, ask yourself,
what can I contribute to today?
If truth is important to you, ask yourself,
how can I make way for wisdom today?
If success is important to you, ask yourself,
what is success today?

If peace is important to you, ask yourself,
what struggle can I let go of today?
If life is important to you, ask yourself,
how can I live well today?

Be Wise

A few years ago, I gave a keynote presentation to the
Annual Mental Health Conference for Wales. At this conference I talked on 'Healing, Listening and Wisdom'. I
suggested that the experience of being listened to wholeheartedly by another person is one of life's richest gifts.
I said that listening is like love in that it unites us, and
that where there is genuine listening separation is over,
fear fades and wisdom begins.

As I began to talk more specifically about the importance
of silence in everyday life, I became aware of how silent the
room was. Everyone was silent, deeply, deeply silent. 'Why
are they so quiet?' I wondered. 'What's with this silence?'
'They're not impressed,' I feared. Other fearful thoughts
came rushing in – 'Change the subject!', 'There's no value
here!', 'Tell a joke', 'You're going to die', 'Make a run for
it . . .', 'Leave Wales now!', etc.

For some reason I decided to trust that everything was
okay. One part of my mind was trusting, the other part was
terrified. Never had I encountered an audience so quiet. I
was tempted at one point to walk among the audience and
check for pulses! I refrained. Somehow, I could see that
what was really happening was that I was coming face

to face with my own fear and uncertainty about silence, listening and wisdom.

I decided to go the whole way. Later, when I listened to the tape of the conference, I listened to the conclusion of my talk on 'Healing, Listening and Wisdom' which ended with these words:

Our greatest fear is that if we were to stop still and listen to our Self, there would be nothing but silence. Be not afraid. For there is a silence in you – an eternal silence that is both empty and full. It is empty of the fear, criticism and judgement that has plagued you; and it is full of the Love that can save you. Trust this silence! This silence is not cold, but warm. Listen to this silence speak to you of your Self that Is, and always will be, wholly free, wholly worthy, and wholly well. Fear not the silence – for it is wise and it brings great peace.

I then said, 'Thank you for listening', and sat down, feeling quite wobbly. What followed was a standing ovation and a tumultuous round of applause. I stood up twice to accept the applause, and still it went on. Looking back now, it was as if the applause was like a reward for me daring to speak my truth even though I was afraid to do so. The applause also felt like a collective affirmation of fresh intent to listen to the *inner-tuition*, to follow the heart more often, and to stand by what is most important.

Immediately after my talk, a man came up to me with a newsletter on mental health which contained the following poem, called 'Listening'. It was written by a user of the local mental health services. His name is Mike, and his poem reads:

When God gave out brains
I thought He said trains
— so I missed mine.

When God gave out looks
I thought He said books
— so I didn't want any.

When God gave out noses
I thought He said roses
— so I ordered a big red
one.

When God gave out chins
I thought He said gins
— so I ordered a large
double one.

When God gave out legs
I thought He said kegs
— so I asked for large fat
ones.

When God gave out heads
I thought He said beds
— so I asked for a big soft
one.

Gosh, am I in a mess!

Life is an act of listening. The quality of your life depends on the quality of your listening[7] In any given moment, you are either listening to the voice of fear (your ego), or the voice of love (your unconditioned Self). Fear always leads to more fear. Love always leads to more love. Learning to switch off the voice of fear is an art. What is unhelpful is to attack fear, resist fear or defend against fear. One answer is simply to focus on love, and to value love more than fear. *The more you value love, the less fear you will hear.*

One of the reasons why we long to be listened to by others is that we do not always listen to our Self. We have stopped listening to our Self because we have learned to believe there is nothing worth listening to. Just as we refuse to believe that happiness is within, love is within and peace is within, so too we refuse to believe that any wisdom is also within. Often in my workshops I will ask, 'Where is wisdom?' My audiences know to say, 'Wisdom is within'. But when I then invite people to stand up and proclaim, 'I am a wise person', very few people do so. Most often whoever dares to stand up gets a round of applause for their courage and their example.

Like the thirsty fish in water, you are surrounded by, immersed in and created with wisdom. However, wisdom is, to your ego, blasphemy. And so too is love, peace and happiness. You can only be wise, therefore, if you first change your mind about yourself. In other words,

> *to accept wisdom and guidance, first you must*
> *be willing to give up your belief in guilt.*

You are not guilty. You are not unworthy. You must be willing to give up what you have learned about yourself. Next, you must also be willing to give up your fearful, limiting beliefs about wisdom and guidance. For instance, wisdom is not special, it is natural. Similarly, guidance is not rare, it is everywhere. Both wisdom and guidance are never deserved, they are merely accepted. If you can possibly accept that your Self is whole, worthy and well, then you will find it easy to accept wisdom for yourself. Even a little willingness can bring untold amounts of wisdom.

Wisdom is unconditional. Wisdom is constant. You are never not wise. Wisdom is everywhere. And all that is ever really going on is that *either you are listening to your wisdom or you are ignoring it.* Wisdom is free. It requires no special techniques, no special learning, and no special 'good behaviour'. Wisdom requires no effort, no sacrifice and no suffering. Those who believe in wisdom find wisdom, for

> ***wisdom is available to those who make themselves available to wisdom.***

How often have you let yourself down because you refused to listen to your own innate wisdom and *inner-tuition*? Many times you have known, with hindsight, that you had the answer all along to the challenges you were faced with. Wisdom was not missing. All that was missing was the belief that you can be wise, you can be free, and you can be happy.

When you make time to listen to the wisdom of your unconditioned Self, you begin to hear a familiar melody. *A Course In Miracles* refers to this melody in an inspired passage of poetry called 'The Forgotten Song'. Here are a few of the lines:

> *Listen, – perhaps you catch a hint of an ancient*
> *state not quite forgotten; dim, perhaps, and yet*
> *not altogether unfamiliar, like a song whose*
> *name is long forgotten, and the circumstances*

in which you heard completely unremembered.
Not the whole song has stayed with you, but
just a little wisp of melody, attached not to
a person or a place or anything particular.
But you remember, from just this little part,
how lovely was the song, how wonderful the
setting where you heard it, and how you loved
those who were there and listened with you.

Believe and know! This is the key to wisdom. If you listen and you have difficulty finding an answer, it is because you are playing out the belief that wisdom is difficult. If you listen and you hear no answer, it is because you are playing out a belief that you have no wisdom. If you listen and are afraid to follow the answer, it is because you are playing out the belief that your wisdom may not be correct. Give up your guilt, take back your projections, and let wisdom be natural to you once more.

People invariably ask me, *how do I know my guidance is right?* Because the ego so firmly believes that you are unworthy it obsesses over 'what is right?' and 'what is wrong?' In the past, I would always pray, 'What's the right thing to do here?' Today, I leave 'right' and 'wrong' well alone, and, instead, I pray, 'What is the most loving thing I can do here?', or 'How can I be the Presence of Love right now?' When in difficulty I always call for love, because love is wisdom.

Walk with love today.

Leap!

There once was a man who went walking along
a cliff-edge. He strayed from the path, lost his
footing, and fell over the edge. As he fell
towards the deep blue sea, he grabbed at a
branch of thorns. Hanging there, daring not
to let go, the man began to pray,
　'Is there anybody there?'
　'Yes,' came the reply.
　'Who is it?' asked the man.
　'God.'
　'Help me, God,' prayed the man.
　'Let go and leap,' said God.
　The man thought for a moment,
and then he prayed,
　'Is there anybody else there?'

The man in this story wants it both ways – he wants to cling
to pain and be free! You cannot do both.

All too often we refuse to let go of our fears until we can
see love; but we cannot see love until we are first willing
to let go of our fears. Similarly, we will not give up our
defences until we are safe; but we cannot be safe until we
are first willing to let go our defences. Again, we cling to
our painful past until we are sure of a bright future; but
there can be no bright future until we surrender our past.
We are so reluctant to give up our suffering before we are
happy again; but happiness cannot happen until we let go
of our suffering.

It is only once you are willing to let go of your illusions

that truth can unfold; it is only once you are willing to let go of your pain that joy can take hold. It is only once you are willing to let go of your grievances that peace will reign; it is only once you are willing to let go of your limitations that you will be free again. Healing is a letting go.

Happiness is a great big let go!

Let ego or let go! To the ego, love, truth and happiness looks like an awfully big risk, but that is because it cannot see straight. Remember, you cannot be in control of your healing, and you cannot be in control and be happy. You have to let go of control and fear. Letting go feels like a risk, but, in truth, the only thing you risk losing when you let go is your ego.

Love is not a risk, not if you are willing to give up guilt. Peace is not a gamble, not if you are willing to give away all thoughts of conflict. Happiness is not unstable, not if you stand firm. Trust is not dangerous, not if you give it unconditionally. Freedom is never broken, not if you accept it wholeheartedly.

It all comes down to where you decide to place your trust. Your unconditional Self is unreasonably joyful because it trusts unconditionally. *Trust is proactive.* Whatever you trust in fully, and that means both consciously and unconsciously, it must come to pass. If, therefore, you trust fully in joy, it must happen; if you trust fully in love, it must happen; if you trust fully in peace, it must happen.

True joy is trust. It is a trust that you are, in spirit, already free and already happy. It is a trust that you are, at heart, wholly innocent and loving. It is a trust that you are, in truth, completely safe and well. It is also a trust that you are, always, blessed with strength, inspiration and power greater than any challenge you meet.

I remember sitting down one afternoon on a crowded beach on a small Greek Island. I was angry and I was nursing my wounds. Miranda and I had just survived a near fatal car crash only a few hours earlier. We had been driven off the road by a drunk driver in a large lorry. We were lucky to be alive. I sat down to pray, and the following dialogue just happened:

> *'What is wisdom?' I asked.*
> *'Wisdom is joy,' came The Answer.*
>
> *'And what is joy?' I said.*
> *'Joy is the knowledge that nothing*
> *that ever happens, in this universe*
> *or any other, can take away your*
> *freedom,' answered The Answer.*
>
> *'Nothing?' I questioned.*
> *'Nothing,' said The Answer.*
>
> *'And what is peace?' I asked.*
> *'Peace is giving up all resistance*
> *to joy,' answered The Answer.*

Walk Free!

> *Be big! You have played small*
> *for too long.*

The following story illustrates perfectly the only 'real key' you need to walk free:

Harry Houdini liked nothing better than digging a hole for himself and then looking for a way out. His ability to free himself from shackles, locked boxes, strait-jackets, handcuffs and all kinds of sealed containers, brought the Hungarian escape-artist world-wide fame. There was nothing he could not escape from. Well, almost nothing.

At the height of his fame, Harry Houdini issued a challenge to the world to build a jail that could hold him. Jail after jail after jail, Harry Houdini would escape within moments. There is a story of one jail, however, where something went very wrong. This jail was like all the rest – concrete floors, concrete walls, a set of bars, no furniture. Harry entered, and the door was shut behind him. The stop-watch started ticking, and Harry got to work on the lock with a piece of metal he had concealed in his clothes.

Harry soon realised this lock was unusual. An hour passed by, no luck. Another hour passed by, and still Harry was imprisoned. Beads of sweat formed upon his brow. Effort upon effort upon effort got the great Harry Houdini nowhere. Cuffed by tiredness, choked with frustration, Harry eventually fell against the door in despair, and . . . the door swung open. The prison door had never been locked.

We have so accustomed ourselves to struggle, suffering and sacrifice that we often overlook the easy option. So frantic is our search for peace that we often miss what is already freely available. When unhappy, we feel hemmed in, trapped and imprisoned mentally and emotionally. The prison bars of pain, fear, guilt and grief feel so real we dare not believe we could simply walk free.

I was once told by a man who had served a ten-year prison sentence that 'The most fearful day of prison for any prisoner is the day before you get your freedom back'. I also remember him telling me, 'My prison bars had become so familiar to me I did not know if I could live without them'. What feels familiar, feels real. What feels unfamiliar, can feel frightening.

If you have felt trapped and imprisoned for a long time, freedom can feel unfamiliar and frightening. If you have been depressed and in pain for any period, joy can be scary. If you have been lonely for too long, love and intimacy can be terrifying. If you have been in sacrifice all your life, then the idea of receiving feels like hell. And if you have played small too often, then the thought of living big will feel exciting, frightening and impossible.

You desire freedom, and you are afraid of freedom. Happiness *now*! is all about feeling the fear of freedom and walking free anyway.

Your unconditioned Self was born free.

You were born free. Despite what you may think, and what you may have learned, you are still free. If you could but believe this, you would see it is so. Like happiness and love, freedom waits on welcome, not on time. Freedom awaits your decision. If only for a moment, now, just let yourself feel free. Feel it. Feel free! Happiness is a decision to be free now. *Be free now.*

Resist yourself no more. Give in to freedom. Accept what is, in truth, already yours, and walk free.

You have suffered enough. Be free now.
You have laboured all your life. Walk free now.
You have searched all over. Be free now.
You have struggled so much. Walk free now.
You have sacrificed too much. Be free now.
You have been guilty too long. Walk free now.
You have waited needlessly. Be free now.

Revel in your freedom. Live wholeheartedly, laugh loud, love much, spread joy, be truthful, give yourself to everything. You, who are already whole, can lose nothing. Your ego may fall from time to time, but you will not. Live big! Think of God, and method act. Pick a role-model like Jesus or Buddha and *be brilliant.* Choose to be happy, for

he who is happy has a gift for this world!

You did not come to add to the madness of this world. You came to be free. And you did not come empty, for you are full of gifts to give. Therefore, do not hide your light now – let it shine. Do not hold back on love now – let it flow. Do not temper your joy – let it inspire. Do not deny your truth – let it be. Do not imprison your imagination – set it free. Do not reign in your creativity – let it go. Do not mask your playfulness – let it play. Do not resist your spirit – let it heal.

The call to live and be free is too powerful to resist for ever. Be loving now, and you will be free of fear; be joyful now, and you will be free of pain; be peaceful now, and you will free yourself of conflict; be forgiving now, and you will be free of suffering; be present now, and you will walk free.

The 'real key' to happiness then is that *there is no key!* This might seem like bad news. Fear not! The good news is that there is no prison, no door and no lock. Happiness is open all hours, and if you are willing to be open to happiness, then you can enjoy happiness *now!*

EPILOGUE

ᗑᗑ

There Is No Future!

ᗑᗑ

What sort of an epilogue begins with the heading, *There is no Future!* – especially an epilogue for a book on happiness.

Well, it's official. The news is out – 'There is no future!' Please understand, this is not a message of despair, it is simply a statement of truth. I repeat, 'There is no future!' Therefore, don't save your best for the future. Do not wait to give your best to the next job, the next time, the next person, or the next opportunity. Give your best *now!*

Some things never change. Your greatest opportunity for happiness has been, will be, and still is, *now*. Unfortunately, you are often too busy 'pasturising' and 'futurising' to see that everything is here already. Give up the past, give up the future, and give in to happiness *now!* It really is all here. It must be, because you are here.

The one piece of good news that is true forever is

the present is here, now!

When in search of wisdom, linguists often refer to roots and connections of words from pre-historic civilisations. They explore ancient languages such as Sanskrit, Aramaic and Latin, to unearth forgotten gems of wisdom. Well, much closer to home and to the present time, it is helpful to note that in the English language the word 'present' has three distinct meanings – 'here', 'now' and 'a gift'.

Is this only a coincidence, or could it be that *the greatest gifts of life are always available to you here and now!* The word 'present' also links to 'presence', 'being' and 'being present'. Here is another clue. Give yourself to *now!* The future is not your answer – it has no true power. Now, right here, is good enough for you. All you need remember is, nothing is missing within you and nothing is missing here now.

Today is brand new. Today is not yet finished. Give today another chance, then. The world has finished with yesterday if you have. And the world cannot tarnish your future if you do not. Be grateful for today. Say 'Thank you' to the present moment. Remember, the gift is,

the more you give to 'now' the more you get from 'now'.

Gratitude is a gift in itself. It inspires you to be open, to be present, and to receive. Gratitude is gold. It takes as much time to appreciate something as it does to curse it or ignore it. And gratitude is a good medicine. One single serving of gratitude is often enough to open the heart, energise the body, warm the bones, make your hair curl, put a spring in your step, start you humming, and make you smile like a baby! Also, it is impossible to be grateful and lonely, grateful and depressed, or grateful and unhappy.

Let your gratitude be unconditional. Be grateful for everything, for no reason. Just be grateful. Before you practise gratitude you are in the dark and there appears to be very little to be grateful for; once you begin, a new light dawns, sometimes a brilliant light, a light as bright as heaven itself[1].

If it appears you have nothing to be grateful for, it is probably because you are not allowing yourself to receive. Just because you do not receive does not mean there is nothing to receive. On the contrary, there is always something wonderful to receive. However you feel, just be grateful anyway, and let yourself be open and present to 'other possibilities'. Never close yourself off.

It is so unfair, *the people who practise gratitude always have something to be happy about!* True gratitude arises spontaneously in us all, however, when we realise that the true gifts come not from the world but from our own heart. In truth,

> *happiness is not something you can get your hands on; it is something you carry in your heart.*

Wouldn't it be wonderful if you could just be happy! Imagine, just for today, giving up the struggle, slowing down a little, cancelling your plans, throwing away your 'to do' list, and simply deciding to be happy. Imagine telling yourself, 'Just for today, I will not struggle,' and 'Just for today, I will not suffer,' and 'Just for today, I will not be in sacrifice,' and 'Just for today, I will stop searching'.

Imagine if you stopped everything, and you simply

allowed yourself to be happy. What a crazy thought! Imagine simply letting yourself *be happy*, for no reason. For a whole sixty seconds, right now, just picture yourself allowing your happiness to bubble up all by itself. You are not meditating on happiness, praying for it, affirming it, visualising it or asking for it – you are simply *being happy*.

My challenge to you is, 'Do not seek love today; merely be loving. Do not seek peace today; merely be peaceful. Do not seek joy today; merely be joyful.' I know it sounds too simple, too silly, too crazy – but, it might just work! Maybe you really can just *be happy*.

Ask not for love today; better still, pray that
you might be the Presence of Love today.
Ask not for rest today; better still, pray that
you might be the Presence of Rest today.
Ask not for kindness today; better still, pray that
you might be the Presence of Kindness today.
Ask not for victory today; better still, pray that
you might be the Presence of Victory today.
Ask not for laughter today; better still, pray that
you might be the Presence of Laughter today.
Ask not for peace today; better still, pray that
you might be the Presence of Peace today.

Further Information

For further information on The Happiness Project and for details on public workshops, books and tapes, the 'Eight Week Happiness Programme', the 'Teaching Happiness' professional certificate training, or the 'Deep and Meaningful Corporate Training Programme', contact The Happiness Project, Elms Court, Chapel Way, Botley, Oxford OX2 9LP Tel: 01865 244414, Fax: 01865 248825, Web site: www.happiness.co.uk, E-mail: Hello@happiness.co.uk

NOTES

Chapter One: Happy Already!

1 Robert H. Schuller has written many inspiring books on the subject of 'possibility thinking'. They include, *Peace Of Mind Through Possibility Thinking, Move Ahead With Possibility Thinking, Daily Power Thoughts* and *Power Ideas For A Happy Family*, all published by Jove Books, New York.

2 For a beautiful treatise on the principle of Attention, see *Wherever You Go, There You Are* by Jon Kabat-Zinn, Hyperion (1994).

3 The words, 'joy waits on welcome, not on time', are inspired by a passage in *A Course In Miracles* which reads, 'Love waits on welcome, not on time, and the real world is but your welcome of what always was' (p 255). For an excellent meditation on this theme, listen to, 'Soul Healing: Accepting Joy', Miranda Holden (1997), available through The Happiness Project.

4 The British press has featured a handful of articles in recent years on: (1) happiness is a dysfunctional response to the world; (2) happiness leads to ineffectiveness at work. Although the media has tried to make much of this, there is very little real support for these ideas.

5 Herbert Spencer, the nineteenth-century English philosopher, and author of *The Principles Of Psychology* (1855), introduced two terms: 'objective psychology', i.e. that which can be observed; and 'subjective psychology', i.e. that which cannot be observed. His work inspired Behaviourism and the study of externals. Also, for research on measuring happiness and subjective well-being, see, *Social Indicators Of Well-Being: Americans' Perceptions of Life Quality* by F. Andrews and S. Withey, New York: Plenium (1976), and the QED 'How To Be Happy' booklet, BBC (1997).

6 'Upanishads' are spiritual teachings from India, the oldest of which were composed between 800–400 B.C. The Sanskrit word, 'Upanishads', means 'sitting at the feet of a Master'. In all, there are over 100 ancient Upanishads that are still in print. The *Mandaya Upanishad* is one of the most popular. There are many excellent translations of these 'sittings', one of which is *The Upanishads*, translated and selected by Juan Mascaro for Penguin Classics.

7 Read *The Uses Of Enchantment – The Meaning And Importance Of Fairy Tales* by Bruno Bettleheim, Penguin Books (1975).

8 For a great anthology of sacred poetry, read *The Enlightened Heart*, edited by Stephen Mitchell, Harper Perennial (1989).

9 See *The Complete Works Of Robert Browning*, edited by J. C. Berkey & Dooley, Ohio University Press (1996).

10 See *Stress Busters* by Robert Holden, Thorsons (1998).

11 Many books have been written on the works of Sri Ramakrishna. I would recommend *The Gospel Of Sri Ramakrishna*, translated by Swami Nikhilananda, edited by Joseph Campbell (1988), and *Sayings Of Sri Ramakrishna*, Amra Press, Madras. Also look up 'Sri Ramakrishna' on the internet.

12 For a good overview of sacred scriptures and world religions, I recommend *The Illustrated Book Of Sacred Scriptures*, edited by Timothy Freke, Thorsons, (1998), *The Complete Book Of World Mysticism*, Timothy Freke, Piatkus (1977), and *The World's Religions*, Huston Smith, Harper San Francisco (1991).

13 A spiritual faith can certainly encourage great happiness. See *The Psychology Of Happiness* by Michael Argyle, Methuen (1986), 'Religious Involvement And Subjective Well-Being' by C. Ellison, *Journal Of Health And Social Behaviour*, 32, pp 80–99 (1991), *Man's Search For Meaning* by Viktor Frankl, Beacon Press (1962), and 'Is There A Religious Factor in Health?' by J. Levin and P. Schiller, *Journal Of Religion And Health*, 26, pp 9-36 (1987). For further information about spiritual faith and perceptions of God, see *A History Of God* by Karen Armstrong, Harper Collins (1993).

14 *A Course In Miracles* is published by Penguin Arkana. First published in 1976, *A Course in Miracles* was scribed, somewhat reluctantly, by Helen Schucman, a psychologist at Columbia University, New York, who one day heard an inner voice which said, 'This is a course in miracles. Please take note'. At first she resisted, but with the help of her colleague, Bill Thetford, she listened to the words dictated to her.

A *Course In Miracles* is a remarkable self-study system which combines perennial wisdom and spiritual psychology principles. The book consists of three parts – a text, a manual for teachers, and a workbook with 365 lessons, one for each day of the year. It emphasises daily practice of its principles, which include letting go of fear, removing the blocks to the awareness of love's presence, practising miracle-mindedness, participating in holy relationship, and experiencing forgiveness.

For further information on *A Course In Miracles*, i.e. newsletters, workshops and mail order, contact The Miracle Network, 12a Barness Court, 6/8 Westbourne Terrace, London W2 3UW, tel/fax: 0171 262 0209; Foundation for A Course In Miracles, 1275 Tennanah Lake Road, Roscoe, New York, 12776-5905, tel: (607) 498 4116; and, Miracle Distribution Center, 1141 East Ash Avenue, Fullerton, California 92831, tel: (714) 738 8380.

15 See *Wordsworth, Complete Poetical Works*, edited by Thomas Hutchinson, University Press (1996).

16 See *A Return To Love* by Marianne Williamson, Thorsons, revised edition (1996).

17 See *The Dhammapada*, translated by Juan Mascaro, Penguin Classics (1987).

18 See *Seasons Of Your Heart: Prayers and Reflections* by Macrina Wiederkehr, Harper Collins, New York (1991).

19 See 10 above.

20 See *Pythagoras And Early Pythagoreanism*, by J. Philip, University of Toronto (1967)

Chapter Two: Giving Up The Search

1 Eddie and Debbie Shapiro are inspirational teachers of healing, spirituality and joy. They are authors of several books, including, *Meditation For Inner Peace: Discovering The Joy Of Relaxation And True Happiness*, Piatkus (1997), and *Out Of Your Mind, The Only Place To Be*, Element (1992). For further information on their workshops, contact 3 Norton Park Cottages, Dartmouth, Devon TQ6 0NH, U.K.

2 In more modern times, the 'pursuit of happiness' was formerly advocated in the American Declaration of Independence, where it is written, '*We hold these truths to be self-evident,*

that all men are created equal, that they are endowed by their Creator with certain unalienable rights, that among these are life, liberty, and the pursuit of happiness.' This Declaration did not cause the 'pursuit of happiness', it merely reflected 'out loud' what most of the world was already thinking, and is still thinking.

3 When people are asked what they need to be happier, the most common answer is 'More money'. There is now overwhelming research which shows that more money does not guarantee more happiness. See *The Sense Of Well-being In America* by Angus Campbell, McGraw-Hill, New York (1981), 'Happiness Of The Very Wealthy' by Ed Diener *et al, Social Indicators,* 16, pp 263–74 (1985) and 'Does Money Buy Happiness?' by R. Easterlin, *Public Interest,* 30, pp 3–10 (1973).

4 See *The Pursuit Of Happiness – Discovering The Pathway To Fulfilment, Well-being, And Enduring Personal Joy* by David G. Myers, Ph.D., Avon Books, New York (1993).

5 There is a large body of evidence which shows that exercise can encourage mental fitness, harmony and well-being. See 'Personality Correlates Of Physical Fitness' by J. Hogan, *Journal Of Personality And Social Psychology,* 56, pp 284–288 (1989), 'The Role Of Aerobic Exercise In The Treatment Of Depression' by E. Martinsen, *Stress Medicine,* 3, pp 93–100 (1987) and 'Physical Activity And Mental Health in USA And Canada' by T. Stephens, *Preventive Medicine,* 17, pp 35–47 (1988).

6 See *Mental Health & Illness – The Nutrition Connection* by Patrick Holford & Carl Pfeiffer, ION Press (1996). For further information, contact Institute Of Optimum Nutrition, Blades Court, Deodar Road, London SW15 2NU.

7 See 'The Effects Of 72 Hours Of Sleep Loss On Psychological Variables' by M. Mikulincer *et al, British Journal Of Psychology,* 80, pp 145–162 (1989).

8 See *Living Wonderfully: A Joyful Guide To Conscious Creative Living – For Today!* by Robert Holden, Thorsons (1994).

9 For an excellent overview of psychotherapy and psychology today, I recommend *Handbook Of Individual Therapy,* edited by

Windy Dryden, Sage Publications (1996), *Innovative Therapy In Britain*, edited by John Rowan and Windy Dryden, Open University Press (1988) and *The Theory And Practice Of Counselling Psychology*, by Richard Nelson-Jones, Cassell (1990).

10 For an excellent introduction to Rumi's work, I recommend *The Essential Rumi*, translations by Coleman Barks with John Moyne, Harper San Francisco (1995),

11 See *How To Be Happy* by John Pepper, Gateway Books (1992).

12 For more information on the development of the Laughter Clinic, read *Laughter, The Best Medicine* by Robert Holden, Thorsons (1998).

13 For more information on workshops, professional training, books and other products, contact The Happiness Project.

14 Copies of the QED 'How To Be Happy' video and programme booklet are available from The Happiness Project.

Chapter Three: Being Good Enough

1 The relationship between happiness and high self-esteem is well documented in psychology research, as is the relationship between depression and low self-esteem. Happiness and Self-perception go hand in hand. See *The Psychology Of Happiness* by Michael Argyle, Methuen (1986), 'Depression And Components Of Self-Punitiveness: High Self-Standards, Self-Criticisms And Overgeneralization' by C. S. Carver *et al*, *Journal Of Consulting And Clinical Psychology*, 92, pp 330–337 (1983), 'Increasing Rates Of Depression' by G. L. Klerman *et al*, *JAMA*, 261, pp 229–35 (1989), 'The Changing Rate Of Major Depression' by G. L. Klerman, *JAMA*, 268, pp 3098–3105 (1992), 'Living Conditions In The Twentieth Century' by D. J. Smith in *Psychological Disorders In Young People* by M. Rutter *et al*, Jon Wiley, London (1995), and *Social Trends* by D. J. Smith, HMSO (1997).

2 For more on the relationship between happiness and achievement, see *Happy People* by Jonathan Freedman, New York:

Harcourt Brace Jovanavich (1978), *The Sense Of Well-being In America* by Angus Campbell, McGraw-Hill, New York (1981), and *Happiness Is An Inside Job* by John Powell, Tabor Press (1989).

3 For more on the relationship between happiness, circumstance and attitude, see 'Environmental And Dispositional Influences On Well-Being' by Costa *et al*, *British Journal Of Psychology*, 78, pp 299–306 (1987), 'Personality Correlates Of Subjective Well-Being' by R. Emmons and E. Diener, *Personality And Social Psychology Bulletin*, 11, pp 89–97 (1985), 'Dispositional Optimism And Physical Well-Being' by M. Scheier and C. Carver, *Journal Of Personality*, 55, pp 169–210 (1987), *The Social Psychology Of Subjective Well-Being*, edited by Fritz Strack *et al*, Pergamon Press (1990), *15 Principles For Achieving Happiness* by A. D. Hart, Dallas: Word (1988) and 'Happiness Is A Decision' by Marianne Williamson, Simon and Schuster Audio Cassette Series (1990).

4 See *Paradise Lost* by John Milton, Longman (1971).

5 For more on the connection between happiness and loving relationships, see relevant chapters in *Britain On The Couch – Why we're unhappier than we were in the 1950s – despite being richer* by Oliver James, Century Books (1997), *Happy People* by Jonathan Freedman, Harcourt Brace Jovanavich, New York (1978), *The Psychology Of Happiness* by Michael Argyle, Methuen (1986), 'The Changing Relationship Of Marital Status To Reported Happiness' by N. Glenn and C. Weaver, *Journal Of Marriage And The Family*, 50, pp 317–324 (1988), and 'The Effect Of Marriage On The Well-Being Of Adults' by W. Gove *et al*, *Journal Of Family Issues*, 11, pp 4–35 (1990).

6 Social Comparison Theory was developed by many psychologists, including Leonard Festinger, in the 1950s. In the last few decades a large body of psychology and sociology research has shown quite conclusively that, unless you are happy with yourself, you will not be happy with what you do, where you are, what you have and who you are with. For the relationship between happiness, wealth and social

comparison, see 'Happiness Of The Very Wealthy' by E. Diener *et al, Social Indicators,* 16, pp 263–274 (1985), 'Will Raising The Incomes Of All Increase The Happiness Of All?' by R. A. Easterlin, *Journal Of Economic Behaviour And Organization,* 27, pp 35–47, (1995), 'A Theory Of Social Comparison Processes' by L. Festiger, *Human Relations,* 7, pp 117–40 (1954), 'Social Comparison And Depression' by F. Gibbons, *Journal Of Personality And Social Psychology,* 51, pp 140–148 (1986), 'Depression And Anxiety In Relation To Social Status' by J. M. Murphy *et al, Archives Of General Psychiatry,* 48, pp 223–229 (1991), 'Physical Attractiveness, Need For Approval, Social Self-Esteem And Maladjustment' by K. E. O'Grady, *Journal Of Social And Clinical Psychology,* 8, pp 62–69 (1989), 'Social Comparison And Negative Self-Evaluation: An Application To Depression' by S. R. Swallow *et al, Clinical Psychology Review,* 8, pp 55–76 (1987).

7 See *The Bible,* St. Matthew 16:26.

8 See *Aldous Huxley, A Biography,* by Sybille Bedford, Papermac (1993).

9 The work of American psychiatrist, Gerald Jampolsky, offers a clear, concise introduction to forgiveness as a tool for self-healing and a choice for wholeness. His Attitudinal Healing programme is inspired in particular by *A Course In Miracles.* See *Goodbye To Guilt: Releasing Fear Through Forgiveness,* by G. Jampolsky, Bantam Books (1985).

Chapter Four: Practising Acceptance

1 Contact The Happiness Project for relevant publications.

2 See *Laughter, A Theological Reflection* by Karl-Josef Kuschel, SCM Press (1994). Also, for excellent reports on the relationship between health, happiness, guilt and simple pleasures, contact ARISE – Associates for Research into the Science of Enjoyment, PO Box 11446, London SW18 5ZH.

3 See *Guilt Is The Teacher, Love Is The Lesson* by Joan Borysenko, Ph.D., Warner Books (1990).

4 For a good introduction to world mythology, see *Gods And Goddesses – 130 Deities And Tales From World Mythology*, general editor Elizabeth Hallam, Blandford Press (1996).

5 The work of Matthew Fox and Creation Centred Spirituality focuses on the concept of original blessing. See *Creation Spirituality – Liberating Gifts For The Peoples Of Earth*, Matthew Fox, Harper Collins (1991).

6 See *The Bible*, John 15:11.

7 See *The Bible*, Matthew 5:14.

8 See *The Bible*, John 10:34.

9 See 'The Protestant Work Ethic As A Cultural Phenomenon' by L. Giorgi *et al*, *European Journal Of Social Psychology*, 20, pp 499–517 (1990).

10 See *Present Moment, Wonderful Moment* by Thich Nhat Hanh, Rider Books (1993). This is one of an excellent series of books published by Rider Books.

11 British Telecom and the 'BT Forum' has collated excellent research on the changing face of work and society in Europe in the 1980s and 1990s. For further information, contact BT Forum, Telephone House, 2–4 Temple Avenue, London EC4Y 0HL.

12 Listen to 'Relaxation For Happiness,' by Ben Renshaw (1997), available through The Happiness Project.

13 See *End The Struggle And Dance With Life* by Susan Jeffers Ph.D., Hodder & Stoughton (1996).

14 See *Psychological And Biological Approaches to Emotion*, edited by N. Stein *et al*, Erlbaum Publishers (1990), which includes a chapter on 'The Influence Of Positive And Negative Affect on Cognitive Organization' by A. Isen; *Emotional And Social Judgements*, edited by J. Forgas, Pergamon Press (1991), and 'Happiness And Helpfulness' by D. Myers, in *Social Psychology*, second edition, McGraw-Hill (1987).

Chapter Five: Living Unconditionally

1 For an interesting read on being, flow and happiness, read *Flow – The Psychology Of Happiness* by Mihaly Csikszentmihalyi, Rider Books (1992).

2 See *Cognitive Therapy And The Emotional Disorders* by A.T. Beck, International Universities Press, New York (1976), *The Cognitive Therapy Of Depression* by A.T. Beck *et al*, Guildford Press, New York (1979), *The Psychology Of Personal Constructs – Vols. I and II*, Norton, New York (1955), *Feel Good: The New Mood Therapy* by David Burns, Avon (1980), *Learned Optimism* by Martin Seligman, Alfred A. Knopf Publishers (1991).

3 See *A Guide To Personal Happiness* by Dr Albert Ellis & Dr Irving Becker, Wilshire Book Company (1982).

4 See 'Joy Is Not A Carrot' by Linda Carpenter, *Miracle Worker*, 19 (Nov/Dec 1997). *Miracle Worker* is published by The Miracle Network, 12a Barness Court, 6/8 Westbourne Terrace, London W2 3UW, tel/fax: 0171 262 0209.

5 See *Britain On The Couch – Why we're unhappier than we were in the 1950s – despite being richer*, Oliver James, Century Books (1997).

6 See *How To Have What You Want* by Timothy Miller, Ph.D., Henry Holt and Company (1995).

7 See *Happiness Is An Inside Job* by John Powell, Tabor Press (1989), *Britain On The Couch – Why we're unhappier than we were in the 1950s – despite being richer*, Oliver James, Century Books (1997), *The Pursuit Of Happiness – Discovering The Pathway To Fulfilment, Well-being, And Enduring Personal Joy* by David G. Myers, Ph.D., Avon Books, New York (1993) and *15 Principles For Achieving Happiness* by A. D. Hart, Word, Dallas (1988).

8 For studies on the relationship between age and happiness, see *Happy People* by Jonathan Freedman, Harcourt Brace Jovanavich, New York (1978), 'Age And Subjective Well-being' by W. Stock *et al*, *Evaluation Studies: Review Annual*, 8 (1983), 'Life-Course And Satisfaction, Equal For Everyone?' by J. J. Latten, *Social Indicators Research*, 21, pp 599–610 (1989),

and *The Sense Of Well-being In America* by Angus Campbell, McGraw-Hill, New York (1981).

9 See *Wordsworth, Complete Poetical Works*, edited by Thomas Hutchinson, University Press (1996).

10 See *How Proust Can Change Your Life* by Alain Debotton, Picador (1997).

11 See *The Joyful Christ: The Healing Power Of Humor* by Cal Samra, Harper San Francisco (1985).

12 See *Quotations To Cheer You Up When The World Is Getting You Down* by Allen Klein, Wings Books (1991).

13 See *Lessons of St. Francis of Assisi* by John Talbot, NAL – Dutton (1995).

14 See *Dialogue On Awakening* by Tom Carpenter, Carpenter Press (1992). For further information on workshops, books and cassettes by Tom and Linda Carpenter, contact The Carpenters' Press, P.O. Box 3437, Princeville, Hawaii 96722.

15 Many of the conversations between Robert and Miranda Holden, and Tom and Linda Carpenter are available on cassette, including 'My Brother; My Self', 'Freedom From Projection', 'Happiness', and, 'Returning To Awareness'. Contact The Happiness Project.

16 See *Laughter, The Best Medicine* by Robert Holden, Thorsons (1998).

Chapter Six: Healing Unhappiness

1 See *Weight Loss For The Mind* by Stuart Wilde, Hay House (1995).

2 See 'Social Comparison And Depression' by F. Gibbons, *Journal Of Personality And Social Psychology*, 51, pp 140–148 (1986), and 'Effects Of Upward And Downward Social Comparison On Mood States' by F. Gibbons and M. Gerard, *Journal Of Social And Clinical Psychology*, 8, pp 14–31 (1989).

3 See *Tao Te Ching* by Lao Tzu, translated by D. C. Lau, Penguin Classics (1963).

4 See 'Exploring The Limits Of Self-Reports And Reasoned

Action' by D. Hessing *et al*, *Journal Of Personality And Social Psychology*, 54, pp 405–413 (1988), and 'The Construct Validity Of Subjective Well-Being Measures' by M. Okun and W. Stock, *Journal Of Community Psychology*, 15, pp 481–92 (1987).

5 From *Solitude* by Ella Wheeler Wilcox (1855–1919).

6 For more on the question of 'drugs or therapy', see *Britain On The Couch – Why we're unhappier than we were in the 1950s – despite being richer* by Oliver James, Century Books (1997), 'Combined Pharmacotherapy And Psychotherapy For Depression' by D. W. Manning *et al*, *American Psychiatric Press* (1990), *Evolutionary Psychiatry* by A. Stevens *et al*, Routledge, London (1996), and 'The Treatment Of Depression: Prescribing Patterns Of Antidepressant Medications' by J. M. Donoghue *et al*, *British Journal Of Psychiatry*, 168, pp 164–168 (1996).

7 See *Hermann Hesse: Pilgrim of Crisis – A Biography* by Ralph Freedman, Cape Publishers (1979).

8 See *The Bible*, John 16:24.

9 See *Feel The Fear And Do It Anyway* by Susan Jeffers, Rider (1997).

10 See *Love Always Answers* by Diane Berke, Crossroad (1994).

Chapter Seven: Lots of Love!

1 See *If It Hurts, It Isn't Love* by Chuck Spezzano, Arthur James Publishers, revised edition (1996).

2 For a beautiful collection of inspirational sayings on love and relationships, see *A Lively Flame* by Eileen Campbell, Thorsons (1992).

3 For more on individualism and well-being, see 'Individualism And Collectivism' by H. Triandis *et al*, *Journal Of Personality And Social Psychology*, 54, pp 323–328 (1988), *Reaching Out: The Three Movements Of The Spiritual Life* by Henri Nouwen, Doubleday Books (1975), *Habits Of The Heart: Individualism*

And Commitment In American Life by R. Bellah *et al*, University of California Press (1996), *Loneliness: A Sourcebook Of Current Theory, Research And Therapy*, edited by L. Peplau and Daniel Perlman, Wiley, New York (1982); 'Psychological Individualism And Romantic Love' by Karen Dion and Kenneth Dion, *Journal Of Social Behavior And Personality*, 6, pp 17–33 (1991), 'Pressures of Modern Life Bring Increased Importance To Friendship' by L. DiStefano, *Gallup Poll Monthly* No. 294 (March 1990), *Individualism And Collectivism* by U. Kim, Sage Publishers (1994), *The Origins Of English Individualism* by A. Macfarlane, Blackwell, Oxford (1978), *Social Trends* by D. J. Smith, HMSO (1997).

4 See *John Donne: Complete Poetry & Selected Prose*, Century Hutchinson (1994).

5 See *The Gentle Smile: Practising Oneness In Daily Life* by Diane Berke, Crossroad (1995).

6 See *William Blake: Complete Poetry & Prose*, University of California (1992).

Chapter Eight: Travelling Light

1 For an excellent introduction to *A Course In Miracles*, see *Gifts From A Course In Miracles*, edited by Frances Vaughan and Roger Walsh, Tarcher/Putnam Books (1995).

2 See 'The Need To Belong: Desire For Interpersonal Attachments As A Fundamental Human Motivation' by R. F. Baumeister *et al*, *Psychological Bulletin*, 117, pp 497–529 (1995), 'Loneliness And Social Contact' by W. H. Jones, *Journal Of Social Psychology*, 113, pp 295–296 (1981), and 'Responses To Social Exclusion: Social Anxiety, Jealousy, Loneliness, Depression And Low Self-Esteem' by M. R. Leary, *Journal of Social And Clinical Psychology*, 9, pp 221–229 (1990).

3 See *Being Peace* by Thich Nhat Hanh, Rider Books (1990).

4 See *The Carl Rogers Reader*, edited by Howard Kirshenbaum and Valerie Land Henderson, Constable (1990).

5 See 'Good Advice for a Happy Life,' edited by Armand Eisen, Ariel Books (1995).
6 See *Carl Jung: Selected Writings*, introduced by Anthony Storr, Fontana (1983).
7 An excellent collection of inspirational sayings on silence and solitude can be found in *A Fabulous Gift* by Eileen Campbell, Thorsons (1994).

Epilogue: There Is No Future!

1 See *14,000 Things To Be Happy About* by Barbara Ann Kipfer, Workman Publishing (1990).